MAORI

MAORI
ART AND CULTURE

EDITED BY D.C. STARZECKA

Contributors

JANET DAVIDSON

NGAHUIA TE AWEKOTUKU

A. T. HAKIWAI

ROGER NEICH

MICK PENDERGRAST

D. C. STARZECKA

ROBERT JAHNKE

PUBLISHED FOR THE TRUSTEES OF THE BRITISH MUSEUM BY

BRITISH MUSEUM PRESS

Acknowledgements

We wish to thank His Excellency Dr Richard Grant, High Commissioner for New Zealand, and his predecessor, Mr John Collinge, for their interest in the project. We are grateful to all the institutions credited in the illustration captions for permission to publish images from their collections, and to Rebecca Jewell and Hans Rashbrook for new illustrations. All the British Museum objects were photographed by David Agar and Michael Row of the Museum's Photographic Service. We thank Jo Doherty (spelling of Maori words and quotations), Pat Brownsey (plant names) and Sandy Bartle (bird names), all from the Museum of New Zealand Te Papa Tongarewa in Wellington, and Sue Beeby of the Department of Ethnography and George Sweetland (voluntary assistant) for their help. We gratefully acknowledge the financial assistance from the British Council in Wellington and the New Zealand Tourism Board in London which made Roger Neich's and Mick Pendergrast's study visits to London possible, and we thank the Director of the Auckland Institute and Museum for granting them leave for these visits. Very special thanks are due to Jill Hasell, Museum Assistant in the Oceanic section of the Department, for her dedicated, intelligent and constructive help with the work on the Maori collections, and to Carolyn Jones of the British Museum Press for her interest, professionalism – and patience – in preparing this book for publication.

Published by British Museum Press
A division of The British Museum Company Ltd
46 Bloomsbury Street, London WC1B 3QQ
First published 1996
Second edition 1998

A catalogue record for this book is available from the British Library

ISBN 0 7141 2540 7

Designed by Roger Davies
Typeset in Great Britain by Wyvern 21 Ltd
Printed in Singapore
by Imago Publishing Ltd

Frontispiece: tekoteko, gable apex figure of a small house, representing an important male ancestor. His face bears male tattoo patterns and his hair is wound up into the male-style topknot. He is decorated with red ochre. Carved in East Coast or Poverty Bay style during the mid-nineteenth century. BM Ethno. 1904–244. H. 65 cm.

Front cover: central image, see frontispiece. Background: detail of the tāniko border of a kaitaka cloak, see fig. 99.

CONTENTS

Editor's Foreword

This revised and expanded edition is issued to accompany the exhibition *Maori* held at the British Museum from 27 June until 1 November 1998. The exhibition, which had been on the Museum's plans for a number of years, had to be re-scheduled repeatedly owing to the preparations for two major rebuilding and reorganisation projects: the Great Court scheme, which – following the departure of the British Library to its own building – will involve a major refurbishment of the main site based around the Reading Room, and the creation of a new Study Centre which will be housed in a newly-acquired building near the Museum. Both these projects are planned to be completed for the millennium and both involve the return of the Department of Ethnography to the British Museum site. The Department's reserve collections, held at Franks House in East London, have been closed to the public since the end of 1996 and are being packed in preparation for the move to the greatly improved facilities at the new Study Centre, and its exhibitions at the Museum of Mankind closed at the end of 1997 and will re-open in the British Museum. *Maori* is the first special exhibition marking the Department of Ethnography's return 'home'. It is also the first major exhibition devoted entirely to the culture and art of the Maori people ever mounted by the British Museum.

The first edition of this book was published in 1996. Its main emphasis is on Maori culture in general (both 'traditional' culture as it was at the time of European contact, and the contemporary expression of it) and on the two greatest achievements of Maori artistic creativity, wood-carving and fibre arts. The authors of the two chapters on Maori culture are themselves Maori and present a Maori perspective, which is so often missing from the literature on Maori topics published outside New Zealand. The chapters on prehistory, wood-carving and fibre arts have been written by Pākehā authors (i.e. New Zealanders of European descent) who have great empathy with Maori culture and exceptional knowledge of their subjects. At the same time, the book is an introduction to the Maori collections in the British Museum, for most of the objects illustrated come from the Museum's own collections.

This edition also includes a new chapter, on contemporary Maori art, by Robert Jahnke, a well-known Maori artist and Co-ordinator of Maori Visual Arts, Maori Studies Department, Massey University in Palmerston North. At first glance it may seem that some of the works illustrated in the new chapter have little to do with what is generally understood as 'Maori art' in the conventional, traditional sense. This initial impression, however, is misleading for, as the author convincingly argues, these works are deeply embedded in Maori culture. Their inclusion is justified – they demonstrate clearly the vitality of Maori creativity and the many different forms in which it manifests itself. Contemporary Maori art which falls within the domain of art galleries (rather than ethnographic museums) is an aspect of Maori culture which is little known outside New Zealand, and a book which aims to present a balanced, rounded view of that culture should not restrict itself to narrowly-defined 'traditional' art.

It is hoped that the book will give readers a better understanding of

Maori people – of the problems they face, of the way they feel about their land and of their special attachment to their art, which they perceive now as imprisoned behind the glass of museum display cases. Maori people are greatly admired abroad for their courage and pride, and are well known for their wonderful singing and dancing, but it is probably safe to say that an average member of the public knows nothing about the complexity and richness of Maori culture. This book is intended to promote a more general understanding that there is more to the Maori than the *haka* and the *poi* dance, that there is a profound philosophy behind their carving traditions, and that there are clear reasons why the issues of the Treaty of Waitangi continue to be so hotly disputed today even though over 150 years have passed since it was signed. The Maori reader is in no need of such elucidations, but he or she may learn more about their *taonga* which are housed in the British Museum. Our own working practices ensure that they are treated with appropriate care and respect.

In a book with several contributors, it is inevitable that there should be a certain amount of duplication and differences in emphasis or points of view. This does not mean that we are at variance among ourselves but rather that, coming from different backgrounds, we all meet on the common ground of appreciation of the significance and uniqueness of Maori culture and are united in our desire to do justice to its complexities.

The book reflects the long-term cooperation on the documentation of the Museum's Maori collections between the Museum staff and our New Zealand colleagues, several of whom know the collections well, having studied them during visits to London. David Simmons, Janet Davidson, Ngahuia Te Awekotuku and, especially, Roger Neich and Mick Pendergrast, have contributed immeasurably to the body of information about objects. Their expertise, combined with the Museum staff's knowledge of the Museum's archives and idiosyncratic practices, produces rewarding results – although in many cases this work is involved, time-consuming and laborious. When it is finished and the results are published in a few years' time as a definitive catalogue of the British Museum's Maori collections, it should be a valuable source of information for anybody interested in Maori culture, but most of all for the Maori people themselves who will know exactly what *taonga* there are in the British Museum and what is known about them.

1

MAORI PREHISTORY

Janet Davidson

Maori prehistory covers a period of less than 1,000 years, from the arrival of the first Polynesian colonists in Aotearoa ('The Land of the Long White Cloud', a contemporary Maori name for New Zealand) to the beginning of sustained contact with Europeans in the late eighteenth century. It is the story of a small group of people from tiny tropical islands who colonised a large temperate land. When they were first described in some detail by European explorers their tropical Pacific heritage was still apparent but their society and culture were uniquely their own. This chapter briefly reviews archaeological evidence about Maori origins and pre-European colonisation and society, and then discusses continuity and change in the various categories of material culture that are normally encountered in archaeological investigations in New Zealand.

Origins

The Maori are closely related in language, culture and tradition to the inhabitants of other islands of Polynesia, the vast triangle stretching from New Zealand to Hawai'i and Easter Island. Their closest relatives and their immediate homeland are in central Eastern Polynesia, a region which includes the Cook and Society Islands. In recent decades, archaeological evidence has provided strong support for long-standing linguistic and cultural evidence in favour of this view (Davidson 1984: 13–28). The settlers of central Eastern Polynesia in turn can be traced west to the islands of Samoa, Tonga and Fiji. This region was first settled approximately 3,000 years ago by people ancestral to present-day Polynesians and Fijians. They had a distinctive, highly decorated form of pottery which archaeologists have called Lapita Ware after an archaeological site in New Caledonia (fig. 1).

Lapita pottery has given archaeologists an important clue in their quest for Polynesian origins. It first appeared, fully developed, in the Bismarck Archipelago at the eastern tip of Papua New Guinea in the mid-second millennium BC and can be traced through Melanesia to New Caledonia and east as far as Samoa. In the Bismarck Archipelago, which had been inhabited since the late Pleistocene, Lapita potters were only one strand in a complex story (Gosden *et al.* 1989). In Fiji, Samoa and Tonga, however, they were the founding population. Many features of Polynesian culture developed in these islands during the first millennium BC (Kirch and Green 1987). During this period, pottery in Samoa and Tonga became plainer and simpler and eventually pottery manufacture ceased. Although a few sherds have been found in Eastern Polynesia, pottery making does not seem to have been successfully established there, and by the time New Zealand was discovered, pottery use had been forgotten. However, developments in other durable aspects of material culture such as stone adzes, fish-hooks and personal ornaments can be traced through Eastern Polynesia to New Zealand (fig. 2).

The exact date of the settlement of New Zealand is unknown. Although some authorities still prefer the mid or late first millennium AD, the weight of opinion currently favours a date around AD 1000 or 1100 (Anderson

1 Fragment of a decorated Lapita pot from the Reef Islands, Santa Cruz Group, Solomon Islands. Photo Anthropology Department, University of Auckland.

2 An archaeological perspective on the colonisation of Oceania and Aotearoa (New Zealand).

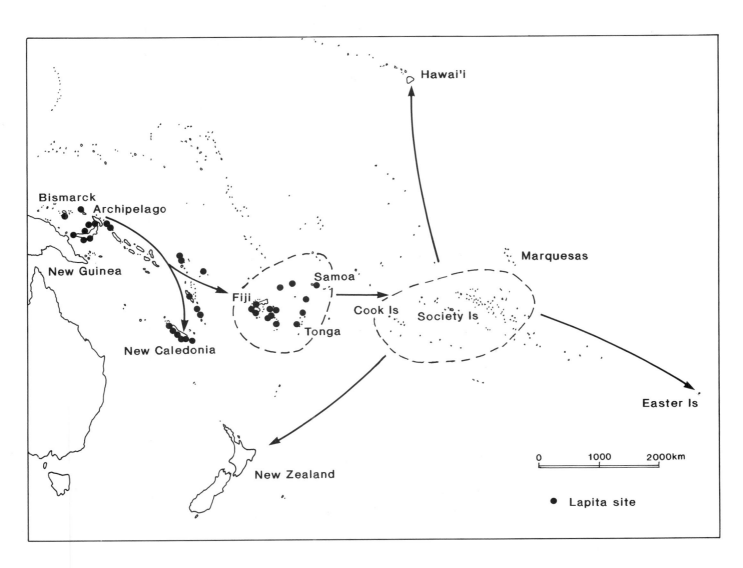

1991), with some arguing for an initial settlement as late as AD 1300. Such a late date, however, demands a large founding population and very rapid population growth to reach the level of settlement evident by about AD 1500. The problem is largely due to the difficulties of using radiocarbon dating to obtain a precise chronology during the short time-scale of New Zealand prehistory (McFadgen 1982).

Rēkohu, or the Chatham Islands, 681 km east of New Zealand, are generally thought to have been settled from New Zealand some time later by a group who then remained largely isolated until European rediscovery in 1791 (Sutton 1980). However, the Chatham Islanders, or Moriori, while very closely related to Maori, also have some distinctive features, and independent colonisation from tropical Polynesia cannot be entirely ruled out (Buranarugsa and Leach 1993).

Settlement and society

The settlement of New Zealand was the result of planned colonisation by people prepared to make long voyages in large sailing canoes in search of a new home (Irwin 1992). The colonists introduced a domestic animal (the dog) and a small rat, and succeeded in establishing a number of food and fibre plants, such as the sweet potato, taro, yam and paper mulberry (used for making bark cloth). By about AD 1300 settlements had been established around much of the coast, especially the more hospitable east coast. The interior had been explored and important stone resources useful for tool manufacture had been discovered.

The Maori immigrants discovered a land unbelievably rich in game. There was a wide range of flightless birds, which were unused to mammalian predators. Most famous are the moa: the smallest the size of a turkey and the largest towering over the men who hunted them. Moa provided abundant meat, large eggs, strong bones for artefacts, and probably also feathers for clothing and adornment (Anderson 1989). An enormous number of seals also frequented the New Zealand coast, providing another major source of protein and raw material. Within a few centuries moa and a number of other birds were extinct and seal colonies were largely confined to remote regions of the South Island. Fish and shellfish, always a significant component of the diet, became even more important (Anderson and McGlone 1992).

Horticulture based on the introduced plants was possible only in warmer northern regions. A major achievement was the adaptation of the sweet potato, a tropical plant, to an annual cycle in temperate New Zealand. The tubers were lifted in the autumn and stored through the winter for food and as seed for planting in the spring. This adaptation permitted an extension of gardening as far south as the north-eastern coasts of the South Island (Yen 1961). Further south the Maori economy remained one of hunting and gathering until the introduction of potatoes and other new food crops by Europeans.

Many archaeological sites contain animal remains, and hunting and fishing at various periods are fairly well documented. Plant foods have been much more difficult to identify. Actual plant remains are rare, although there have been finds of charred berries and very occasionally carbonised remains of sweet potato tubers and bracken fern rhizomes (an important gathered plant resource). The study of prehistoric horticulture has focused on field systems and on structures assumed to have been for crop storage (Leach 1984). It has been difficult, therefore, to establish the relative importance of plant foods in general and cultivated plants in particular. Moreover, there is still disagreement as to the importance or otherwise of horticulture, even in the north, during the early centuries when wild game was abundant. There is no doubt, however, that northern regions of the country were on the whole far more favourable to Maori occupation. By the eighteenth century, the bulk of the population was concentrated in the northern half of the North Island, with extensions down the coasts as far south as Hawkes Bay and Wanganui (Pool 1991: 38, 51).

The settlers of the Chatham Islands did not succeed in establishing the dog or any of the cultivated plants. There were no moa, although seals were abundant. The Moriori economy was always dependent on hunting and gathering and was very heavily oriented towards marine resources.

The first colonists of New Zealand established their settlements in sheltered coastal locations, often adjacent to large harbours or estuaries. Relatively little is known of the layout of these settlements. No evidence has been uncovered to suggest that they were fortified. Food was cooked on hot stones in the ground, either in the open or under a shelter set apart from the dwelling house. This practice is typical of Polynesian societies. Details of houses of any age are seldom uncovered. Among the most complete house plans are those from two different sites in Palliser Bay at the southern tip of the North Island (fig. 3). These have been dated to the twelfth, and the fifteenth or sixteenth centuries, although the radiocarbon dates, on wood charcoal, may be somewhat older than the actual buildings. Both houses had the rectangular plan with porch at one end which is still seen in the meeting houses of today, suggesting that the spatial organisation of Maori houses has considerable antiquity (Prickett 1979; Leach

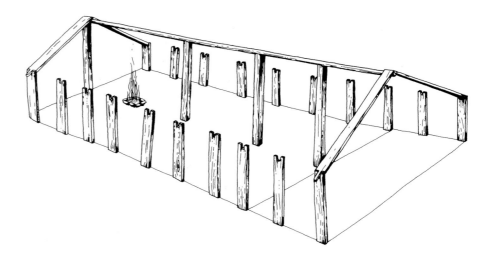

3 Partial reconstruction of a fifteenth or sixteenth century Maori house in Palliser Bay at the southern tip of the North Island, based on archaeological evidence. From Davidson 1984.

1979). Often there was a cemetery on the edge of the early settlements. One of the most famous of these early sites is at Wairau Bar in the northern South Island, dated to between the eleventh and thirteenth centuries, which seems to have been a centre of stone tool making (fig. 4). Grave goods from Wairau have been important in defining the material culture of the early period (Duff 1956).

As the population grew and resources in some areas became scarcer, intergroup tensions increased. Fortified settlements suddenly appeared in most parts of the country shortly before AD 1500 (fig. 5). It is possible that earlier settlements were fortified by palisades, although no evidence of this has yet been found. By 1500, however, fortifications included complex arrangements of ditches and banks as well as palisades. More than 6,000 *pā* (as these fortified settlements were called) have been recorded. They are concentrated in areas of high population; fewer than 200 are in the South Island. The majority are pre-European in age; they range in size from tiny sites which can be described as fortified homesteads to huge complexes of earthworks covering many hectares (Fox 1976; Davidson 1987). It has recently been argued that in the world context, these large sites can be considered to be urban settlements (Bulmer, in preparation). Although the threat of war was always present, at least during the last three hundred years of prehistory, there were quite long periods when particular regions enjoyed relative peace and fortifications fell into disuse. There were no *pā* in the Chatham Islands; the isolated Moriori were not involved in warfare when their islands were rediscovered in the late eighteenth century, although their traditions referred to former wars.

Settlement patterns varied from region to region. In late prehistoric times, small groups of hunter-gatherers in the far south ranged over large territories, whereas northern groups were more sedentary. However, most if not all social groups moved about a defined territory, to seasonal fishing and hunting camps, while maintaining a central settlement which might or might not be fortified. Social organisation was fluid and flexible; Maori throughout New Zealand held similar concepts of social organisation and land tenure, despite considerable differences in economy and settlement pattern from north to south.

Changes in social and religious life and settlement pattern are more difficult to document than changes in economy and material culture. Particularly in northern regions, there are a great many archaeological sites, ranging from *pā* to small hamlets. Only a few are remembered in oral traditions and the limitations of dating methods make it extremely difficult to determine which were contemporaneous. In some areas there were marked changes in land use and settlement pattern through time, while in others a similar way of life marked by similar types of settlements seems to have continued for centuries (Davidson 1984: 163–71). Detailed regional studies are documenting this variation (e.g. Leach and Leach 1979; Sutton (1990).

The appearance of fortifications was a major change, but in many cases fortifications were superimposed on an existing settlement pattern, rather

4 The setting of the Wairau Bar archaeological site, a typical early settlement at the mouth of a large estuary. The excavation was on the inner (right hand) side of the boulder bank, beyond the trees. Photo Kevin Jones, Department of Conservation, Wellington.

5 Rangihoua Pā, Bay of Islands, Northern New Zealand. Rangihoua, a terraced *pā* on a cliff edge, was inhabited in the early nineteenth century. The setting is typical of many coastal fortifications. Remains of ditched field systems can be seen to the left of the *pā*. Photo Kevin Jones, Department of Conservation, Wellington.

than representing a new departure. In the late prehistoric period *pā* represented the heart of the community territory and were symbols of *mana* (prestige) and strength. Although the restricted space within most fortifications precluded the inclusion of a *marae* (ceremonial ground) as we know it today, the essential elements of this type of open space in front of a principal building, built to the same general plan as the modern meeting house, were probably present. *Pā* are one of the features that distinguish Maori from other Eastern Polynesian societies. Large fortifications are found in Fiji, Tonga and Samoa, but not in the Society or Cook Islands, where warfare was practised in different ways. On the other hand, New Zealand lacks the large, formal religious edifices that characterised many Eastern Polynesian societies in the late prehistoric period: the *marae* of the Society and Cook Islands, the *ahu* of Easter Island, or the *heiau* of Hawai'i. Communal labour and communal prestige were invested in *pā*, rather than in religious structures.

This is not to suggest that religion was unimportant in Maori society. On the contrary, it permeated all aspects of life. But just as the early explorers were unable to recognise evidence of religious practice, archaeology has been able to contribute little to the understanding of Maori religion. Most conspicuous is a change in burial practice from the cemeteries associated with the early settlements to the custom of hiding bones in caves and other secret places after temporary interment or exposure followed by ritual scraping of the bones (Davidson 1984: 172–7). This two-stage cycle of mourning is perpetuated today in the ceremonial unveiling of a memorial stone one or more years after burial. Archaeologically documented examples of religious practice include the ritual disposal of items which were *tapu* (ritually dangerous) in a special place in a swamp adjacent to a settlement; the ritual burial of a dog jaw beneath the principal post of a house; and the deposition of obsidian flakes in a pool beneath a freshwater spring (Davidson 1984: 172).

The first European sighting of New Zealand was in 1642 by Abel Tasman, who left a tantalising account of his brief and unhappy contact with Maori in the northern South Island. Far more detailed records were left by English and French visitors in the late eighteenth century: Cook, Surville and Marion du Fresne. Their accounts and those of later visitors provide a rich source of information about some aspects of Maori life at the close of the prehistoric period (Salmond 1991). It was these visits that shattered Maori isolation and began the process of interaction which culminated in British colonisation in the nineteenth century.

Although Maori were quick to adopt aspects of European material culture along with pigs, potatoes and other crops, tribal life continued relatively unchanged in most respects well into the nineteenth century. A notable exception was the upheaval caused by intertribal warfare using muskets, which was intense during the 1820s and 1830s. This resulted in changes to the location and nature of fortifications and led to both temporary and permanent population movements.

Tools and *taonga* ('treasures')

In studying pre-European material culture, archaeologists have often contrasted early archaeological assemblages from excavated sites such as Wairau Bar with the range of objects described in the late eighteenth century and preserved in museums but not well documented by modern excavation. This approach resulted in a polarisation which did not help in understanding the processes of adaptation and change that were at work in Maori society. Moreover, until recently there has been a tendency to assume that changes in art and material culture were associated with economic changes and were spread by tribal conquest and migration. The view taken here is that innovations in material culture may have taken place at different times and places, and are more likely to have spread through friendly contact and gift exchange than through conquest.

Stone tools

A Maori saying, *he iti toki, e rite ana ki te tangata* (though the adze be small, yet does it equal a man), reflects the pre-eminence of stone adzes and chisels among Maori tools. Large tools were needed for making canoes and shaping the timbers of buildings while smaller ones executed intricate decorations on wooden objects.

Maori ancestors brought with them from tropical Polynesia a well-developed technology for shaping adze preforms by conchoidal flaking and finishing them by hammer dressing and grinding. In New Zealand they found stone resources eminently suited to this technology. Major manufacturing centres grew up on the Coromandel Peninsula at the source of a fine-grained basalt similar to that of the island homelands, and in the northern tip of the South Island where there were numerous outcrops of altered argillites and mudstones. Other suitable sources were found in the far south and in the Auckland area. Products from these manufactures were transported by trade and exchange over large distances (Davidson 1984: 195–200). The Chatham Islands also had sources of high-quality stone for adze making.

The early adze kit in New Zealand and the Chathams was varied, and archaeologists have identified a number of formal types similar to those of tropical Eastern Polynesia (Duff 1956). Cross-sections include rectangular and triangular, and some adzes show a marked tang or reduction of the butt to facilitate lashing to the wooden handle (fig. 6). A major change in adze technology in New Zealand was a shift to a more uniform, untanged blade of rounded quadrangular section. These later adzes were usually not flaked, but shaped by hammer dressing a suitably shaped cobble. The raw material was often a dense rock such as gabbro. Numerous different local sources were used and products were not exchanged over such large distances as the earlier adzes. The exception was adzes made from *pounamu* (New Zealand nephrite), which in more recent times were the most highly prized of all adzes. *Pounamu* is found only in relatively remote western and southern parts of the South Island, but *pounamu* adzes reached all parts of the country (fig. 7).

6 Stone adzes of the early period. BM Ethno. Left to right: NZ 13. L. 29.6 cm; NZ 12. L. 20.8 cm; NZ 11. L.24.6 cm.

7 Hafted adzes of nineteenth-century age. The smaller one has a blade of *pounamu* (nephrite). BM Ethno.
TOP: 54.12–29.66. L. 64 cm. Grey collection; BOTTOM: LMS 157. L. 55.5 cm. London Missionary Society collection.

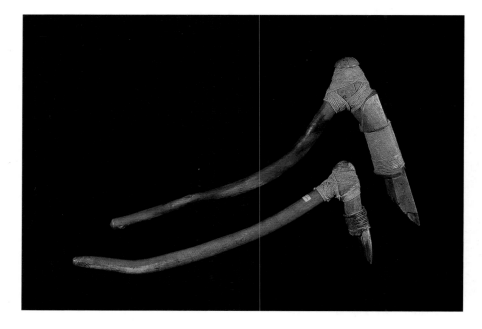

Many reasons have been advanced for the decline of the earlier adze forms and the cessation of widespread trade from the early manufactures, but no single cause has been generally accepted. The working out of the best-quality rock, the inability of the major early quarries to supply an ever-growing population, and a change in consumer preference as craftsmen learned to use other kinds of rocks in different ways may all have played a part. However, a hypothesised breakdown in trade networks as a result of warfare is unlikely, because trade in *pounamu* and other materials continued unabated. The networks did not die out, they adapted to handle other goods.

Pounamu is hard, strong and beautiful. It seems to have been valued first for its ability to take and maintain a sharp cutting edge, for the first *pounamu* items to appear in the archaeological record were adzes. Only later were its aesthetic properties exploited for personal ornaments. Although it was sometimes worked by flaking, particularly in earlier times, the more usual method was by sawing and grinding.

Obsidian (volcanic glass) and other rocks that fracture conchoidally were used extensively for knives and scrapers, but the skills of the early adze makers were not applied to the production of formal flake tools to any extent. An exception is seen in the southern South Island where large blades struck from prepared cores are found in early sites (Leach 1969) and are thought to have been associated with moa butchery. A large tanged flake tool, known as a *matā*, is found mainly in the Chatham Islands and has parallels in distant Easter and Pitcairn Islands (Jones 1981). Another specialised stone tool is a flat, polished stone knife, confined to early South Island sites and found mainly in the far south. These have often been interpreted as moa-processing tools but their use has not been demonstrated experimentally. The value placed on obsidian was probably second only to that of *pounamu* and it was traded throughout the country from

8 Carved stone pounder from Taranaki on the west coast of the North Island. Such a finely decorated object is likely to have been used ritually. BM Ethno. 1896.11–19.5. L. 29.5 cm. Presented by W. Strutt.

a number of sources in the northern half of the North Island. Obsidian from one of the main sources, Mayor Island in the Bay of Plenty, has also been found in the Chatham Islands and the Kermadecs, 755 km north-east of New Zealand (Leach *et al.* 1986).

Stone was used for a variety of other tools, such as hammers, grinders and files, which are common in sites of all ages. Stone beaters or pounders for preparing the fibre of *harakeke* (New Zealand flax) are a formal tool type not often found in excavations. Elaborately carved examples from Taranaki are a significant regional variety (fig. 8). Most of the few examples of stone beaters from excavations are from relatively late sites. However, two of rather different shape from early sites and samples of prepared *harakeke* from early contexts in a central North Island cave show that Maori quickly learned to process this valuable material (Davidson 1984: 103, 110).

Fishing and hunting equipment

Fishing was a major economic activity throughout New Zealand prehistory and fishing rights remain extremely important to the present day. Maori fishing gear included nets (sometimes of enormous size) and traps as well as a wide range of both bait hooks and lures. Relatively few fragments of nets and traps have been recovered from archaeological sites, but fish-hooks and parts thereof are common finds. In New Zealand, as elsewhere in Polynesia, they are among the most useful archaeological indicators of relative chronology. Net fishing was also important in the Chatham Islands, where only a restricted range of bone fish-hooks is found.

As with stone tools, the colonists brought with them a well-developed set of fishing gear. In the tropical Pacific this consisted of trolling lures, which usually had a pearl-shell shank and shell or bone point, and one-piece bait hooks which were often of pearl shell. The lack of pearl shell in New Zealand prompted some early adaptation. Lure shanks were made initially of bone or stone and one-piece bait hooks mostly of bone, although some use was made of local iridescent shells, both the *pāua* (*Haliotis* spp., a New Zealand form of abalone) and a gastropod of the Turbo family. Suitable bone was abundant in the form of moa bone and, to a lesser extent, sea mammal bone and ivory. Very large hooks could be fashioned from moa bone. As this resource dwindled, other materials had to be used, and one-piece hooks were progressively replaced by two-piece hooks with a separate shank and point lashed together with fine strong fibre. The shanks were often of wood, sometimes of bone or shell, while the points were predominantly of bone but sometimes of shell (fig. 9). Dog bones and teeth were popular materials. Human bone and marine mammal bones and teeth were also used. Complete specimens in museums show that the size of the point may not be a good indication of the size of the complete hook. Small one-piece hooks continued to be made of bone and shell. The development of two-piece bait hooks appears to have begun in the south and spread north, although there may have been a tropical Polynesian antecedent (Davidson 1984: 62–71).

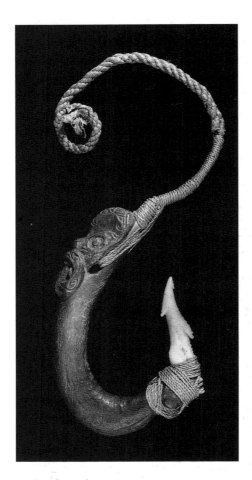

9 Two-piece fish-hook of eighteenth or early nineteenth century date, with carved wood shank, bone point and fibre snood and lashing. BM Ethno. 9356. L. 12.5 cm (excluding snood).

Trolling lures also changed through time. In northern regions, forms utilising the iridescent properties of *pāua* developed. At first these had a shank made of the thick rim of the shell, but in the nineteenth century a highly standardised form consisting of a wooden shank with a thin *pāua* shell plate became widespread. In the south a wooden shank and bone point were used. Metal points replaced bone ones in both kinds of lure during the nineteenth century, and large iron hooks were modelled on traditional styles of wooden and bone two-piece bait hooks.

Fish-hooks provide a clear archaeological reflection of a growing preference for decoration in Maori art. Early bone and shell fish-hooks were mostly plain. There was a steady increase in notching and other ornamental features which came to predominate in late prehistoric and early post-European times. Fish-hooks of this period are sometimes described as 'baroque'.

Stone sinkers were an important component of fishing gear but have been little studied. The vast majority are utilitarian, with pecked grooves to facilitate lashing, but there are some intricately carved examples. A recent find from the excavation of a late prehistoric *pā* in the far north carries a miniature expression of the distinctive northern Maori wood-carving style.

Items of hunting equipment are less often found and seem to exhibit little chronological change. Bone harpoon points were introduced by the earliest arrivals and used throughout the sequence. They are generally considered to have been used to take dolphins. Barbed bone spear points attached to long wooden shafts were used to take certain forest birds. Two examples from a site in Hawkes Bay each carry a tiny carved human figure; this is another case where small durable artefacts provide concrete archaeological evidence of motifs more often seen in wood carving. Metal versions of bird spear points, replicating the earlier bone forms, were made in the nineteenth century. Bone bird spear points are also found in the Chatham Islands.

Personal adornment

Fashions in personal adornment are another area in which marked chronological changes can be seen. The best evidence of early ornament styles comes from Wairau Bar, where complete ornaments were found with burials (Duff 1956). These included necklaces of large bone or ivory beads (known as reels) with a central pendant of real or imitation whale tooth (fig. 10), and necklaces and bracelets of 'imitation whale tooth units' in bone. Similar units have been found in many early sites throughout New Zealand, in the Chatham Islands and in contemporaneous Eastern Polynesian sites, but only rarely is there evidence of how they were worn. It is often said that there was a major change from necklaces in the early period to single pendants or clusters of pendants in later times. This argument depends largely on the archaeological evidence from Wairau Bar and the early historic records.

Among the most distinctive Maori ornaments in the eighteenth century

10 Necklace of sea mammal ivory beads and central sea mammal tooth pendant from Wairau Bar. By permission of the Museum of New Zealand Te Papa Tongarewa, Wellington. ME006315. L. of central pendant 10.8 cm.

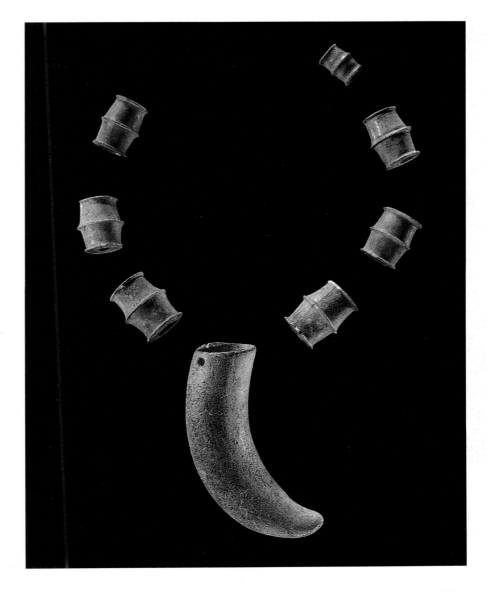

were breast and ear pendants of *pounamu*. Most famous is the *hei tiki*, a squat, stylised human figure worn as a breast pendant (fig. 29). Other formal breast pendants are rare and probably confined to certain regions: *hei matau*, or stylised fish-hooks, which were predominantly southern, and anthropomorphic or zoomorphic forms related to carving motifs, which seem to have been confined to the north. Associated with the breast pendants were bone toggles, usually made from the bones of large sea birds such as albatrosses, which were used to secure the cord at the back of the neck. Ear pendants included both straight and curved forms (fig. 28) as well as a variety of less formal and pebble shapes. These distinctive forms of Maori ornament are not found in the Chatham Islands, where whale-tooth breast pendants seem to have continued in vogue.

Pounamu pendants first appear in the archaeological record in the South Island around AD 1500. Because of their value and rarity they were seldom lost or discarded and they may therefore have originated somewhat earlier.

11 *Rei puta* or carved whale-tooth pendant with fibre cord and bone toggle, collected on Captain Cook's voyages. BM Ethno. NZ 159. L. 13.5 cm (excluding cord).

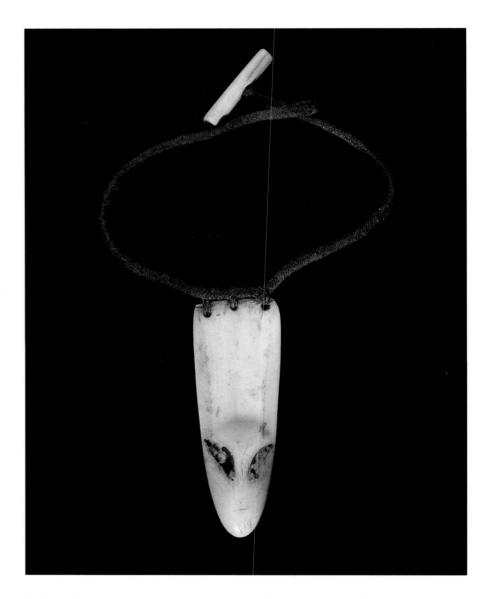

Only a few simple pendants have been found in controlled excavations in the North Island in recent decades. Although there are *hei tiki* from rich sites such as Oruarangi near Thames, turned over by curio hunters in the 1930s (Furey 1996), none has been found by an archaeologist in the last forty years.

Another rare but important form of pendant is the so-called *rei puta* (fig. 11), a shaped whale tooth with eyes, illustrated by Sydney Parkinson, an artist on Cook's first voyage (fig. 12). No *rei puta* have been found in controlled excavations, although there are examples from known archaeological sites. The *rei puta* is far more akin to the earlier Polynesian whale-tooth ornaments than are *hei tiki* or other specialised *pounamu* pendants. New Zealand museums contain other ornate and unusual pendants in stone and ivory which differ from both the archaeologically documented early types and those described in the eighteenth century. The fact that authorities are not in agreement about their likely age is a reflection of how much remains to be learned about personal ornaments.

Most ornament forms seem to have been worn by both men and women, although perhaps more often by men (fig. 12). Ornamental head combs, however, seem to have been particularly associated with the long hair and topknots favoured by men. The combs are of two sorts, a one-piece comb of bone or wood, and a composite form in which wooden tines are bound together by fibre worked in an ornamental pattern. An extremely important find of wooden combs in a waterlogged site at Kauri Point in the Bay of Plenty gives them an antiquity of at least two or three hundred years before European contact (Shawcross 1976) (fig. 13). Both one-piece and composite wooden combs have also been found in undated but pre-European contexts in dry caves, and bone combs were recovered in some numbers by curio hunters from known sites, including Oruarangi, in the earlier twentieth century. Archaeological evidence of combs before about AD 1500 is elusive, although it is likely that combs were brought to New Zealand by the earliest settlers, as they are quite widespread elsewhere in the Pacific.

There were many other forms of personal ornament: perforated teeth of dogs, seals, dolphins, sharks and humans, beads of bird bone and small tusk shells (these last particularly associated with children), pendants of shell, bone and stone and, in historic times, various perishable materials including feathers, seeds and other plant materials. Despite the apparent shift in emphasis from necklaces to single pendants, there were probably some single pendants in early times, just as some necklaces were described in historic times. There was considerable continuity in the use of items such as bird bone, tusk shell beads and perforated teeth.

A rather difficult category to identify archaeologically is the *aurei* or cloak pin, a slender curved pendant-like object of bone or ivory, perforated at one end (fig. 28). These were used to secure the cloak at the shoulder, but were also ornamental. They were well described by early explorers and nineteenth-century examples, sometimes in ivory, often carry decorative carving at the midpoint. Archaeological examples, however, are difficult to distinguish from ear pendants on one hand and the range of bone 'needles' on the other.

Any small item of value might be perforated or notched and worn as a pendant. This was particularly true of small chisels of *pounamu*. An early response to first contacts with Europeans was to convert trade goods to ornaments. Some archaeological sites which date to the early nineteenth century and have only small amounts of European material contain items such as small pieces of china and pigs' teeth which have been perforated for use as pendants. At least one of the known examples of the *Resolution* and *Adventure* medals distributed by Cook on his second voyage has been perforated for suspension.

Tattooing was (and in some parts of Polynesia still is) a major component of adornment and identity. Bone tattooing chisels are found in archaeological sites of all ages in New Zealand, as well as in early sites in Eastern Polynesia. The Moriori do not seem to have practised tattooing. In New

13 An ornamental wooden head comb from the archaeological excavations at the Kauri Point Swamp, Bay of Plenty. By permission of the Waikato Museum of Art and History, Te Whare Taonga ō Waikato, Hamilton. 1973/50/405. Photo Anthropology Department, University of Auckland. L. 10.3 cm.

12 'Portrait of a New Zeland Man', pen and wash portrait of 'Otegoowgoow' of the Bay of Islands by Sydney Parkinson, 1769. This chief's son is wearing a *rei puta*, an ear pendant of *pounamu*, and a *heru* or ornamental head comb, as well as a finely woven cloak of *harakeke* (New Zealand flax). His tattoo is typical of the northern region. By permission of the British Library. Add. MS 23920, f. 54.

Zealand, the widest blades are found in early sites, and it has been suggested that this may reflect a preference for more rectilinear patterns in earlier times. However, narrow blades seem to have been used at all periods. Museum collections contain some interesting examples of nineteenth-century tattooing sets which contain both bone and metal blades, neatly arranged in leather containers.

Other objects

Various other bone objects have been recovered from archaeological sites. Needles range from fine slender items only a few centimetres long with perforations of less than 1 mm in diameter to long robust specimens often described as thatching needles; they include less formal, perforated slivers of bird bone sometimes interpreted as fish threaders. There are also awls and pickers of various kinds. The fine delicate needles from early sites suggest fine sewing on plaited or woven garments, although actual examples have not been recovered.

Bone chisels, made of moa bone in early times and later of human or sea mammal bone, are thought to have been used to make lashing holes in the timbers of canoes and buildings and perhaps also the perforations for suspension cords on weapons. There is little chronological change in most of these items other than a shift from moa to other bone and an increase in the use of human bone through time.

Excavations in several waterlogged sites over the last thirty years have produced a range of wooden objects not normally recovered by archaeologists (Davidson 1984: 110). These include house timbers and canoe parts, agricultural implements, beaters, wooden and bark containers, weaving sticks, spears and rare examples of other wooden weapons, and a few examples of the *pūtōrino*, a musical instrument which can be played either as a flute or as a trumpet. None of these sites is older than about AD 1500 and the items they contain are for the most part comparable to those of the early historic period. However, some unusual forms serve as a reminder that the range of late prehistoric material culture was probably wider than what has been documented by early European visitors or preserved in museum collections.

Musical instruments are seldom found. An exception is the small bone flutes made from the wing bones of large sea birds, which are common in southern sites and found also at the famous northern site of Oruarangi. This site was also the scene of considerable experimentation with the manufacture of *nguru* (short flutes) in a variety of different stones (Furey 1996).

In view of the intense archaeological interest in the prehistory of warfare in New Zealand, finds of weapons have been very disappointing. Wooden spears and the longer wooden clubs can be expected only in waterlogged sites, but the short fighting clubs or *patu* in stone and whalebone, if not the highly valued examples in *pounamu*, might be expected in normal sites. Despite finds of wooden and whalebone clubs very similar to Maori *patu* in an early site in the Society Islands, no whalebone weapons have been

14 A stone club, probably used for killing seals, from the Chatham Islands. These 'bird-shaped' stone clubs are unique to the Chatham Islands, although they have some resemblance to wooden and whalebone *wahaika* clubs from mainland New Zealand. BM Ethno. +4345. L. 29.5 cm. Presented by the Rev. W. Greenwell in 1889.

found in secure early contexts in New Zealand, although some South Island finds, particularly, are often considered likely to be early. The distinctive *patu ōnewa* or stone club, which was a standard item of equipment for warriors in the eighteenth century, is represented by only a small number of finds in late prehistoric sites. The origin and age of the apparently related stone clubs of the Chatham Islands are unknown (fig. 14).

Archaeological perspectives on Maori art

Archaeology has so far contributed little to our understanding of the development of Maori art. Finds from a dated swamp site in south Taranaki show that figurative sculpture and the double spiral motif were present by about the fifteenth century. Spirals and the *manaia* motif (in which figures are shown in profile) were being applied to wooden combs at the Kauri Point swamp by the late sixteenth or early seventeenth century. However, the majority of important wood carvings from swamps are casual finds which are undated and without context (Davidson 1984: 209–14).

As noted above, the progressive increase through time in ornamentation on bone and shell fish-hooks appears to be a reflection of a general trend towards more decoration. Rare archaeological finds of elaborately decorated objects, such as stone fishing sinkers and bone bird spear points, offer some hope that elements of regional carving styles may become datable through such finds in future.

The only substantial corpus of early artistic expression is a large number number of rock drawings in limestone shelters in the central South Island (fig. 15). Deposits in the floors of a number of these shelters have been dated before about AD 1500 and there is little evidence of later use. The majority of motifs are human or animal figures (dogs, birds, fish) (Trotter and McCulloch 1981). Rock engravings, thought to be more recent, occur sporadically in shelters in the North Island. Canoes are a favourite subject. Rock engravings and tree carvings are found in the Chatham Islands (Skinner 1923).

It has often been assumed that the art tradition brought from Eastern Polynesia was rectilinear in emphasis and involved work in small design fields. However, curvilinear motifs can be found both in the Lapita decorative system and in the art of other parts of Eastern Polynesia (Davidson 1984: 209). The South Island rock drawings show a freedom of expression, a cursive style and a use of large design fields. The numerous finds of small chisels as well as large adzes from early New Zealand sites hint at a wealth of artistic expression in wood carving of which we are woefully ignorant.

Conclusion

It may appear from this review that there was a major milestone in New Zealand prehistory around AD 1500. It is certainly the case that by this time many typical features of eighteenth-century Maori culture were already present, including *pā* and some distinctive artefact forms, while most of the characteristically Eastern Polynesian forms had disappeared.

15 Examples of typical motifs from South Island rock drawings. TOP: dog and birds; CENTRE: human figures; BOTTOM: 'bird men'. After Trotter and McCulloch 1981 and Davidson 1984.

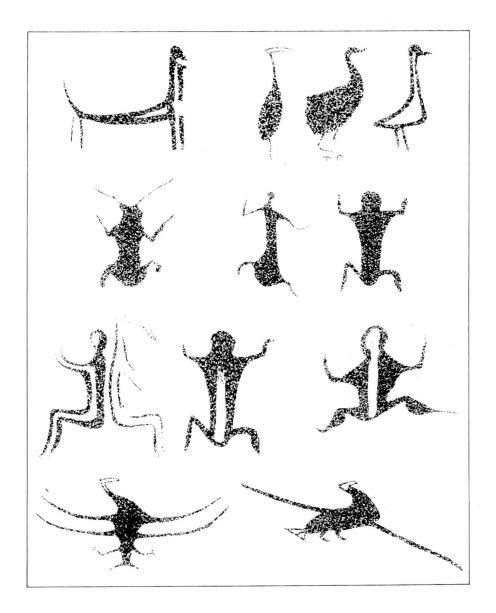

There is no evidence, however, of a sudden or dramatic change, apart perhaps from the appearance of *pā*. With more precise dates and a far better sample of artefacts from controlled archaeological excavations, we would be in a better position to document the progressive shift from Eastern Polynesian to Maori, of which at present we have only a crude and broad picture. Similarly, further archaeological work in the Chatham Islands would expand our knowledge of this most isolated Polynesian outpost. Even without additional work, however, we have some insight into the remarkable cultural adaptations of the Polynesian colonists who settled some of the most remote outposts of the world, Aotearoa and Rēkohu.

2

MAORI: PEOPLE AND CULTURE

Ngahuia Te Awekotuku

The unseen realm: deities, spirits, ancestors

He wairua kore, te Pō, te Ao	Without spirit, Darkness: Light
He wehenga rua, ka awatea;	Dawning from Their separation,
Ka puta, ko Hauora.	Emerged the Breath of Life
Ko te ao whakatupu, ka puawai.	As the world, growing, blossomed
Kua tau, kua tau . . .	And was realised . . .

(Maori text by Mamae Te Rangiaroha Takerei, 1995;
translated by Ngahuia Te Awekotuku)

They were Ranginui, the Sky Father, and Papatuanuku, the Earth Mother, both sealed together in a close embrace. Crushed between the weight of their bodies were their many children, whose oppression deepened. They yearned to be free; they fought their parents and each other to break loose. Tūmatauenga, virile god of war, thrust and shouted; Tangaroa of the oceans whirled and surged; Tawhirirangimātea howled with many raging winds; Haumiatiketike and Rongomātane, of wild foods and cultivated crops tried their best but were not successful; and Ruaumoko, god of earthquakes, yet to be born, struggled in the confinement of his mother's womb. Of them all, Tāne Mahuta, the god of the forests, was the most determined; he set his sturdy feet upon his father's chest, and braced his upper back and shoulders against the bosom of his mother. He pushed; and they parted. So the world, as the Maori understand it, came into being.

From the progeny of Papatuanuku and Ranginui came many offspring – the various inhabitants of earth, sky and water; the first humans, and the rare half-human demigods of whom Māui the Trickster has been the most acclaimed. Māui features throughout Polynesia; he netted the sun, slowing its daily course across the heavens; he fished up entire archipelagoes; he captured and commanded the essence of fire, and most ambitious of all, challenged Hinenui-te-Pō, the goddess of death – his last mission, his first and only failure.

The world was thus populated by humans, who ventured across the vast ocean to explore and enjoy the many islands. They wished to explain for themselves and their descendants the realities of the world itself. Understanding the deities – the gods and goddesses of the forest, the weather, the ocean, war-making, horticulture – also involved the understanding of the godliness in one's human self, and the need for balance among all living things. This sense of the divine, and the need to balance and engage the spiritual realm with the physical, or human, is demonstrated by the significance of two pivotal elements – *tapu* and *mana* (Te Rangihīroa 1950; Makereti 1986). Through these elements, a humble human being may relate to the divine; to the ancestors and spirits beyond one's reach, but within one's memory.

Tapu has many meanings, references and interpretations. It may be a descriptive or prescriptive condition, making an object, person or environment restricted and inaccessible to human contact, prohibited and out of bounds. It may also be a framework defining particular behaviours or sensations, ensuring a certain response. Sacred items may be regarded as *tapu*;

for example, those associated with death ritual (see below), or the body parts of a chiefly person, particularly the head. Similarly, a menstruating woman may be seen as being in a *tapu* state, at the peak of her arcane power as a breeding female.

Personal ornaments – hair combs, earrings, and pendants – were *tapu*, and especially so if they adorned an aristocrat, for they carried his or her vital essence, and, if handled inappropriately or malevolently, could cause considerable harm. Unless taken with deliberate malice, an item was usually safe from casual theft, because *tapu* was an effective sanction. Similarly, *tapu* related to certain types of knowledge – of genealogy, of chant forms, of navigational mnemonic and astronomic devices, of healing techniques. Within the framework of *tapu*, information and its dissemination were regulated and controlled, and only people properly trained and initiated gained access. On a more mundane level, again as a protective function, such places as burial caves, sites of the disposal of miscarriages, afterbirth or incidental remains of hair and nail clippings, menstrual napkins and medical dressings, were acutely *tapu* and sacrosanct.

Balancing the notion of *tapu*, though not in perfect dichotomy, is the notion of *noa*. This pertains to mundane, ordinary objects and functions – household and serving utensils, the acts of preparing and eating food, the many small and common interactions of everyday life. *Noa* is safe – without preternatural sanction or restricted association, it is demonstrated by the lifting of the condition of *tapu* from a particular environment or object. A newly built house, ornamented and fresh, would be considered *tapu* – unsafe, prohibited, raw with spirit and inaccessible to the common touch of people. Making the place *noa* – 'blessing' it in current terms – would involve ritual, and the crossing of the threshold, usually by a high-born woman. Her special form of *tapu* would counter the energies within the house, and thus render it *noa*, and safe for general entry. Such ritual continues to be observed today; even in the context of an ethnological or fine arts exhibition, these procedures are followed, to appease the ancestral forces who may generate *tapu*, which imbues the objects with dread or beauty. It also renders the space safe for mere curious mortals, most of whom may not otherwise have the *mana* to cope.

Mana, like *tapu*, is a pan-Pacific concept. It has layers and levels of meaning: primarily, it is about power and empowerment, about authority and the right to authorise. Charisma, personal force, social status, princely charm, leadership inherited or achieved are all forms of *mana*; it is a subjective human quality, measured by various means. Two of the most important were *mana whenua* and *mana tangata*. *Mana whenua* implies stewardship of vast acreages of land in which one controls the economic resources – fisheries, horticulture, rat runs, bird snaring and related activities. *Mana tangata* reflects the importance of people, of the complex social and political relationships that secure a community's alliances and effective leadership; a successful chief would embody *mana tangata*.

Just as they are rich with the *tapu* of their former owners or makers, objects – *taonga* or treasures – may also carry their *mana*. *Toki poutangata*

16 Ceremonial adze, *toki poutangata*, an emblem of chiefly authority and spiritual power. The highly polished nephrite blade is lashed to the carved haft with flax braided cord. BM Ethno. 1900.5–19.1. L. 50 cm.

(ceremonial adzes) (fig. 16) are specific emblems of chiefly power; their adze shape may symbolise building for the future and they represent *mana* and authority. *Hei tiki* (nephrite neck ornaments) are not only *tapu* by their intimacy with the wearer, but they absorb the person's *mana*, and in some instances may be associated with the collective or accumulated *mana* of succeeding generations. Another example is weaponry; like ornaments, they may have personal names. These names indicate their lethal nature; they also consume the *mana* of those whom they slay, and are treated with considerable reverence and caution.

Management of the potent energies of *mana* and *tapu* required adepts trained in a specialised system of knowledge, skilled in the complexities of ritual and the protocols of mediating between the realms of spirit and humankind. Such training occurred in the *whare wānanga*, the college of priests or higher school of learning, attended by carefully selected young people. They emerged as *tohunga* – priestly experts, shamans or specialists. The oral records describe such institutions as being single-sex, for males or for females, though only the male establishments occur in the written accounts (Best 1924; Te Rangihīroa 1950; Makereti 1986). Certainly, their graduates impressed early visitors from the northern hemisphere: Robert

Graves describes the *tohunga* Maori as an ollave (a Gaelic equivalent) in *The White Goddess* thus:

among the Maoris of New Zealand ... the capacity of the ollave to memorize, comprehend, elucidate and extemporize staggered Governor Grey and other early British observers. (Graves 1971: 457)

Maori society was highly ritualised, although the rituals occurred within flexible parameters – they presented a form of theatre, invited and ensured the presence of the deceased and the relevant deities, and protected the welfare of the community, guarding against the profane or hostile. Rituals could be humble yet sublime, like the harvesting of flax for garment making in which Huna, the flax goddess, was invoked in friendly conversation; or they could be complex and choreographed. Examples of the latter include the elaborate procedures undertaken by a canoe designer, his working crew and the shaman *tohunga* in approaching a majestic forest tree marked for felling and transforming into a sea-going vessel.

Rituals of encounter, dialogue and farewell were also important, and continue to be enacted even in the 1990s, though with minor adaptations (Karetu 1977). The basic structure has remained: the keening chant of women, addressing the deceased, identifying the living; the exchange of poetic orations, usually between learned men; and the resolution of the dialogue by music and chant. Often, this is preceded by a warrior's aggressive martial challenge to the leaders of the visiting party. Members of the British royal family have experienced this on a number of occasions, in both ceremonial and quite literal, contexts. In ancient times, the practice was to ascertain the intent of the party approaching; if the potential for any unpleasantness was revealed, the ritual would then become a rout.

Critical points in one's life were also ritually observed (Te Rangihīroa 1950, Makereti 1986). In some tribal areas, it is said that a child would be dedicated at birth to a particular deity, such as Tūmatauenga (war), Rongonui (peaceful pursuits) and Hine-te-Iwaiwa (midwifery and healing). Certainly, at the time of death strict protocols were followed to ensure the deceased enjoyed a swift, unencumbered flight to the world of spirit, and reunion with the ancestors and other, familiar, departed. This ritual was *tangihanga*: the deceased lay in state, to be visited, mourned over and spoken to; the ceremonies often continued for many days, even weeks, as people came from throughout the land to pay their respects, especially for someone of great *mana* (Dansey 1977). Related to the death ritual and mortuary custom was the practice of decapitation and head-preservation, allowing the very visage of a beloved leader, consort, father or warrior chief to remain with the family and community long after death. This was done, however, at the risk of theft and defilement. At the time of European contact, a nefarious trade began in preserved heads – such *taonga* became more than battlefield trophies; they became collectible artificial curiosities (Robley 1896).

Tangihanga remain a prominent cultural practice today; they continue to determine who, and what, is Maori, since they retain the recitation of genealogical chant that is the true source of Maori community. They link the people to the gods and goddesses, who were their primal parents.

Whiringa tāngata: the patterns of Maori society

E hara taku toa	My strength comes not
i te toa takitahi	From one source
Engari takimano	But from thousands;
nō aku tupuna.	From my ancestors.

(Maori proverb,
translated by Ngahuia Te Awekotuku)

Māori, according to Williams (1975), means clear, fresh or natural, as in *waimāori* – a fresh-water spring; it also means usual or ordinary, not distinctive (Williams 1975). In their encounters from the eighteenth century onwards with voyagers and settlers from the northern hemisphere, the original inhabitants recognised themselves as ordinary, as belonging to a collective group different from the new arrivals. To these people they described themselves as Maori.

The Maori trace their descent to the arrival of the first canoes from Eastern Polynesia; during the centuries that followed more arrived and communities flourished in the coastal margins and explored the hinterland, settling in arable valleys. These early voyagers were linked with their *waka*, great voyaging canoes, of which Arawa, Tainui and Mātaatua are three famous examples. Over succeeding generations extensive societal networks evolved and formed the most broadly defined social grouping. In many instances this was known as a *waka*, and was named in memory of the founding canoe.

Waka further divided into *iwi*, or tribes, descended from individual crew members; thus Arawa, Tainui and Mātaatua may be described as three separate confederations, each one embracing a number of loosely associated tribes who were often adversaries, particularly on the issues of territorial boundaries. *Iwi* segmented into *hapū*, sub-tribes or tribal sections, whose members were descended from the same founder. *Hapū* were the most visible and economically distinctive association. Political and economic alliances and accords were made with other confederate *iwi*, but the *hapū* functioned primarily as an autonomous unit, living within its own vigilantly maintained and guarded domains. Illicit trespass and the poaching of economic resources – birds, fish, rats, nephrite – caused armed confrontations that sometimes took decades to resolve.

Whānau were the smallest social unit; a number of *whānau* or extended families constituted a *hapū*. They were inter-generational, consisting of grandparents, their children and their grandchildren, and lived, if not in the same group of dwellings, then in close proximity to each other. Movement between households varied; women usually went to their husband's *whānau*, although men shifted around too, particularly those who enjoyed multiple relationships. If a *whānau* numbered more than two or three hundred people, across generations, it evolved into a *hapū*, and thus assumed a political identity. This development is anticipated by the word *whānau* itself which means birthing, implying the birthing of new generations. The terms *iwi* and *hapū* also reflect the Maori world view: *iwi* literally translates as bones, and *hapū* means gestation, pregnancy. Together these terms – *iwi, hapū, whānau* – present a metaphor of the visceral relationships that bind people within Maori society.

Genealogy, or *whakapapa*, was crucial to the institutions of leadership and aristocracy. *Whakapapa* was the recitation of the (literal) making of layers of descent: the naming of original voyagers from Eastern Polynesia, and beyond to the gods and goddesses themselves. Every Maori person familiar with her or his *whakapapa* could claim this exalted ancestry, despite the mean realities of possible enslavement in war or conquest of land. No conqueror or coloniser had the power to deny Maori their *whakapapa*, though they could, and often did, deny them descendants. *Whakapapa* recitation was often aided by a specially designed mnemonic staff (fig. 17), through which successive personalities and their various adventures could be narrated.

Within these parameters, social classes did exist, but they could be quite mobile, as many factors shaped effective chieftainship. Being the first born of the first born was an impressive line of descent; but the concept of exclusively male primogeniture may have been introduced with Christianity, since in many genealogies gender is often disputed. Primogeniture, however, defined the *ariki*, or paramount chief's, family; such a family enmeshed the descent lines of all the principal ancestors in an *iwi* association, exerting political influence over the *iwi* as a whole. Such leadership was, however, comparatively rare, although in the nineteenth century charismatic chiefs of this calibre emerged in direct response to the threat of invasion by remote, alien forces – the colonial settlers and militia. The most notable example was Pōtatau Te Wherowhero, who was elevated as the first Maori King in 1858. His direct linear descendants dominated nineteenth- and twentieth-century Aotearoa/New Zealand as warriors, visionaries and negotiators of awesome talent, through the Kīngitanga, or Maori King Movement, which continues to this day (Mahuta 1978).

Principal responsibility for *hapū* leadership, direction and defence rested with the *rangatira*, or chiefs (Winiata 1967). Unlike the status of *ariki*, *rangatira* status could be either inherited or achieved. *Rangatira* were essentially managers, distinguished by the capacity for hard work, inventive thinking, martial prowess and diplomatic skills that were considered chiefly attributes, as well as the maintenance of food resources and the storage of surplus that ensured contentment in the community, and provision in case of war. Although the ethnographic record declares that most *rangatira* were male, oral and genealogical accounts describe the achievements of many women, both in the horticultural settlements and on the battlefields (Mahuika 1977). Through descent lines, women were *rangatira* in their own right, as Maori traced descent through both parents, and they were of equal importance in reckoning inheritance of property and clan affinity.

The *tohunga* stood apart from other people. They were usually *rangatira*,

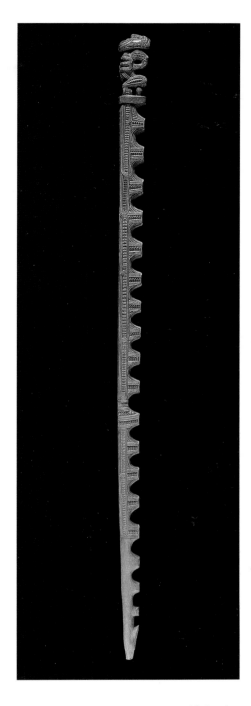

17 Genealogical staff, a memory aid for the ritual recitation of *whakapapa*, or genealogy. This staff counts eighteen successive generations preceding the original owner. BM Ethno. 1854.12–29.22. L. 103.5 cm. Grey collection.

as selection for the *whare wānanga* (higher school of learning) occurred in this class. *Tohunga* were experts in a range of specialities which included tattooing, carving and house construction, medicine, healing and midwifery, sorcery, music, weather casting and astronomy, and the encyclopaedic storage of information. They mediated between the realms of human and divine, recording their insights and experiences in both narrative recitation and simple story-telling. Some *tohunga* were itinerant, travelling from settlement to settlement within tribal boundaries, and they were highly respected and sometimes deeply feared. Since particular traits, such as prodigious memory, talent in design, clairvoyance and verbal creativity, were regarded as inherited, *tohunga* families tended to intermarry.

Social relationships were fluid. Hard work, martial talent, exceptional weaving ability, fine design skills and inspiring oratory never went unnoticed; everyone had leadership potential, just as they had *rangatira* descent. *Mana*, and recognition, accrued by achievement. And *mana* could also be lost, irretrievably, by enslavement as a prisoner of war. Slaves were a labouring underclass within the community; the more comely became concubines and, very rarely, consorts whose children assumed the free parent's status. As well as keeping rare prisoners of war, some *hapū* subjugated their neighbours, reaping the benefits of economic control and production and, eventually, assimilating the vanquished. Resistance was fatal, but often chosen in preference to the prospect of ownership by and subjection to another *hapū*.

Marriage was flexible, depending on the couple involved (Makereti 1986; Biggs 1960). Political alliances were frequently confirmed by arranged marriage between leading families. Monogamy was not an established convention, for *rangatira* had many spouses, a practice enjoyed mainly by chiefly men, although oral history and genealogy record polyandrous relationships, too, for aristocratic women. Dissatisfaction was enough to dissolve a liaison; the parties simply moved apart, unless there were issues of *mana*, property and alliance at risk. In these instances, the proceedings involved complex rituals of confrontation and retribution in which the slighted party's family claimed compensation and redress. Their demands were usually satisfied by the presentation of valued items – fine textiles, nephrite ornaments and chiefly weapons (Te Rangihīroa 1950: 371) – though in some instances such items were forcibly taken rather than volunteered.

Sexuality was enjoyed in many forms. People chose partners of either sex for pleasure, and same-sex love was not condemned or vilified (Te Awekotuku 1991). Continuing one's line – having children – was nevertheless a priority. High performance and erotic skill were greatly admired, and accomplished individuals, both male and female, feature prominently in chant poems of their time, their physical attributes and relevant behaviours fondly detailed (Ngata 1959, 1961).

One class of person was sheltered from excessive carnal adventures. This was the *puhi*, a young aristocratic female whose role included receiving guests and appropriate suitors, and participation in ritual activities; it is not clear if she was forbidden sexual contact with just men, or both sexes, though she had at least one intimate female attendant at all times (Makereti 1986). *Puhi* featured in many famous stories as headstrong and charismatic individuals – Hinemoa of Arawa, Puhihuia of Tainui, Wairaka of Mātaatua and Ruapūtāhanga of Taranaki – proving that they were perceived, and perceived themselves, as much more than makers of peace through exogamous marriage.

The role and status of women may have varied in pre-Christian Maori society, differing from *iwi* to *iwi*, and *hapū* to *hapū*. However, the high incidence of female representation in art (fig. 18), and the related narrative in chant poems and genealogy, indicate a complementary, not inferior, relationship to men, and acknowledgement of a woman's singular status as *whare tangata* – the 'bearer of the house of humankind', the 'progenitrix of people' (Te Awekotuku 1991).

Elderly people were revered, and they contributed to the community until well into their dotage. They came from the past and shaped the present; their counsel was respected, and the wisdom of their accumulated experience was listened to. *Kaumātua* (old men) and *kuia* (old women) were deeply involved in child-rearing; they looked after and taught the young, often from birth, a situation which continues today in rural communities. They never actually retired from working, though as age may have slowed them down, the engagement of one or many *mokopuna* (grandchildren) as helpers or apprentices ensured the jobs were done and the skills passed on. In this relationship, direct links of descent were not absolute; children and old people were drawn to each other, and just as different children were breast-fed by different mothers, so a child could be more emotionally attached to an aunt or a grandmother, than to her or his biological mother. Responsibility for the nurturing and raising of children was shared, both between age-peers and across generations (Ritchie 1979).

The enduring land

Whatungarongaro te tangata: Humankind fades away:
toi tu te whenua.   The land endures.
(Maori proverb)

Papatuanuku is the Earth Mother, combining all elements of the planet; her immediate form is *whenua*, the land. Continuing the organic metaphor, *whenua* is also the Maori word for the placenta, which is promptly buried with simple ritual after birth. The practice is still observed today, even in cities; thus the word itself reflects the relationship between people and the land, clearly stated in the concept of *tangata whenua* (Te Awekotuku 1991).

To be *tangata whenua* is to claim stewardship and economic use and settlement of a defined area. The words translate as 'people of the land', people whose afterbirth is buried there, and whose kinship to each other is described in the preceding section. For this reason, and the reverence for Papatuanuku as Earth Mother, there was no concept of land as a marketable commodity or object to be owned in the European sense, and sub-

18 *Tekoteko*, gable apex figure of a small house, representing an important female ancestor, carved in the Hawkes Bay style of the early nineteenth century. BM Ethno. 1642. H. 35 cm.

sequently much strife arose during the early Pākehā (European) settlement period, and continues to this day.

To reinforce the *hapū*'s association with the land, *rangatira* often named certain sections of land after their own body parts, extending the *tangata whenua* concept. Te Pane-ō-Horoiwi (the Head of Horoiwi) and Te Rae-a-Rangikawhata (Rangikawhata's Forehead) are examples (Kelly 1949, Stafford 1994), made potent by their reference to the head or parts of the face. If such places were threatened by invasion, the descendants of the original name-giver were fiercely motivated to defend it and retain its stewardship.

Boundaries were determined by prominent features of the landscape – rivers, mountains, streams, lakes and coastlines – and individuals identified themselves by naming these features. Thus a speaker of Tainui heritage could introduce herself at a gathering: *Ko Tainui te waka, Taupiri te maunga, Waikato te awa, he piko he taniwha* ('Tainui is the nation, Taupiri is the mountain, and Waikato is the river where a dragon dwells at every bend'). The dragon here is a chiefly warrior and the recitation clearly states the speaker's background. In oratory or prose-poetry and chant an *ariki* might be alluded to not by her or his personal name, but by a distinctive geographic feature, enhancing her or his *mana* accordingly; for example: *Kua tae mai a Tongariro* ('The mountain, Tongariro, has arrived'). Here the image refers to the paramount chief Te Heuheu who lived beneath the smooth cone of this sleeping volcano.

Land – the tribal estate – was the prime economic resource of the people. It represented their collective *mana*, but more importantly it provided their livelihood (Firth 1959; Kawharu 1977). Fresh- and salt-water fisheries, shellfish beds, bird-snaring groves, rat runs, and acreages of sweet potato cultivation and fern root grounds defined the wealth of a community. Conservation practices were observed with regard to both fisheries and birdlife through the *rāhui* system, which warned people to observe seasonal restrictions on food gathering and fishing. Penalties were severe when poaching did occur. To appropriate another *hapū*'s resources was seen as a declaration of war, and boundaries were frequently marked by plain or carved posts or staffs driven into the ground. Surplus food was kept in *pātaka*, or storehouses (fig. 46), often ornamented with visual references to human fertility (couples embracing) or an abundant food supply (symbolised by whale motifs on the bargeboards). Crops of *kūmara* (sweet potato, the most important food in the Maori diet) were stored in cool underground pits with expertly fitted doorways.

Stewardship of land implied the exploitation of other resources as well. Plantations of *harakeke* (*Phormium tenax*: New Zealand flax) were highly valued, as were the elevated forest vaults of *kiekie* (*Freycinetia baueriana*) used extensively in basketry and matmaking. Some areas had unique resources, such as *pounamu* (nephrite) and obsidian. Whalebone was another coveted material found in some coastal areas. All of these commodities were traded from island to island and *kāinga* to *kāinga* (Firth 1959), being carried across land in sturdy backpacks or conveyed by canoe along extensive waterways and over the sea.

Kāinga, meaning a place to eat, is the word for village or settlement. Usually located near or upon a fresh-water source – springs, a stream, lake or riverside – they were within easy running distance of a *pā*, or hill-top fort with natural and constructed defence systems. *Pā* and *kāinga* often assimilated each other, as the populations changed seasonally. Areas of food cultivation were often some distance from the *hapū*'s permanent village, and makeshift dwellings were common (Makereti 1986). Populations varied – many villages supported only a few households, totalling no more than a hundred folk, others were densely occupied, with thousands of people. Such villages displayed their wealth with ornate storehouses, magnificent war canoes, rare weaponry and fine houses; their people were also fashionably attired, with fine jewellery and body adornment.

Community business was conducted on the *marae*. Larger settlements had more than one such site, but one was always the most prestigious. A *marae* is the open plaza or forecourt of a meeting house (figs 37, 38), community house or the leading chief's personal dwelling. Visitors are received on the *marae* – challenged and welcomed and embraced; negotiations occur there, disputes are conducted and (most of the time) resolved. Even today, the *marae* remains the pivotal site of Maori political and economic negotiation. It is also the location of ceremony and celebration; it is a place to rest one's feet, to make a stand, to claim one's rights. It is a place that pulsates with the *mauri*, the essential spirit or metaphysical sense of being part of the community and of the land. *Mauri* can be manifest within a natural object or an artefact – a carved stone, sculptured wood, talismanic nephrite. Thus it may travel, even across the world, so that the *marae*, as a physical venue or site, may be constructed in the galleries of an overseas institution (Mead 1986a). For it is Maori belief that wherever Maori people gather for Maori purposes and with the appropriate Maori protocol, a *marae* is formed at that time, for that time, unless it is contested.

Contesting the stewardship of land – claiming prior rights of bird snaring or harvesting, or simply coveting the natural resources of healing mineral springs, nephrite rivers or stands of *kauri* pine forest – was cause for war, as was the desire for retribution, *utu*, over a real or alleged slight or an unresolved difference. *Utu*, the avenging of a wrong, was a powerful influence in the making of war, and war was a seasonal way of life for the ancient Maori.

The ways of war: the way of the warrior

Tūmatauenga was worshipped as the god of war; his season was the summer months between late November and early April, when wild food was bountiful in the forests and fisheries, and days were long, thus ensuring sufficient nourishment and time for a war band on the trail.

Traditional Maori warfare – fighting technique, military strategy and leadership structures – puzzled Western observers and ethnographers (Vayda 1960; Best 1927; Smith 1910). They judged the Maori at war as lacking effective and visible command, capricious and poorly organised; they seldom acknowledged that they witnessed a corruption and drastic

19 War Dance at Maketu, Bay of Plenty, watercolour by H.G. Robley, 1864. This image captures the synchronised vigour and ferocity of a war party preparing to go into battle. Weapons include long and short clubs, and the recently introduced tomahawks, long axes and firearms. A palisaded fort, with a carved gateway, is in the background. By permission of the Museum of New Zealand Te Papa Tongarewa, Wellington.

upheaval of traditional systems caused by firearms and Pākehā military advisors. Reconstructing the ancient methods of warfare necessitates a scrutiny of primarily the oral record – chant poetry and genealogy.

War parties (fig. 19) comprised members of a *hapū*; almost all were mature males, though women were trained in martial arts, especially for the final defence of home and children. Many tribal histories celebrate the triumphs of female war chiefs, but they are outnumbered by their male counterparts (Mahuika 1977). A fighting party led by a *rangatira* contained around seventy members, the average complement of a *waka taua* (war canoe), though some canoes carried as many as a hundred and forty warriors; such a company was called '*Te Hokowhitu ā Tū*', the chosen contingent of Tū (Tūmatauenga) himself. *Rangatira* motivated rather than commanded the Maori fighter, who was essentially a volunteer not a conscript; he chose to go into battle for his own reasons (Gardiner 1992).

In the field the deployment of smaller groups proved most effective; these highly mobile, compact units of warriors engaged the enemy in short, fast skirmishes, attacking by surprise. Dawn was the preferred time for such ambuscades; stealth, then alarm, was a favoured tactic, aided by the heavy rainforest environment of narrow trails and natural camouflage. Attack, engagement and hasty withdrawal formed the most common field strategy; few captives were taken, unless they had political, nutritional or symbolic value. The aim was to leave no one alive to seek vengeance.

Palisade fighting – the attack and overwhelming of fortified villages – was much more carefully orchestrated on both sides, and prolonged sieges

20 ABOVE Detail of a whipsling, *kōtaha*, a device for the launching of sharp darts and fiery projectiles. The design is deliberately provocative: with her feet pressed beneath her large head, a female figure exposes her vulva between two spiral-ornamented thighs. This example was collected on Captain Cook's voyages. BM Ethno. NZ 75. H. of figure 12.5 cm.

21 ABOVE RIGHT Long clubs, three of wood and one of whalebone. Left to right: plain *pouwhenua*; *taiaha*, with decorative wool binding and tassels of dog hair; *tewhatewha*, with ornamental bunch of feathers; *hoeroa*, with finely carved end. BM Ethno. 4877, L. 158.5 cm; TRH 24, L. 159.5 cm, Royal Loan 1902; 1854.12–29.78, L. 155 cm, Grey collection; 1903.11–16.3, L. 128.5 cm, Bequest of Francis Brent.

did occur, though it was more common for the aggressor to withdraw if the omens or conditions seemed inauspicious, and to return at another time (Te Rangihīroa 1950; Best 1927). Combat was immediate and hand-to-hand, and individual 'heroes' could be 'called out' and challenged, or marked by an ambitious opponent. This style of fighting is lucidly demonstrated by the range of weaponry; apart from the whipsling, *kōtaha* (fig. 20) for propelling darts, possibly used in firing the palisades, the ancient Maori had no projectiles.

There were two principal types of weaponry – the short club and the long club or staff. The latter were made of wood and used with both hands. They included colourful *taiaha*, ornamented *tewhatewha* with an axe-like head, and plain but effective *pouwhenua*. There was also the *hoeroa*, made from elegantly curved whalebone (fig. 21). Measuring between 1.5 and 2.7 m long, depending on the height of the wielder, these long weapons thrust, parried and sliced, maintaining a defensive radius. If this radius were broken, the short club was engaged. Some fighters preferred to use only

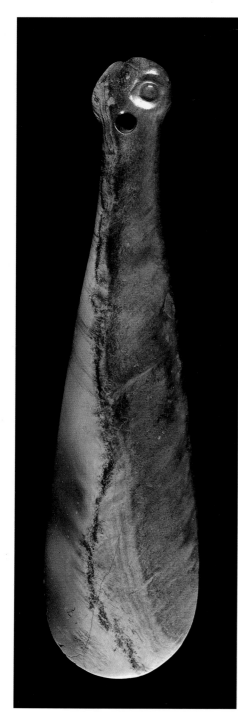

22 Short nephrite club, *mere pounamu*. This was manipulated like a cleaver, with slicing motions to the head, neck and joints of the enemy's body. It was considered the most prestigious of chiefly weapons. This specimen is unlike any other known example as the grip is carved into a *manaia* instead of a plain finish. BM Ethno. 1907.12–23.1. L. 37 cm. Presented by C.H. Read.

short weapons, though both types were carried into combat, the staff in hand, and the club tucked into a folded fibre belt. Short clubs were grasped in either hand, and struck, jabbed and sliced in swift, dance-like motions. The most prestigious were *mere pounamu* of nephrite (fig. 22), whose spatulate shape was also worked in whalebone as *patu parāoa*, and stone as *patu ōnewa*. Others were made of wood or bone: *wahaika*, with a crescent-like profile, and the figure-of-eight shaped *kotiate* (figs 23, 24). The most popular woods were *maire* (*Nestegis cunninghami*), *mānuka* (*Leptospermum scoparium*) and *pōhutukawa* (*Metrosideros excelsa*), hardwoods that could be further tempered by fire (Makereti 1986, Te Rangihīroa 1950).

Weapons were regarded as precious heirlooms, passed from one generation to the next. They were also coveted battlefield trophies, and many of the most acclaimed carried personal names, such as 'Kaitangata' ('Man-Eater'), 'Te Ngaheretoto' ('Forest of Blood') or 'Te Ngakimate' ('Vengeful Death'). Being intimately associated with the god of war and the shedding of blood, they were highly *tapu* and were concealed when not in use; possession of such treasures was a weighty responsibility.

The raising of a war party and its dedication to Tūmatauenga required considerable ritual, initiated by the accompanying *tohunga*. It involved the strict observance of different prohibitions, among them a ban on intercourse and the handling of cooked food. This created a protective sphere of *tapu* around the warriors. These practices focused concentration, prepared the warrior for the fight ahead and engaged him in the spiritual dimension of making war (Gardiner 1992). On the return of the war party cleansing ceremonies were undertaken, and the warrior resumed everyday activities.

To ensure a permanent peace between adversaries, marriage was arranged between formerly hostile *rangatira* families. Young *puhi* women were married with the appropriate ceremony; the offspring from such sharing of bloodlines were seen as a deterrent to war. In many instances, significant *taonga*, treasured possessions of great *mana*, were exchanged as tokens of goodwill; personally named treasure boxes and prestigious weapons were popular offerings. One famous example is the staff called 'Te Pīpīwharauroa' ('Shining Cuckoo'), which symbolised the peace made between the tribes of Northland and the Waikato Valley. Such gifts were also presented in friendship or to avert potential trouble.

In times of peace or restful retirement hostilities could be sustained by more subtle activity. This included sorcery, involving the composition and chanting of virulent cursing poems of which many famous examples are women's work, and the manufacture of small, portable items from the skeletal remains of the vanquished, such as ornamental toggles, needles, birdspear barbs, fish-hooks, bird-leg rings, jewellery, clothes pins and musical instruments.

Music – the stamping rhythmic ferocity of the *haka* or war dance to intimidate the enemy and stir the blood; the haunting echo of the *pūtātara* conch trumpet or *pūkāea* war horn; the resonant booming of the *pahū* tree gong – contributed to the arts of Tūmatauenga, the god of war, though

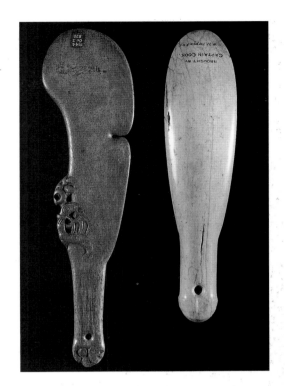

23 ABOVE Short clubs, one of stone and two of wood. From left to right: *patu ōnewa*, collected on Captain Cook's voyages; *kotiate*; *wahaika*. BM Ethno. NZ 80, L. 40 cm; 1934.12–1.27, L. 31.5 cm, presented by E.A.L. Martyn; 9335, L. 30.5 cm.

24 Two whalebone clubs. The *wahaika* (left) stained from many seasons on the battlefield, carries the three-dimensional representation of a fierce female ancestor and is a particularly fine example. The *patu parāoa* was collected on Captain Cook's voyages. BM Ethno. 1944 Oc.2.820, L. 37 cm, Beasley collection; St 827, L. 32.5 cm.

they were all but muted by the musket fire of the nineteenth century. And one art form, contrived consciously to terrify and bewitch, to conceal and entice, disappeared entirely – the art of *ta moko* or tattoo.

The arts of personal adornment and fashion

A person anxious to follow the fashion to its highest level would need to dress his hair into a topknot, place a decorative comb beside it and stick two or three white feathers into the knot; have greenstone pendants and white feathers hanging from his ears; have the rei puta pendant suspended from his neck, have a dogskin cloak around his body; a belt around the waist and a string tied to his penis; have elaborate indelible tattoo designs over his face and forehead, and over his buttocks and thighs . . . (Mead 1969: 82)

Of all the aspects of high fashion, the most singularly impressive for its permanence and design was *moko*, tattoo. Its mythic origins begin with a young man, Mataora (whose name means 'Face of Vitality'), who fell in love with Niwareka, a princess of the underworld. He beat her, and she fled back to her father, Uetonga's, realm. Contrite and heartbroken, Mataora followed; after various trials, he reached her family home with his face paint messy and spoiled. There he met Uetonga, whose stern countenance was engraved with fine, curving lines. Mataora's in-laws mocked him for his ludicrous appearance, and thus humbled, he begged Niwareka's forgiveness. She eventually accepted him again, and her father offered to tattoo Mataora and teach him the art. During this time, Niwareka acquired the skills of *tāniko*, plaiting cloak borders in multiple colours. Together, they returned to the world of humankind, carrying the treasures of *ta moko* and *tāniko*.

25 Pigment pot, which contained a mix of soot and thin oil for tattooing. Such crafted containers were passed from generation to generation, and the pigment was duly added to and enriched. BM Ethno 1944 Oc.2 809. H.8 cm. Beasley collection.

Archaeological evidence has revealed that the practice of tattooing came to New Zealand as part of the cultural template from Eastern Polynesia. Excavations have unearthed tattoo equipment dating from early settlement times, and the preferred sites of the body adornment suggest a continuation of Eastern Polynesian design tradition, in which the puncture technique (of piercing the skin with bone chisels that had a serrated edge to hold and apply the pigment) was also practised. Often exquisitely finished, these implements resemble a miniature hafted adze; they were tapped rhythmically by a small wooden mallet, and blood seepage was wiped away with flax fibre swabs.

Pigment was produced by mixing soot with light fish or dog oil, or spring water, depending on the density and texture of the soot. This was prepared by the burning of resin or the vegetable caterpillar. These sticky substances produced an indigo blue-black or greenish black, and were kept in highly prized containers (fig. 25). Often beautifully figured, these little pots became heirlooms, their contents refilled and greatly valued, colouring the faces from one generation to the next. Most such containers were wooden, but pumice stone was also used (Robley 1896). Because of the high risk of infection and disfigurement, tattooing was a profoundly *tapu* procedure. Sexual intimacy and consumption of solid food were prohibited the person being tattooed, particularly in the application of facial tattoo for which a special feeding and watering device, *kōrere* (fig. 26), was invented. This funnel-like object supplied broth and fresh water to the patient. It thus ensured that no contaminating substances touched the traumatized skin. To hasten the skin's healing, slit leaves of the *karaka* tree were placed over the incisions.

As well as the puncture technique, which ideally suited the laying in of dense amounts of pigment, the ancient Maori had another, unique, way of inscribing the skin. This form closely followed the development of curvilinear patterning on wood and involved a different type of chisel. Still made from bone, and more rarely nephrite, the chisel was finely honed and unerringly sharp, with a straight cutting edge. This sliced lines which caused textured scarification, into which the pigment was applied by the serrated implement. Thus, the double spirals and the precise curves on chin, forehead and nostrils took form as incised parallel lines ridged into the surface of the skin, markedly different from the silky smooth finish of tattoo in Samoa and the Marquesas. As the Maori scholar Te Rangihīroa observed: '. . . in addition to supplying art motifs, carving influenced the mechanical process of reproducing these motifs on flesh' (Te Rangihīroa 1950).

Ta moko is the process; *moko* is the product. *Moko* sites and design, as well as extent, varied between men and women, though in both sexes it marked rites of passage and significant events in one's life, besides being a premier fashion statement (fig. 27). Men were tattooed between the waist and knees, this permanent decoration usually being completed while a person was comparatively young. Looking like snug bicycle shorts, this waist-to-knee tattoo involved swirling double spirals on either buttock,

26 Feeding funnel, *kōrere*. The funnel was used to feed broth and water to a person undergoing facial tattoo; most funnels were ornately carved, possibly as a visual distraction for the patient, as is this fine example with a vigorous female figure in high relief. BM Ethno. 1915.2–17.4. L. 20.5 cm.

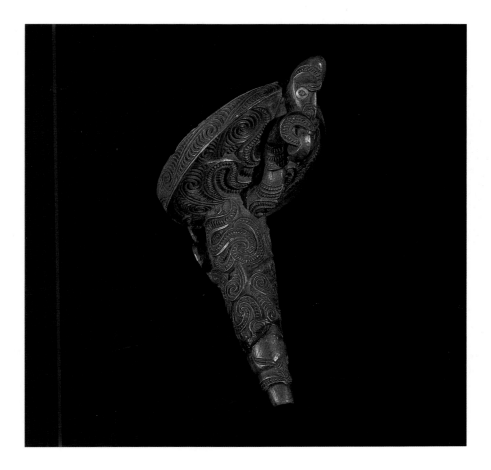

stretching down to the knees in an oblique, more angular, design. The full face *moko* was much more exacting and time-consuming, as a competent and experienced tattoo specialist considered the subject's bone structure, unique features and even such 'flawed' attributes as squinting deep-set eyes, a low forehead or a broken nose. Work could also be done on other parts of the body – the arms, shoulders, lower calves and back, but this was a matter of individual taste and preference.

Women generally had much less *moko* visible. It occurred on the upper lip and chin, with deep colouring of the lips, and the nostrils were also finely incised. Another favoured site was between the eyebrows, on the central forehead. Like the chin *moko*, the basic motif comprised linked crescents and spirals balanced symmetrically on either side of a blank, narrow median. Full face *moko* in women was exceptional but is noted in oral history and recorded by Robley (1896: 34), and partial patterning on the forehead has also been illustrated; *moko* was also observed on the neck and shoulders. Other marked parts of the body included the limbs and shoulders, and the hips and lower abdomen, but the chin *moko* remained the most popular, surviving even into the 1970s as a potent symbol of Maori identity and cultural resilience.

Moko provided natural camouflage in times of war, and gave the warrior the confidence of an intimidating, even awesome, appearance. It also dis-

27 Panel of tattooed faces, commissioned by the Dominion Museum in 1894 and carved by Tene Waitere. Primarily an example of the different tattoo designs for men and women, this carving is notable for the oblique aspect of the female portrait, sheltered by *manaia* figures. By permission of the Museum of New Zealand Te Papa Tongarewa, Wellington. ME 4211. H.77 cm.

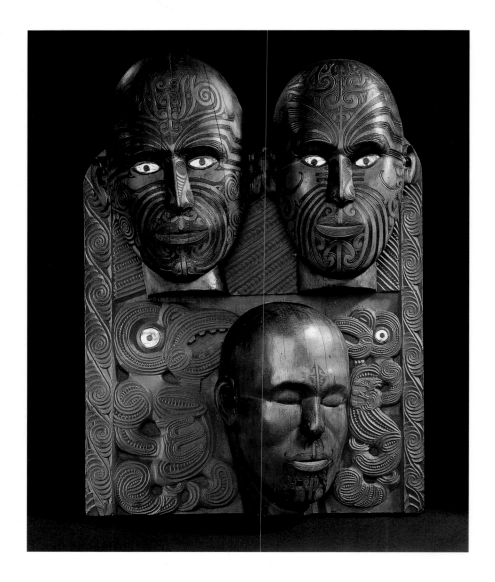

played one's capacity for pain and endurance, and it enhanced the carrier's erotic appeal quite considerably. Each art work, each 'canvas' had a singular design, as Banks commented:

... it is impossible to avoid admiring the immence Elegance and Justness of the figures in which it is form'd, which in the face is always different spirals, upon the body generaly different figures resembling something the foliages of old Chasing upon gold or silver; all these finishd with a masterly taste and execution, for of a hundred which at first sight you would judge to be exactly the same, on a close examination no two will prove alike; (Beaglehole 1963, II: 13–14)

Face and body paint was also worn, with the generous application of *kōkōwai*, or red ochre, to the face, body and hair. In some areas, powder blue was also popular (Neich 1993).

Ornamental feathers were affected by both sexes, the spatulate tail feathers of the now extinct *huia* (*Heteralocha acutirostris*) being the favourite chiefly emblem. They were blue black, with the uppermost quarter stark white. Flowing plumes of the white heron and the downy feathers of the albatross were prized for earrings, and the elegant narrow tails of the red-tailed tropic bird were also popular. Whole bird carcasses, particularly *huia*, were worn suspended from the ears. This decorative element also occurred in carved figures.

Like the other peoples of Polynesia, the Maori enjoyed garlands of flowers in season, and threaded necklaces of seeds and shells. Little sachets of scented leaves and grasses were also worn to perfume the body. Human teeth, usually of a parent or grandparent, were displayed, in clusters of two or three, or arranged with other items. Small pieces of wood, stone chips and sherds were looped around wrists or suspended from the neck, as were more conspicuously sophisticated and glamorous objects.

The ancient Maori supported the conscious and highly skilled crafting of jewellery in various media from the time of the earliest settlement. Whalebone and wooden forms were brought from Eastern Polynesia, and with the discovery and working of *pounamu* other forms developed, employing the technology of sandstone, grindstones and rasps. This involved three operations – sawing, grinding and drilling the stone, the last process accomplished by the rotating flywheel drill, mechanised by the rhythmic pulling of balanced cords. The drill points were made from a variety of stones – quartz, argillite, flint and obsidian were the most frequently used (Beck 1984).

Polished nephrite chips, pebbles and offcuts were often worn, and the simplest forms of pendants – *whakakai* or long earrings, *kuru* or elegant straight-lined pendants, and *kapeu* with a curved lower end – were also prized (fig. 28). More complex carving produced bat-shaped *pekapeka*, spiralling miniature eels (*koropepe*), and the subtle bird-shaped/fish-hook form, *hei matau*. Also worn as pendants but crafted specifically to tether pet birds, the *pōria kākā* rings were functional yet attractive. The simplest forms were also produced in *tangiwai*, or bowenite, which shattered easily and was difficult to work, yet was deeply appreciated for its luminous transparency.

The most famous of all Maori jewellery items is the *hei tiki* (fig. 29), the humanoid figure described in many contradictory accounts (Best 1952: 230; Te Rangihīroa 1950: 295; Skinner 1932: 202–11) and attributed with 'fructifying properties', or with having the appearance of 'Tiki, the First Man'. The latter attribution is unlikely, as *hei tiki* are emphatically female or quite sexless. The pronounced and often dilated vulval area, splayed hips with arms akimbo, bulging eyes and hugely gaping open mouth might represent a woman in childbirth, and thus the birthing goddess Hine-te-Iwaiwa; but like the theory suggesting the ornament represents an embryo, this is still speculation. Oral and family history nevertheless records instances of women, previously barren, who conceived on being given *hei tiki* by their husbands or parents. The *hei tiki* shape represented on a drastically reduced scale the upright figurative form in wood carving; this shape appeared in the earliest nephrite examples and probably developed from bone and wood prototypes long since lost. From these, the two

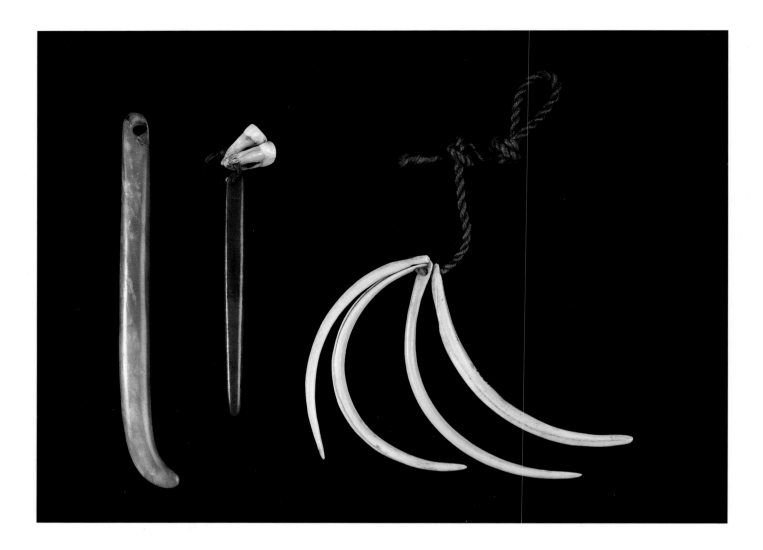

28 Two nephrite pendants and a cluster of cloak pins of pig tusks. The curved pendant, *kapeu*, was also used as a teething ring by babies. The pendant with two human teeth was worn as an earring; the teeth may have belonged to a parent or grandparent and had a protective function. This pendant was collected on Captain Cook's voyages and is probably illustrated in Parkinson's drawing (fig.12). Cloak pins, *aurei*, secured the garment to the shoulder or chest, but were also worn in clusters as an ornament, or suspended from ears. BM Ethno. TRH 1, L. 14 cm, Royal Loan 1902; NZ 162, L. 9 cm; 7987, L. 9.5 cm, presented by A.W.Franks.

principal types evolved. One type features a head/body ratio of 30–70 per cent, small round eyes, clearly discernible ears, elbows and sometimes knees, asymmetrical shoulders, smooth brow, and the head tilted at almost forty-five degrees. It measures between 5 and 12 cm in length. The other type, developed more recently, has a 40–60 per cent head/body ratio, an incised brow above pronounced eyes, the head tilted very slightly sideways above even shoulders, and arms usually akimbo; it can be between 5 and 17 cm long. In the early nineteenth century, with the introduction of metal, many adzes were recycled as large, impressive *hei tiki* of the second variety, and were worn proudly, despite their prodigious weight and unconventional origins. Some *hei tiki* also carried personal names, and were presented as oath gifts – one outstanding example is the *hei tiki* 'Te Pirau Kakai Matua', acquired by Governor Grey from Hone Te Paki of Waikato; another is the exquisite, enigmatic friendship token Titore of Ngāpuhi gave to Captain Sadler in 1834 (fig. 116). This second example demonstrates the genius and versatility of the ancient Maori lapidary and jeweller. At the same time, many nephrite pendants were also used as flax fibre scrapers and small knives. Nephrite was thus the medium for decorative, talismanic and functional devices.

Hei tiki in human or whale bone are rare but a few were produced in the nineteenth century. Curved, elaborately carved pendants were fashioned from cranial bone, and finger bones were sometimes transformed into toggles to secure the loop of a jewel's suspension cord. More commonly, toggles were made from albatross bone.

At the time of Cook's arrival one item very much in vogue was the *rei puta*, a whale-tooth pendant. The upper two thirds were scooped into a fine curve, finishing in a straight edge with suspension holes for a braided cord. The lower section swelled into a blunt, eel-like face on which two slanted eyes were carved and painted, with elegant yet eerie effect (fig. 11).

Aurei, or curved pins (fig. 28), fastened garments together, and were often worn in ornamental bunches; they were made from *pāua* shell, whale bone and teeth, and seal's teeth. Shark teeth were also popular as earrings, and are still, even to this day, though now worn mainly by women.

Men in the ancient Maori world favoured long hair; women's hair was usually short, as it was cropped in times of mourning, though younger women let it grow long. For fashionable men the *heru*, or comb, was an essential accessory; it was made from either wood or whalebone (fig. 12), carved from a single piece of material, or formed of separate slivers of wood held together by a complex assemblage of plaited fibre.

With this elaborate and tastefully designed array of jewellery and other ornaments, including the permanently inscribed indigo-black patterning of *moko*, the Maori were acutely conscious of personal appearance. This was observed even more in the cut and design of garments, the dyeing and preparation of fibre, and the deliberate flattery of shape, all for the purpose of enhancing *mana* and making the maximum visual impact. Even the most mundane dress or humble ornament was aesthetically pleasing or tasteful; the most successful fashion statement implied harmony of function, texture and design, as well as glamour.

29 Nephrite pendant, *hei tiki*. The strongly defined features and robust manner of this example date it to the classic period of Maori art. Female *hei tiki* were worn as talismans of fertility and easy childbirth. BM Ethno. St 825. L. 13.8 cm.

The arts of peace and pleasure

Taku pūtōrino
no wai ra ngā ngutu
hei whakapā ki ōu
hei puhi i te hau ora
Kia rangonahia anō te reo?

My *pūtōrino*,
whose lips will touch yours,
whose living breath
will give you voice,
again?

(Hirini Melbourne, 1991,
on seeing a *pūtōrino* in a museum display case)

Words were like food for the Maori – riddles, word puzzles and proverbs were continuously used and new ones invented daily, for as the saying states, *Ko te kai a te rangatira, he kōrero* ('oratory is the sustenance of chiefs'). Simple word games and story-telling also conveyed the *hapū*'s history and values to the young. They were informal devices for instruction as well as bedtime stories or tales told by one generation to another. People

30 *Poi* ball, made from plaited flax fibre ornamented with haliotis shell and stuffed with bullrush down. It was swung rhythmically around the body and tapped for percussive effect to the accompaniment of chant. This is one of only three known surviving examples from the early nineteenth century. BM Ethno. 5870. DIAM. 11.5 cm. Presented by A.W.Franks in 1869.

enjoyed playing and working with words, and the oral arts were important.

Oratory – the art of *whaikōrero* – was an exacting and scholarly pursuit. An accomplished orator was an alumnus of the higher school of learning, and his address would include a multitude of references, quotations and intriguing subtleties, enhanced by extensive genealogical citation, and often some contrived theatrical performance. In recent times oratory has become almost exclusively a male practice, the most noted exceptions being the Ngāti Porou and Whānau-a-Apanui peoples, who have presented fiery and talented female orators in the last few decades. In the Arawa region, where the ceremonial protocol has been rigidly upheld, elderly women retain the right to judge an orator's performance, comment on the content, and publicly correct any errors, misapprehensions or inconsistencies in delivery; this is also likely to have occurred before European contact (Te Awekotuku 1991).

Oratory was rarely rehearsed; it was a spontaneous rendition, but the speaker frequently consulted other experts about specific subject-matter and for information. It followed a loose structure, opening with an invocation that could be either quoted or extemporised. After this lyrical or stirring prelude had set the tone, the speaker gave ritualised greetings to the deceased and the assembled living, and identified himself, though this was not always necessary. The issues to be addressed followed next, usually forming the main body of the speech, which then concluded with a series of poetic references. Not all orations had such focused linearity – circular argument, and the layering and spiralling of ideas, facts and images, also occurred. Spontaneous dance, involving the audience, was also a possibility (Dewes 1977). Contemporary practice resolves an oration with a relevant chant poem, some of which may be longer and denser in meaning than the oration itself (Karetu 1978).

Waiata, or *mōteatea*, were chant poems that formed the canon of Maori oral literature. They ranged from the potent incantations and charms of sorcerers (Te Rangihīroa 1950) to complex and instructive geographical accounts and virulent recitations of contempt and derision (Ngata 1959, 1961). Of the recorded and annotated works collected, the majority with known authorship were composed by women, which suggests that women excelled in the literary creative arts across a variety of genres. These include laments, love songs, lullabies, *poi* chants (see below), and songs of challenge and contempt. Related to the last type are passionate war chants to heat the blood and rouse to action, which also fall into the *haka* or posture dance category. *Waiata* were chanted, rather than actively performed or postured to, the impact coming from the voice and the lyrical or inflammatory nature of the words; performance, tone, rhythm, gesture and volume would vary according to the text (Karetu 1993).

Haka were active performance items composed intentionally to demonstrate the fitness, agility and ferocity of warriors, and to intimidate or confuse the enemy. They had a high ritual element, and invoked Tūmatauenga, the god of war, while informing the adversary of what awaited them. A mixture of almost military precision of movement, and outbursts of tongue-jabbing, eye-bulging spontaneity, the *haka* disarmed more than a few enemy troops on the battlefields of World War II (Gardiner 1992), as well as gentlemen travellers in former times:

Imagine a body of about 3,000 nearly naked savages, made as hideous as possible by paint, standing in close ranks, and performing a sort of recitative of what they would do with their enemies if they could lay hold of them. They stood in four close lines, one behind the other, with a solitary leader (as it appeared) in front at the right end of the line. This leader was a woman who excelled in the art of making hideous faces (viz, poorkun). The feet had but a small part of the work to perform as they did not break their lines, but merely kept up a kind of stamp in excellent time with one foot; their arms and hands had plenty to do, as they were twisted into all possible positions to keep tune with the recitative; their eyes all moved together in the most correct time it is possible to conceive – and some possessed the power of turning them so far downwards that only the whites were visible. This was particularly the case with the woman whom I have spoken of as the leader; she was a remarkably handsome woman when her features were in their natural state, but when performing she became more hideous than any person who has not seen savages can possibly imagine: she was really very much like the most forbidding of the Hindoo idols – the resemblance to a statue being rendered more perfect by the pupilless eyes, the most disagreeable part of sculpture. (Bidwill 1841: 32)

Haka were performed by both men and women, often with weapons flashing and quivering in stark visual accompaniment. In dramatic contrast to the stamping, body slapping aggression of the *haka*, the *poi* chant was a graceful, fluid dance involving the rhythmic manipulation and gentle tapping of the *poi*, a fibre ball attached to a plaited cord (fig. 30). Now performed exclusively by women, this dance form strengthened the wrists and forearms, increased co-ordination and hand/eye skills, and was excellent training for wielding traditional weapons.

Puppetry (fig. 31), string figures, hand games, word puzzles and baton-tossing matches were all diversions; they were for fun but also trained the eye and mind in alertness, speed and timing. Timing – rhythm – was important; for every human activity – crop planting, tattooing, fire making, oratory, plaiting and weaving – moved to a specific rhythm within the community, or was accompanied by devices that made music.

The *poi*, castanet-type clickers and short sticks were among the few percussive instruments in the Maori musical repertoire. There were no membranophones, or drums, despite their dynamic presence in Eastern Polynesia (Te Rangihīroa 1950).

Flutes, the gifts of the goddess Hineraukatauri, whose figure appears on many instruments, featured prominently in entertainment. Some were simply leaf blades and tiny snail shells, others were fashioned from wood into items of great beauty (Melbourne 1991). Short, straight *kōauau* flutes (fig. 32) were made from wood, albatross or human bone, some embellished with carved narrative and shell or even human tooth inlay, others exquisitely simple. They were blown with the mouth across the open upper end, accompanying chants. Small, curved *nguru* flutes (fig. 34) were played with the mouth, *kōauau*-style, but could also be played with

31 Wooden puppet with moveable arms, manipulated by flax fibre cords. These ornately carved figures entertained both adults and children. This example is unusual as it combines a full-face male tattoo with a visibly female body. BM Ethno. 1921.10–14.2. H.47 cm. Acquired from Captain F. Vernon RN in 1824.

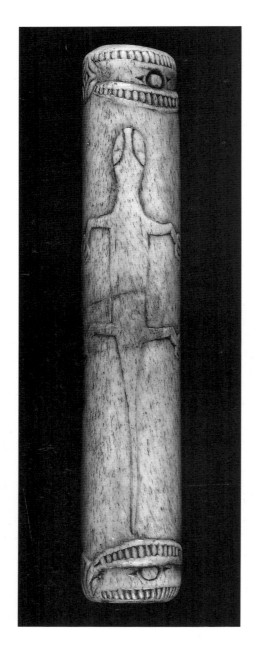

the nose. The latter technique produced a less resonant, sobbing, effect; much would no doubt depend on the musician playing and the arrangement preferred. Like *kōauau*, *nguru* could be either simple or elaborate, crafted in wood, stone and the aptly shaped sperm-whale tooth.

Much larger than *kōauau* and *nguru* were the famous bugle flutes, or *pūtōrino*, which measure between 25 and 55 cm in length (fig. 33). They were made from two pieces of hollow wood, bound together by the aerial roots of the *kiekie*. Forming a single elliptical shape, the *pūtōrino* had two distinct voices, 'female' and 'male', brought out by the technique of the flautist. Some instruments could be played at either end.

Kiekie roots were also used in the binding of massive war trumpets or *pūkāea*, usually ranging in size from 135 cm to 280 cm (fig. 33). Two separate lengths of wood were cut, hollowed and sealed together, and

32 *Kōauau*, flute of human bone. Fallen enemies often provided the material for various items, including musical instruments. This fine example further recalls human mortality in the carved lizard form, as many tribes believed the reptile was a symbol of death and misfortune. *Kōauau* produced a melancholy sound and were played during tattoo ritual, healing, childbirth and funerary occasions. BM Ethno. LMS 145. L. 14.2 cm. London Missionary Society collection.

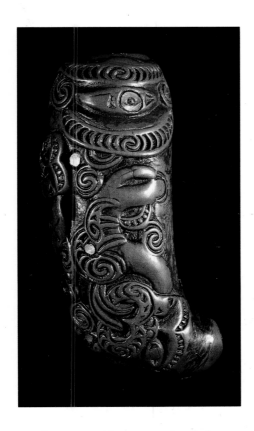

34 Flute, *nguru*. Flutes were played alone or to accompany songs and chants. With its *pāua* shell inlay and fine patinated carving, this flute has attained a fine jewel-like quality. Three sinuous-bodied figures cover the surface with one of their bodies forming a lug for a suspension cord; the mouthpiece is surrounded by a Janus face. Carved in Bay of Islands style during the later eighteenth century. BM Ethno. +7926. L. 11 cm.

33 Bullroarer, war trumpet and bugle flute. The bullroarer has painted *kōwhaiwhai* patterns on both sides. Attached to a long cord, it was spun in rituals of weather divining and preparation for battle. The war trumpet, *pūkāea*, has lashing of *kiekie*. It is a superb example but smaller than average. The flute, *pūtōrino*, could be played at either end. Elaborate *manaia* forms encircle the middle aperture on which stands a depiction of Hineraukatauri, goddess of music. BM Ethno. 4878, L. 34.3 cm; LMS 147, L. 58.5 cm, London Missionary Society collection; 1692, L. 55 cm.

sometimes separate insets were added to widen the flare of the funnel, like petals on a flower (Te Rangihīroa 1950). The *pūtātara*, or conch shell, was another trumpet type, with a carved mouthpiece and occasionally *pāua* inlay. Such instruments were restricted to martial use.

Music was also a factor in healing; flute music and chant poems soothed the pain of tattooing. Small elliptical discs attached to cords were spun over the faces and congested chests of bronchial patients, and the arthritic joints and aching backs of the elderly (Melbourne 1991). They moved through the air, changing the energy currents, as did the bullroarer (fig. 33). This whirling instrument, tied to a cord, invoked the goddesses and gods, cast various enchantments, and summoned the desired weather; like *pūtātara* and *pūkāea*, they were probably played only by a trained and erudite few.

Kites were flown and enjoyed by various age-groups; children played with simply constructed triangular forms, sorcerers and weather diviners employed the more complex forms, often accompanied by music or chant (fig. 113).

The air, the breath − *te hā* − was regarded as the essence of life in the ancient Maori world; thus it was claimed, celebrated and controlled through instruments and music.

Concluding thoughts

Reconstructing the way people lived, how they felt, what they thought, remains a challenging process. In the case of the Maori, it is densely layered with evidence and assumption, coloured by traditional sources, Western comment and oral history. *Taonga* − treasured material artefacts − inform this process too. Each one tells a story, comes from a particular community, and holds the creative, making, power of human hands, of human thought. Maori society at the time of Captain Cook's arrival was dynamic and adaptable, a society which appreciated knowledge, applauded beauty, admired martial courage, and appeased the unseen presences of ancestors and deities; these qualities are recalled in the phrases of a contemporary composer, Te Rangiaroha:

Hoki atu ki te tapuwae parekura
ō te tini, ō te mana.
Kei reira ke te tino taumata tapu
ō taku mana.

Who we are is what
our ancestors made us.
And made,
for us.

3

MAORI SOCIETY TODAY: WELCOME TO OUR WORLD

A.T. Hakiwai

Te tangi a te Mātui	*The Call of the Mātui*
Kia Whakarongo ake au	As the very senses of my being
Ki te tangi a te manu nei	Are drawn to the cry
A te Mātui	It is the Mātui
Tui-i-i, Tui-i-i, Tuituia	Calling Tui-i-i, Tui-i-i, Tuituia!
Tuia i runga	That it be woven above
Tuia i raro	That it be enmeshed below
Tuia i waho	That it be entwined without
Tuia i roto	That it be embraced within
Tuia i te here tangata	Interlaced as with the strands of
Ka rongo te pō!	humanity
Ka rongo te ao!	Reaching the very senses by night
Tuia e te muka tangata	And by the light of day
I takea mai i Hawaiki-nui	Embodied in the image of all beings.
I Hawaiki-roa	Born from Great-Hawaiki
I Hawaiki-pāmamao	Born from Long-Hawaiki
Ki te whaiao	From the merging of the spirits
Ki te ao marama	Out into the light
Tihe Mauriora.	Into the world of light
	Behold the essence of life
	The ethos of life
	The principle of life.
	Tihe Mauriora!!

This ancient *karakia* or chant is sometimes used as an introductory saying on speech-making occasions to focus and guide the speaker before any major undertaking. The term *Hawaiki* refers to the Maori ancestral homeland, while *tuia* means to bind or knit together. This chant was used as the introduction to a 1990 publication commemorating the 150th celebration of the signing of the Treaty of Waitangi calling for people to unite together in the common bond of fellowship.

Today I recall these ancient words as a reaffirmation of our cultural origins and as a celebration of our tribal ancestors and their *mana* (power, authority) as represented by traditional Maori artefacts, or rather our *taonga* (treasures). Therefore, like my ancestors before me, I welcome these treasures back into the world of light: I greet them, I weep for them, I pay my respects to them. Together we are one and together we face the future. *No reira, Tihei Mauriora! Mauriora ki te whaiao, ki te ao marama! E ōku tīpuna hoki wairua mai ki a mātou i tēnei wā* (Awaken, and return to this living world of ours. To our ancestors, return in spirit to us, your many descendants).

The *haka* which the New Zealand All Black rugby team performs is well known on rugby fields throughout the world, sending shivers down the spine of their opponents. Dame Kiri Te Kanawa enthrals all with her heavenly operatic voice. The world has caught a glimpse of the highly successful travelling Maori art exhibition *Te Maori* which toured the USA in 1985–6. However, people quite often see the outward signs but are ignorant of the inward messages, and of the symbols and meanings of the culture they represent.

He toi whakairo   Where there is artistic excellence
He mana tangata   There is human dignity

(Maori saying)

As a young Maori who works for the Museum of New Zealand Te Papa Tongarewa, I take much pleasure in writing about 'Maori Society Today'. Maori treasures occupy a special and important place in Maori cultural identity, and the feelings Maori people have for their cultural heritage are strong, intimate and real. 'When a descendant holds one of these pieces, all the power, awe and authority of the ancestors flows into the living person. Tears flow, and a living bridge is built between the living and dead, the past and the present' (*New Zealand Geographic* 5,1990: 75). The carvings, textiles, paintings and other creations of Maori culture reach across generations and, whether elaborately decorated or plain and simple, speak of a way of life peculiar to Aotearoa, the 'Land of the Long White Cloud', New Zealand. To find out that the All Black's *haka* has a deeper cultural and historical meaning, and that Dame Kiri Te Kanawa has a *whakapapa* (genealogy) that reaches back to the origins of creation suggests something unique about Maori culture, something very different from other cultural experiences.

We as Maori people have our own timeless rhythms and group dynamics. We trace descent from the ancestors who travelled on their voyaging canoes across the ocean pathways of the Pacific Ocean from the homeland of Hawaiki (generally regarded as being somewhere in Eastern Polynesia). The basic building block of Maori society is the *whānau*, or extended family, which involves the most intimate of social relations. The *whānau* is where the fundamental development of the individual occurs and where he or she is nurtured in knowledge, customs, tribal histories and traditions. The *whānau* consists of three or four generations and includes grandparents, parents, children and grandchildren. It can number as many as fifty or more, and some *whānau* today number more than a hundred. The extended family is bound together by *whanaungatanga* or kinship, which to the Maori means the warmth of being together as a family, sharing the joys and pains of life. In former times the *whānau* was the basic household unit in each village and today its significance is still paramount in our culture. As when cultivating flax we have to make sure that the seed is nurtured and nourished properly for it to grow and blossom, so we must cultivate and nurture our traditions to meet the challenges and opportunitites of the future.

Whanaungatanga, or kinship, has provided a sheltering embrace for the Maori family since time immemorial. However, many of the social problems facing Maori people today stem from the long-standing inequality and lack of understanding of the relationship between Pākehā and Maori, and from the changes facing Western and Westernised societies the world over. Shifting populations, urbanisation, unemployment, cultural imperialism and the erosion of common 'traditional' values, like the 'breakdown' of the family, have all contributed.

How are the Maori placed in today's world? The statistics for Maori people are alarming and reflect poorly on a land of rich resources which has become known as 'God's own country'. As a minority within our own country we are facing particular economic and social disadvantages. In 1991, 39 per cent of Maori children lived in single-parent families, compared with 16 per cent of non-Maori children. Of these Maori single parents 12 per cent were in full-time paid employment, 78 per cent received an income of less than NZ$15,000, two-thirds had no school qualifications and over half lived in rented accommodation. Access to good health, education and employment are, therefore, serious concerns for Maori people. In the area of education alone statistics show that, although there have been significant improvements in Maori educational achievement at all levels in the past decade, in most areas wide gaps still remain between the performance of Maori and non-Maori.

Past, present and future: space and time in the Maori world

According to a New Zealand historian, 'History is the umbilical cord that connects us to the past and nourishes the present by making that present understandable. Unless we know where we come from — as individuals and as a nation — we cannot know where we are. And if we don't know where we are, we cannot know in which direction we are heading' (King 1990: 10). For Maori people these words ring particularly true. The poetic chant at the beginning of this chapter expresses something of our world view, revealing the connections with our living past. To understand Maori society today we must first understand the significance and value that our past has in our present lives and culture.

Why, whenever Maori people meet, do they talk about their ancestors, who in many cases may have lived hundreds of years ago? Why do Maori people talk to, greet and lament over their ancestors as represented by treasures in exhibitions of Maori art in Aotearoa and overseas? Why do Maori people travel thousands of miles to be with their treasures, which to many an outsider are merely objects of primitive, tribal or native art? The answer lies in the dynamic relationship of past, present and future in Maori culture — the Eternal Now.

The Maori world is a world of unity and coherence. People, the universe, stars, mountains, rivers, rocks and fish are all connected through genealogy, demonstrating the intimate relationship between the Maori and the world around us. Through genealogy we identify our kin, relationships are known, and expectations and responsibilities stem from it. The world is a big family tree where everything has a place and position of importance. Within the context of this genealogical tree there is an important dimension of the Maori world which must be understood — the composite notion of time and place. Genealogy is the common thread or principle of the Maori world by which people, events and history are linked, and the reason why Maori people behave as they do. Maori *taonga*, like real people, are important because they too are regarded as having a genealogy and a *mauri* or life-force which generates, regenerates and upholds creation. Many represent specific ancestors who may have travelled in the ancestral canoes as well as others who occupy a special position in their tribal history and identity.

This genealogical relationship also commemorates the creators of these treasures as they too are fondly remembered in today's world. Maori people and our artworks – what is the connection? In the words of one elder:

We treat our artworks as people because many of them represent our ancestors who for us are real persons. Though they died generations ago they live in our memories and we live with them for they are an essential part of our identity as Maori individuals. They are anchor points in our genealogies and in our history. Without them we have no position in society and we have no social reality. We form with them the social universe of Maoridom. We are the past and the present and together we face the future. (Mead 1985: 13)

For the Maori the past is an important and pervasive dimension of the present and future. Often referred to as the 'ever-present now', Maori social reality is perceived as though looking back in time from the past to the present. The Maori word for 'the front of' is *mua* and this is used as a term to describe the past, that is, *Ngā wā o mua* or the time in front of us. Likewise, the word for the back is *muri* which is a term that is used for the future. Thus the past is in front of us, it is known; the future is behind us, unknown. The point of this is that our ancestors always had their backs to the future with their eyes firmly on the past. Our past is not conceived as something long ago and done with, known only as an historical fact with no contemporary relevance or meaning. In the words of a respected Maori elder: 'the present is a combination of the ancestors and 'their living faces' or genetic inheritors, that is the present generations. Our past is as much the face of our present and future. They live in us . . . we live in them' (Mead 1985: 16). Therefore, to understand and appreciate Maori treasures one must realise that they continue to stand tall in *front* of us today.

Maori *taonga* speak of real people, their lives and accomplishments, their ways and traditions, their understandings of the world around them, and all those cultural nuances that collectively make up what is now known as Maori culture. The relationship of these treasures to successive generations of descendants remains essentially the same, although in the context of a different moment of time. Maori people display passion, emotion and intense feelings for their treasures because they are as real to them as their parents, grandparents and children. In a sense they are people and many have personal names and genealogies. They are revered as if they were the ancestors themselves and they are referred to as *taonga tuku iho* or treasures handed down (from our ancestors). Many of these treasures carry the *mana* of those who made them as well as the messages and symbols which have relevance in today's world.

Tō te kanohi tōna kite   The eye, the mind, the soul –
Tō te hinengaro tōna kite   Each has its own perspective.
Tō te wairua tōna kite.

(Maori saying)

Art is a pervasive presence in the Maori world, seen and appreciated in all walks of life. There are many manifestations of it, such as oratory, carving and weaving, but what is it that makes Maori art unique? As the Maori scholar Professor Mead said while talking within a carved ancestral meeting house: 'The Art of the Maori is people-based. You sleep here, you talk here, you sit here for hours. Here, we are very close to our ancestors. We delight in looking at them and transforming them into themes that give us meaning' (Mead 1990a: 144). To understand the significance of Maori art for Maori cultural identity it is necessary to look at the wider cultural context and to reflect on what has happened in the past and what will continue to develop and grow in the future.

Taonga or treasures embody all those things that represent our culture. The histories, myths and traditions, memories, experiences and stories, all combine to help define and identify us as Maori people – the indigenous people of Aotearoa, New Zealand. The Maori live in a living past which is as real to them as the world of today. Our treasures are much more than *objets d'art* for they are living in every sense of the word and carry the love and pride of those who fashioned them, handled and caressed them, and passed them on for future generations.

Messages and *kōrero* or stories associated with *taonga* provide the meaning and significance that are central to Maori art. Whether it is carving, weaving, painting or sculpture, Maori art is a manifestation of a larger whole. Tribal traditions, the stories of ancestors, genealogical relationships, symbols and metaphors, the *taha wairua* or spiritual element that unifies our world are among the essential elements of Maori art. Maori artworks are like history books brought to life and transformed through the creative process to provide meaning and significance.

Pāki Harrison, a well-respected master carver of the Ngāti Porou tribe, says that the most important element in carving is, *te kupu*, the word, or *ngā kōrero*, the message. 'Without the kōrero you have nothing to carve. Without the kōrero you have nothing to learn. Without it you have nothing to understand' (Winitana 1994: 14). 'The principal component of carving is kōrero. Many people think it's how it looks, but that's just one consideration. Your carving has to say something to people' (Winitana 1994: 20). He further says that *taonga* like those from the exhibition *Te Maori* had the balance right. They had the technique and the *wairua*. 'You could feel them. They were beautiful. You just knew they captured everything' (Winitana 1994: 14).

Identity and belonging

Ehara taku toa i te toa takitahi   My prestige comes not from me
Engari takimano nō āku tīpuna.   alone
                                            But descends from my ancestors

                (Maori saying)

The outsider will ask what is Maori culture? What is a Maori and what does it mean to be a Maori? Let me share with you my personal thoughts. A culture is:

a unity . . . an abstract unity, which can be comprehended by the mind but cannot be seen or touched. It is made up of many elements, some of which are material and observable, for instance objects and behaviour patterns, while others are abstract and invisible, for instance language, ideas and values. These elements are related to each other in a complex and more or less coherent system: they get their meaning from their interrelations and cannot be properly understood out of that context. (Metge 1980: 63)

My feeling of identity is a direct result of my upbringing, my education and those things I believe in. I find it almost impossible to isolate any one element of my culture, but rather, see it as a greater whole. 'What makes a culture distinct is not the elements taken separately but the way they are related to each other in the total pattern' (Metge 1980: 64). Knowledge of my tribal histories, traditions and customs, protocols and etiquette of the *marae*, the language – these things are important for me and my family because they are the continuing life-force of generations past and provide meaning and relevance to generations to come. Growing up in a Maori environment involves observance and participation, although with many Maori moving to the cities this has become extremely difficult and has resulted in a degree of isolation from their cultural roots. I carry within me all my ancestors of generations past. We as Maori people face the future with a solid foundation from the past. Whatever the occasion, I know that when I attend a *hui* or meeting I am comfortable in the knowledge that all my ancestors are there with me.

What is a Maori? This name distinguished us from the new arrivals to this country who were different from us and today it is still used as a word that collectively refers to us all, notwithstanding the many tribes in Aotearoa. Similarly, the word *Māoritanga* has been used to talk about those common or shared elements that make up our culture, for instance, customs and traditions. However, Maori people are a tribal people and many consider their own tribes of more importance. One highly respected elder had this to say: 'My being Māori is absolutely dependent on my history as a Tūhoe [a particular tribe] person as against being a Māori person. It seems to me there is no such thing as Māoritanga because Māoritanga is an all-inclusive term which embraces all Māoris. And there are so many different aspects about every tribal person. Each tribe has its own history' (Rangihau 1981: 174).

35 In the last twenty years there have been serious concerns about the Maori language and its ability to survive beyond the year 2000. With the establishment of *kōhanga reo* or early Maori language 'nests' which have been set up with assistance from the Government and strong Maori input, the Maori language is assured of its rightful place for the future. This *kōhanga reo* is based at the Takapuwahia *marae*, Porirua, and was photographed in September 1990. Photo J. Nauta, Museum of New Zealand Te Papa Tongarewa, Wellington.

My *Māoritanga*, or rather my tribal identity, is expressed in a number of ways. First, in acknowledging that language is the key to understanding any culture, I make sure that I speak my language in as many places as possible and pass this on to my children. I want them to learn their language and to know who their ancestors are, their tribal histories, as well as the customs and traditions we have. Knowledge of my language enables me to move comfortably amidst my people and to participate more fully when the occasion arises. The Maori language is the lifeblood of our culture. As expressed by the late John Rangihau, elder of the Ngāi Tūhoe tribe, 'Maori language is the means by which I celebrate birth, teach and chastise my children, work and feed my family, mourn my dead and communicate with my god. Without it I am nothing. I don't belong, I can't relate, I am lost' (Muru 1990: 99). In 1982 the first *kōhanga reo* or language nest programme was set up in New Zealand to provide early childhood education based on immersion in Maori language and culture. *Kōhanga reo* (fig. 35) are like kindergartens for pre-school children where only the Maori language is spoken and where the child is brought up in an environment that reflects our cultural values and traditions. In 1992 there were already 719 *kōhanga reo*; at the time of writing there are over 800.

Secondly, my 'Maoriness' is in the belief that I must bring up my children in ways which will help them develop and grow in the knowledge of who they are. I consider it important to support my *marae*, tribe and sub-tribe because to me they are all essential parts of the extended family and those things dear to me.

Thirdly, there are many 'outward' expressions of Maori identity. Wearing a carved bone or nephrite pendant or ear ornaments in the form of fish-hooks and other Maori motifs, or possessing *kete*, or plaited baskets, are all visible expressions of Maori identity. On special occasions you see the elders wearing beautiful cloaks, nephrite pendants and other finery. These are worn as much to express one's tribal identity as they are to enhance the occasion. When Maori people meet, they greet each other in the traditional way by pressing noses together, the custom known as the *hongi*. This connects the two people both physically and spiritually.

Finally, my identity also lies in understanding that our *taonga* form an important part of my cultural heritage, my birthright. The successful *Te Maori* exhibition of 1985–6 highlighted how little understood and appreciated our artworks had become, and provided an outlet for the general dissatisfaction and disillusionment Maori people felt towards museums. Calls for the repatriation of treasures, for greater Maori control over and access to their own cultural property, and issues of ownership and indigenous rights have created a need to examine the role and function of museums. While some museums have responded by creating successful partnerships with tribal groups, some tribes have begun to set up their own tribal museums or culture centres. This is understandable as 'Maori art has become a means of enculturation, of education in one's own culture' (Mead 1990b: 168).

The *marae*: a place to stand, a place of the heart

Maori people are acutely aware of the spirit of the land, and the *marae* is an expression of this attachment. The *marae* is the place where Maori values, customs, protocols and knowledge are fully expressed (fig. 36). The *marae*, according to Williams's *Dictionary of the Maori Language*, is 'Enclosed space in front of a house, courtyard, village common'. A *marae* has an ancestral meeting house, either carved or uncarved, decorated or undecorated, a dining hall and an ablution block. Some *marae* also have

36 The *marae* with its ancestral meeting house is a recognisable feature of New Zealand's landscape. As a *tūrangawaewae* or 'place to stand' for all Maori people, it is like a home away from home. Weddings, christenings, birthdays, family reunions, tribal meetings, funerals, etc., can all be held on *marae*. Here a group of people are welcomed on to the Omahu *marae*, Fernhill, Hawkes Bay, to celebrate the opening of the Ruatapuwahine dining hall on 29 September 1990. Photo A. Marchant, Museum of New Zealand Te Papa Tongarewa, Wellington.

37 Maori art is vibrant, ever-evolving and developing. Modern meeting houses combine all the elements of Maori art – carving, painting and lattice-panel weaving. Artistic innovation is part of Maori tradition and historical experience, and this meeting house is no exception. This is the Ngāti Hawea meeting house, Te Matau-a-Māui, which stands on the Matahiwi *marae*, Haumoana, Hawkes Bay. Its name refers to the fish-hook of Māui, the great Polynesian demi-god. Photo A. Marchant, Museum of New Zealand Te Papa Tongarewa, Wellington.

other buildings, such as *kōhanga reo* (language nest centres), flats for the elderly, sporting clubs, etc. However, quite apart from the physical make-up of the *marae*, there are the spiritual and cultural dimensions which signal to the world the importance of the *marae* for all Maori people.

A *marae*, like a home away from home, is a place where Maori people can meet to celebrate the rituals of life as well as to say farewell to those who have passed on. It is regarded as a *tūrangawaewae* or 'place to stand', for all Maori people who have their own *marae* by right of genealogy and belonging. Hiwi Tauroa, former school principal and Race Relations Conciliator, tells us that the *marae* is a special place because of its high level of *wairua* (spirituality), *mana* (prestige), and *tikanga* (customs) and that 'Here they [the people] are able to stand upon Earth Mother and speak. Here they may express themselves, they may weep, laugh, hug and kiss. Every emotion can be expressed and shared with others – shared not only with the living but also with those generations who have gone ki tua o te arai (beyond the veil)' (Tauroa 1986: 6).

Usually people are called to a *hui* or meeting on the *marae*, and these occasions can range from tribal discussions relating to land, to family matters like weddings and *marae* committee meetings. *Hui* literally means to congregate, come together, meet, and it is a term used often by Maori people. *Hui* are like any other meeting except that they are often run according to Maori protocol. When people attend *hui* the discussions are often beneficial and constructive, involving a hearing of both sides of the argument and coming to some sort of recommendation based on consensus at the end. If, as in many cases, an agreement has not been reached, then another *hui* is called to debate the issues further.

The meeting house which stands proudly on any *marae* deserves special mention as it is a powerful symbol of identity and community. All over New Zealand there are hundreds of meeting houses, carved and uncarved, large and small, which grace the landscape of Papatuanuku our Earth Mother (fig. 37). The meeting house symbolically represents an ancestor, its ridge-pole is likened to the ancestor's backbone and the *heke* or rafters to the ancestors' ribs. Meeting houses provide shelter and comfort to those who step inside and are 'places of the heart' for relaxation and peaceful contemplation.

With its carvings, lattice panels and painted rafters, each offering its own story or message, the meeting house embodies the tribal history (fig. 38).

38 Interior of Te Hau-ki-Tūranga, the oldest carved meeting house in existence, carved by Raharuhi Rukupō in 1842 and re-assembled in the Museum of New Zealand. Painted rafters are supported by carved ancestral figures which stand between panels of lattice weaving. The effect is one of space and harmony. By permission of the Museum of New Zealand Te Papa Tongarewa, Wellington.

When we approach a fully carved meeting house we feel its presence immediately. Entering, we feel pride in knowing that our ancestors may be represented in it and from seeing the beauty and artistry of its adornments. Inside a meeting house history becomes real and personally relevant.

The Maori language is supreme on the *marae*, and it is this that gives the *marae* its fullest expression of life and vitality. 'The thought of a marae in the future denuded of its own tongue is a tragedy beyond comprehension. For many of us who are city dwellers, the yearning is always there to be enveloped by the ancestral house and to bathe in korero and waiata. To hear a kaumatua's healing powhiri' (Muru 1990: 106).

The Treaty of Waitangi

Ko te atakau ō te whenua i riro i a te Kuini,	The shadow of the land is to the Queen,
Ko te tinana ō te whenua i waiho ki ngā Māori.	But the substance remains with us.

(Said by the Te Rarawa tribal leader Nopera Panakareao about the Treaty of Waitangi, Kaitaia, 28 April 1840)

The Treaty of Waitangi has a special place in New Zealand's history, but misunderstanding and ignorance have created tension and uneasiness around it. Variously described as our 'nation's founding document', the 'Maori Magna Carta' and a mere 'fraud and nullity', the Treaty and its history tell an interesting story about the relationship of one nation and two peoples and their determination to live in Aotearoa, New Zealand. The British thought that, by virtue of the Treaty, they had acquired sovereignty over New Zealand, but to Maori people the Treaty had a different significance (after Orange 1987).

In January 1840 Captain William Hobson arrived in New Zealand to draw up a treaty with the Maori, and his instructions from the Colonial Secretary, Lord Normanby, were to get the 'free and intelligent consent' of the Maori (Orange 1990: 11). The Treaty was drawn up in two versions, English and Maori, but with important differences between the two texts due to an inadequate translation of English into Maori. It contained three articles of which a recent translation of the Maori text is as follows:

The First

The Chiefs of the Confederation and all the chiefs who have not joined that Confederation give absolutely to the Queen of England for ever the complete government over their land.

The Second

The Queen of England agrees to protect the Chiefs, the subtribes and all the people of New Zealand in the unqualified exercise of their chieftainship over their lands, villages and all their treasures. But on the other hand the Chiefs of the Confederation and all the Chiefs will sell land to the Queen at a price agreed to by the person owning it and by the person buying it (the latter being) appointed by the Queen as her purchase agent.

39 The carved meeting house, *Whare Runanga*, at Waitangi, Bay of Islands. It does not belong to one particular tribe but represents all Maori people. It was built between 1934 and 1940 at the instigation of Sir Apirana Ngata, then Minister of Maori Affairs, as the Maori people's contribution to the centenary of the signing of the Treaty of Waitangi. Photograph D.C. Starzecka.

The Third

For this agreed arrangement therefore concerning the Government of the Queen, the Queen of England will protect all the ordinary people of New Zealand and will give them the same rights and duties of citizenship as the people of England. (Orange 1990: 39)

After a day of speeches and discussions by those chiefs who had assembled at Waitangi, Bay of Islands, the Treaty was signed on 6 February 1840 by Hobson, on behalf of the British Government (Crown), and various Maori leaders present at the meeting (fig. 39). The Treaty was then taken around the country to secure other signatures from leaders in other tribal areas. Although over 500 Maori chiefs signed the Treaty, many Maori leaders never signed it because they either refused to do so or were not given the opportunity.

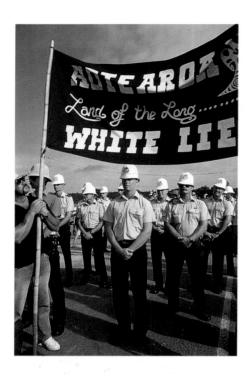

40 The Treaty of Waitangi continues to be the subject of great debate and controversy. This protest march, held at the Waitangi Day celebrations at Paihia, Bay of Islands, in 1990, illustrates the frustration and ambivalence the Treaty holds for various groups of people. Photo A. Marchant, Museum of New Zealand Te Papa Tongarewa, Wellington.

As one commentator has said: 'The Treaty of Waitangi therefore created a dynamic, ongoing relationship between Crown and tribe. The chiefs entered into a "partnership" with the Crown, giving the latter overriding power on intertribal matters and recognising its authority over the settler population. Tribal property rights, the authority of the chiefs under Maori customary law (rangatiratanga) and optional tribal access to the benefits of European culture were recognised by the Crown' (McHugh 1991: 6). Many chiefs and leaders believed that the Treaty was a personal agreement between the Queen herself and the chiefs. However, the 'very differences between the two cultures – the Crown on the one hand and the various tribes on the other – meant that the interpretation of the Treaty of Wait-angi would become an issue even before the ink was dry on the roll of parchment' (McHugh 1991: 1). The distinction between *kāwanatanga* (governorship) and *rangatiratanga* (chieftainship), two key words and con-cepts in the Maori version, is central to any interpretation of the Treaty of Waitangi, and the most obvious and fundamental problem relates to the question of what it was that the chiefs were ceding.

Equally crucial to the Treaty of Waitangi is the land and its value and importance to both cultures, Maori and Pākehā. To Maori people the *whenua* or land is a treasure handed down by our ancestors to be held in trust for future generations (fig. 41). The land is held sacred and is seen as the sustainer of life, precious because it is life. It is Papatuanuku or Mother Earth, who resembles the human mother who nourishes her child in the womb and then upon her breasts (Marsden 1988). The spirit of the land lives in the person, and physical and emotional ties with the land are strengthened through song, myth, dance and ritual.

Retention of Maori land in Maori ownership has always been a desire of Maori people. In 1840 when the Treaty of Waitangi was signed, Maori owned 66,400,000 acres of land. By 1891 they owned a little over 11,000,000, and in 1975, when the Waitangi Tribunal was set up, only 3,000,000 acres. Today half the land of New Zealand is owned by the Crown or reserved for public purposes, 47 per cent is freehold land under European title, and 3 per cent is Maori, owned by thousands of Maori shareholders (Naumann *et al.* 1990: 55). It is not surprising, therefore, that a huge effort should now be put, not only into retention and better utilis-ation of land but, more importantly, into halting the continued fragmen-tation of land holdings, which has been occurring generation by generation (Gardiner 1993).

In the last 150 years the Treaty of Waitangi has meant different things to different people, but for many Maori the main objectives have not changed. Struggles for land grievances to be addressed, calls for the Treaty of Waitangi to be honoured (fig. 40), and initiatives towards Maori self-determination and sovereignty are some of the events of the nineteenth and twentieth centuries that have shaped, and continue to shape, our nation.

The nineteenth century was a time of upheaval and struggle for Maori people. The period before 1830 was one of adjustment. The missionaries

41 Mountains, rivers and other geographical features of Aotearoa are important tribal markers and anchor points for Maori tribal identity and sense of belonging. The Whanganui river has a special cultural and spiritual significance for the Maori people of Whanganui, and in former times it was a lifeline of transport and trade in the area. Photo J. Nauta, Museum of New Zealand Te Papa Tongarewa, Wellington.

were working hard to set up their mission stations, to provide a Christian example to the Maori, and to learn the language (Elsmore 1989: 16), and the years 1830–50 saw great changes in cultural beliefs and attitudes. The spread of Christianity extended to remote corners of New Zealand, the introduction of the printed word meant new opportunities for both cultures, and the demand for land for the arriving settlers was increasing, putting great pressure on the owners to sell.

The formation of the *Kīngitanga* or Maori King Movement in 1857–8 was a Maori attempt to counteract Pākehā demands and to hold on to the prestige of the Maori race. Maori were excluded from the political decision-making process, and setting up their own form of government was a natural response against the colonial system and land sales. Pōtatau Te Wherowhero of the Waikato tribes was the first Maori king. He had the allegiance of various Maori tribes, such as those of Waikato and Taranaki, which put their land under his protection and refused to sell. This conflict over land ultimately ended in the New Zealand Land Wars of the 1860s. 'In the interests of the safety of the settlers, no challenge to European power would be tolerated; the Maori had to adopt the culture of the now dominant people – if this wasn't accepted voluntarily then it must be forced upon them' (Elsmore 1989: 161).

The wars started in Taranaki and Waikato and soon involved almost all North Island districts. They were a direct result of the alienation of Maori land by the government and the emerging settler colony, and involved British and colonial troops. Disputes escalated into warfare between the two races, and also among the Maori themselves as some chose to support the government (Elsmore 1989: 161). Land confiscations for those who had opposed the government's policies was the aftermath of the wars. Legislation (e.g. The New Zealand Settlers Act, 1863) authorised the confiscation of lands from those in 'rebellion' in any district in New Zealand.

The Land Wars were fought over a ten-year period and the 'result of the warfare of the 1860s was the rise of even more bitter feeling among the Maori, and reaction from the settlers' (Elsmore 1989: 162). For museums this period is significant, since many of the Maori treasures were collected during this time as 'spoils of war' and relics of what was still widely believed to be a dying race. The Land Wars were followed by a period of 'Millenarian or Prophetic Movements', when Maori people turned to leaders who offered a way of life and political organisation which attempted to reconcile Maori and Pākehā ideas in a manner that reasserted Maori identity. One such leader was Te Kooti Arikirangi Te Tūruki.

Believed to have been born in 1814 in the Gisborne area, Te Kooti was educated in the traditions of his people and at the Whakatō school of the Church Missionary Society, where he was considered one of the more promising pupils. In 1865 he was unjustly accused and arrested 'on suspicion of being a spy' and in the following year was sent to a penal settlement on the Chatham Islands. While there, he had a divine revelation commanding him to found a church. This he did, and acquired many followers. In 1868 he escaped back to the mainland and immediately began a five-year campaign of revenge against all who had wronged him. From 1873 to 1883 Te Kooti lived in relative peace and evolved the rituals of his church. He was pardoned by the government in 1883 and died in 1893. 'The religion of Te Kooti was first known as Te Hāhi ō te Wairua Tapu (The Church of the Holy Spirit), but was soon given the name Ringatu, the upraised hand, which referred to the characteristic gesture of the prophet and his followers of raising their hand in blessing' (Elsmore 1989: 232). 'Like all prophet-leaders he was a man of friction. His goal was the collective redemption of the people and the recovery of their land into their own hands. His belief was that God had made a promise not to forget those who were lost and whose land had been taken. Te Kooti sought to direct all his followers' actions in this world towards the fulfilment of this vision' (Binney 1995: 6).

Other prophetic movements in the nineteenth century included the Parihaka Movement, centred around two Taranaki leaders, Te Whiti-ō-Rongomai and Tohu Kākahi, which protested against land sales. It was a campaign of passive resistance. Tohu commanded the people 'Be patient and steadfast. Even if the bayonet is at your breast, do not resist!'. Te Whiti and Tohu were arrested without trial and served a period of detention in the South Island during 1882–3 (Elsmore 1989: 242), and the movement was finally crushed in 1889.

Characteristic of this period were the innovation and creativity of the art world, which produced some of the most distinctive and vibrant expressions of Maori art. 'Among people under Te Kooti's influence, art became innovative, direct, and powerfully expressive' (Davis 1976: 27).

The increase in legislation relating to Maori land, and the government's indifference to the plight of the Maori, created a climate in which plans were made for the setting up of a Maori Parliament or *Kotahitanga* (unity or oneness) which would involve all tribes coming together in the spirit of unity. The first session met in 1892 and an annual parliament was held, each year in a different venue, until 1902, although the government refused to give it official recognition (Orange 1990: 81).

Towards the end of the nineteenth century the Maori population was at its lowest ebb culturally, spiritually and economically. But the twentieth century ushered in a new breed of Maori leaders who continued to challenge the status quo. Well-educated young Maori men such as Apirana Ngata, Māui Pōmare and Te Rangihīroa entered parliament and, collectively known as the Young Maori Party, were committed to working towards the betterment of the Maori race. Improved health, better housing conditions, and the need to address long-standing land issues occupied their attention after the turn of the century. On another level, Maori participation in both World Wars showed the commitment of Maori people to play their part – a special Maori battalion was established, which served with honour in wars overseas. However, throughout this period Maori discontent, resulting from the alienation of Maori land and the inability of Maori tribes to maintain the *mana* over their lands, forests, fisheries and other prized possessions as guaranteed in the Treaty of Waitangi of 1840, continued.

The twentieth century has also been characterised by the birth of new political parties, such as the Rātana Movement of the 1920s, led by the prophet and faith healer Tahupōtiki Wīremu Rātana, who sought to unite the tribes and to have the Treaty of Waitangi recognised by the government and the courts. This period is one of adjustment, protest and change. The Waitangi Day celebrations, which are held annually, evoke mixed responses from both Maori and Pākehā, and land marches, land occupations, court battles, and government–tribal negotiations have become the order of the day. Eventually, after over a century of political, statutory and judicial debate the government finally set up the Waitangi Tribunal in 1975, a court of justice and legal advisory body that makes recommendations to the Crown based on the Treaty of Waitangi, to investigate Maori grievances. A law change in 1985 enabled the Waitangi Tribunal to investigate grievances going back to 1840, instead of grievances dating from after 1975.

What does the Treaty mean today? For Edward Taihakurei Junior Durie, the Chief Judge of the Maori Land Court and Chairperson of the Waitangi Tribunal, four qualities describe the importance of the Treaty.

The Treaty is first and foremost our national birthright. It is evidence of the foundation of our modern state in accordance with the most basic principles of law. Our nation was neither conceived from the ravages of conquest nor did it result from the illegitimate influx of settlers. Our nation was founded upon an agreement. It is well to recall Lord Normanby's instruction to Captain Hobson that:

'The Queen . . . disclaims for herself and for her subjects, every pretension to seize on the Islands of New Zealand, or to govern them as part of the Dominion of Great Britain, unless the free and intelligent consent of the Natives, expressed according to their established usages, shall be first obtained.'

Secondly, the Treaty is not just a Bill of Rights for Maori but belongs to everyone in New Zealand. It is the Treaty of Waitangi which gives Pākehā the right to be in these islands. The Treaty also preserves the inherent rights of the original people to maintain their own land, their treasures and their inheritance. Durie's final point contains the essence of the previous three in that the Treaty symbolises the joining of two peoples in a common enterprise to the expected advantage of each. Maori assimilation is not assumed. The Treaty established a regime for the development of two peoples who shared a common goal (after Durie 1990: 18).

Conclusion

| Ko te pae tawhiti whāia kia tata | Seek the distant horizons |
| Ko te pae tata whakamāua kia tīna. | And those that you attain, treasure them. |

(Maori saying)

Although there are many problems facing Maori people in the areas of health, education and employment, there are indications that a better future and a healthier society are emerging in the Land of the Long White Cloud, Aotearoa, New Zealand. Although some symbols and expressions of our identity may have changed, the main values of the Maori culture continue in this ever-revolving world of ours – *Te Ao Hurihuri*.

Maori *taonga* or treasures are not seen as relics of the past but rather as powerful symbols of pride and identity today. As the master carver Pāki Harrison stated, the messages contained in these treasures remain as an enduring legacy from our past and speak to us in different ways. Their value and importance remain steadfast and impervious to the passing of time (Winitana 1994).

While the struggle for retention and return of the land remains a major concern for Maori people, grievances are being heard and slowly addressed by the government through judicial advisory bodies such as the Waitangi Tribunal. Unsure of what the future holds, we can only hope and pray that justice will prevail. At the same time the Maori language has undergone a renaissance and new initiatives have developed – for example, the establishment of Maori childcare centres, and Maori radio stations, which give hope and confidence in keeping our language alive. Maori striving for

42 While some contemporary Maori artists are experimenting with different media and cross-cultural ideas, there are still those who practise the more traditional art forms, such as carving and weaving. If the vitality of a culture is indicated by the strength of its arts, then Maoridom is in a healthy state. Here we see students of the Manu Kopere Arts Centre at Hongoeka, Plimmerton, one of the many centres dedicated to the continuation and development of Maori art. Photo J. Nauta, Museum of New Zealand Te Papa Tongarewa, Wellington.

self-determination is increasing, and many Maori tribes and individuals are entering the business world with confidence and a determination to succeed.

The arts are healthy and strong and new artists are emerging from all walks of life. Contemporary Maori artists are drawing strength and inspiration both from modern influences and from their own tribal traditions and experience (fig. 42). Maori cultural competitions are held in all tribal areas, and the growing number of groups participating emphasises the importance of our songs, speechmaking and other forms of the performing arts (fig. 43). The importance of the Maori language, of holding on to our customs and traditions, of learning our histories, are some of the key messages contained in these songs. However, amidst all the clamour and confusion of the modern world the *marae* still remains a steadfast bastion for the fullest expression of Maori identity and belonging.

I hope that for those who read this book our art can be the mediator and bridge to a greater understanding of our culture. Maori treasures are a tangible expression of this culture, to be shared and enjoyed by all privileged to see them. I hope that one day soon these *taonga* will travel home

43 The phrase 'Reaching back to go forward' described the momentous occasion of the building of twenty-two tribal war canoes to coincide with the 150th anniversary of the signing of the Treaty of Waitangi. Symbols of enduring strength and purpose, these war canoes have re-awoken the spirit of Maoridom and they act as a focus of tribal pride and *mana*. Here a group of paddlers from one of the canoes performs a *haka* on the beach. Photo A. Marchant, Museum of New Zealand Te Papa Tongarewa, Wellington.

to Aotearoa to be once again greeted, enjoyed and appreciated by the living descendants of their creators and kinfolk. To be fully understood and appreciated these treasures must be 'liberated' from the stifling atmosphere of academia and museology, and from those who insist on explaining and describing them from 'outside' the culture. Our art is an important dimension of our strength and cultural wealth. I feel reassured that we are able to face the future secure in the knowledge of our past and quietly confident of what is to come. Therefore, I invite you to share with us the *mana* of our *taonga* or treasures, to journey with us through histories and memories, past experiences and future aspirations. Like the spirit of our ancestors we ask you to open your heart, clear your mind, and learn about another people and culture that sees things differently. In the words of Ngahuia Te Awekotuku: 'The wairua lives on: a new beginning ... and another story' (Te Awekotuku 1990: 97).

4
WOOD-CARVING

Roger Neich

Introduction: Art in Maori culture

Maori culture is distinguished by a rich repertoire of many varied and complex arts, each carried to a high degree of refinement. This extreme variety and refinement of art forms marks Maori culture as exceptional among the cultures of the Pacific region. Art pervades the whole culture, and aesthetic concerns are apparent in nearly all activities of both men and women. The arts of oratory, dance, song and music were, and still are, highly regarded. Each of these performing arts had its famous exponents of the past who continue to inspire the practitioners of today. Similarly, in the visual arts of weaving, painting, latticework, carving and tattoo, the achievements of the past still provide models for the present, sometimes modified, sometimes discarded and partially revived after long disuse. Much of the accumulated knowledge and skill required for these arts is retained by living experts, passed down from generation to generation and kept alive by teaching and practice.

Traditionally, the great majority of artefacts were decorated to some extent or at least shaped according to canons of good taste. Fine form and design imparted supernatural power to the artefact, enabling it to carry out both its practical and symbolic functions with efficiency. As mediator of this supernatural power, the artist was respected as much for his ritual expertise as for his technical skill. The specialist wood-carver or tattoo expert, along with the religious ritual expert, were known as *tohunga* and regarded as vehicles through which the gods expressed their power in the human domain.

Because art is so all-pervasive in Maori culture and so integrated into all activities, there is no single word equivalent in meaning to the English term 'art'. No Maori carver in the old traditional world set out to 'make art' in the same way as a European artist does. The Maori carver set out to make a canoe or a storehouse or a container, and the artistic element was an integral aspect of the task. Most Maori words for art describe the special knowledge of both ritual and practical techniques required, the activity of employing these techniques or the product that results.

The most general word used in relation to art is *whakairo*, which simply means a design; it is also a transitive verb meaning to ornament with a pattern, used of carving, tattooing, painting and weaving. *Whakairo* is, therefore, often qualified to make the reference more specific, as in *whakairo rākau* for wood-carving or *whakairo tangata* for tattooing. However, there is also a very strong tendency (especially when the context makes it obvious) to use the unqualified term *whakairo* to refer to wood-carving specifically.

Wood-carving is certainly the most spectacular and prominent of the Maori arts, although in the past facial and body tattoo, especially on men, would have been equally prominent and impressive. On closer acquaintance, painting on architectural structures such as houses and mausolea, carving on stone and bone artefacts, and small carved nephrite personal ornaments worn by men and women all demonstrate the importance of art and aesthetic values in this society. Nevertheless, it is wood-carving that figured most in the oral traditions, that caught the attention of foreign visitors, and that consequently became the most thoroughly recorded art form. For an outsider trying to understand Maori art, a study of their wood-carving provides the best avenue into the rich diversity of art forms and traditions in this culture. And even though the actual techniques of working stone and nephrite were different, the figurative conventions of wood-carving also operated in the composition of stone and nephrite figures.

Mythological origins

In different tribal areas, certain mythological personages are associated with the origin of the art of carving, obtained for humanity from Tangaroa, god of the sea. The most prominent of these, especially among the Tūhoe and Ngāti Porou tribes, is Rua (Best 1898; 1925: 775–7; 1928; Mead 1984: 64–9; 1986b: 8–12). In these myths, Rua's son offends Tangaroa, who then carries the son away beneath the sea and sets him up as a *tekoteko* carving (frontispiece) on Tangaroa's house. Searching for his son, Rua finds the house under the sea and is surprised to hear the carvings talking to each other. In revenge, Rua sets fire to the house of Tangaroa but rescues his son and some of the carvings (fig. 44) from the porch (these carvings happen to be ones that cannot talk). Back in this world, the carvings became models for all later wood-carving taught to mankind by Rua. But sadly, like their models, carvings made by men cannot speak.

These stories of talking carvings set up an ideal in the traditional Maori aesthetic of efficient communication through the art of carving to which all carvers aspire. Poor carvings are criticised in terms that imply ideas of dry, withered, dull, stammering, stupid and ultimately poor communication. Efficient communication now occurs through the gaze of the carved figure, just as the speechless *tekoteko* could only convey his appeal for help to his father by his intense stare. This communicative gaze is intensified by representing the eyes of carved figures with glistening *pāua* shell, taken from Tangaroa's realm of the sea where carvings once could talk.

By his actions, Rua is seen as a culture hero who brought the art of carving away from the supernatural world of the gods into the world of humanity. This progressive desacralisation of carving knowledge is continued down through the generations from Rua to the famous artist–carver Hingangaroa who built a house of learning named Te Rawheoro at Tolaga Bay in about 1500 AD. Hingangaroa is considered to have been a historical figure, and is credited with teaching his art to chiefly students from other areas of eastern North Island (Ngata 1958). In this way, traditional accounts of the spread of carving styles around the country are expressed in legendary narratives and songs about the travels, teaching activities and marriages of ancestral carving experts.

About four generations after Hingangaroa, two very high-born students came to Te Rawheoro to learn the art of carving and its ritual lore. One of these was Tūkaki from Te Whānau-a-Apanui tribe of the eastern Bay of Plenty, the other was Iwirākau from the Waiapu valley at the northern

44 *Poupou* panel from the interior side wall of a meeting house depicting a male warrior ancestor holding his *wahaika* fighting weapon. The spiral patterns incised on his face allude to his male facial tattoo, while the small figure between his legs probably indicates succeeding generations of his descendants. This panel was carved by an expert from the Ngāti Pikiao tribe of the Rotorua area in the mid-nineteenth century. BM Ethno. 1894.7–16.2. L. 146.5 cm. Sudeley collection.

45 Frontal carving of a raised storehouse, *pātaka*, from Te Kaha, East Cape district. Carved in the later part of the eighteenth century by artists of Te Whānau-a-Apanui tribe, this magnificent set of carvings was hidden in a coastal cave to keep them safe from northern Ngāpuhi raiders in the 1820s. Both bargeboards feature the classical Bay of Plenty storehouse motif of a whale being dragged upward tailfirst by frontal human and profile *manaia* figures, all bearing an early form of *taratara-a-kae* surface decoration. The figure over the doorway represents a tribal origin deity guarding the threshold between two states of existence. By permission of the Auckland Museum. 22063. Right bargeboard, L. 360 cm; doorway, H.246 cm. Photo K. Pfeiffer.

end of the East Coast. They gave a famous cloak to their teacher in exchange for the knowledge of carving which they took back to their respective home areas.

Among Te Whānau-a-Apanui, Tūkaki and his descendants refined their style of carving which culminated about three hundred years later in the magnificent storehouse carvings from Te Kaha (fig. 45). In the Waiapu valley and further north at Te Araroa, the work of Iwirākau was carried on by a distinguished school of Ngāti Porou carvers, who eventually produced such famous carved houses as Porourangi and Hinetapora which still stand in that district. One of the last carvers trained traditionally in the Iwirākau school was Hone Ngatoto, who died in 1928. At Tolaga Bay, the Rawheoro school of learning continued into the early nineteenth century, taking its last students in 1836 before succumbing to the competition of Christianity.

Tools and materials

By trial and experiment, Maori woodworkers soon discovered that the best native timbers for their way of carving were the *kauri* tree (*Agathis australis*), which is restricted to the northern forests, and the more wide-ranging *tōtara* tree (*Podocarpus totara*) of lowland broad-leaf forests. *Kauri* and *tōtara* trees grow to a very large size, so tall and straight that single-hulled dugout war canoes up to 25 m long could be shaped from one tree. As moderate hardwoods with straight fine grain, *kauri* and *tōtara* were amenable to the sharply detailed curving cuts of Maori surface decoration.

Other timbers were also used for carving, especially some with tougher resilient qualities needed for specialised purposes, for example as weapons. However, *kauri* in the north and *tōtara* throughout the country quickly became the preferred timbers for wood-carving and have remained so to the present day.

With their great size and symbolic properties (they are considered to represent revered ancestors), *kauri* and *tōtara* trees themselves were invested with noble qualities. Great chiefs were referred to as *tōtara* trees and their deaths likened to the falling of a *tōtara* in the forest. As two of the largest species of forest trees, they are also associated with Tāne, god of the forest, who separated the Sky Father and Earth Mother by standing on his head and pushing them apart to let the light of life enter the world. The tall trees still continue this process, and in so doing form a living link between earth and sky. Wood for carving was referred to figuratively as Tāne himself. When carved into posts for a house, the timbers (now as named ancestors) continue to form this link: with their bases in the earth, they reach up through the rafters to the ridge-pole, the place where spirits appear and depart for Te Reinga, the abode of the dead. The *tāhuhu*, the ridge-pole of the house, also represents the main line of tribal ancestry.

Tōtara especially was very much a noble tree, being the child of Tāne and the forest goddess Mumuwhango. Rituals were necessary to appease Tāne before one of his children could be cut down. A *tohunga* or ritual expert, who was frequently also the head carver for the intended project, presided at these rituals in the forest before and after the tree was felled.

As on all Pacific islands, Maori carving tools were originally made from stone of various types. Metal tools were not used in the Pacific until after the introduction of metal by the first Europeans. The first Polynesian settlers in the islands of New Zealand apparently explored the whole country very quickly and soon gained a good practical geological knowledge of the wide range of rock types available. The most important event for the future development of wood-carving in New Zealand was the discovery of nephrite in the South Island, on the west coast and in inland Otago (Beck 1984). It is often difficult to decide whether an old carving has been done with nephrite or metal tools, since they produce similar cuts. Working blades were sharpened on sandstone grindstones, either small portable grindstones or large suitable outcrops near to running water.

Larger blades were hafted as adzes in a wooden haft, while smaller blades were mounted and lashed as chisels into a straight wooden handle. Chisels usually had a straight cutting edge, but a rounded gouge chisel was also developed. Both chisel types were driven into the wood with blows from a mallet, made either of wood or whalebone. Smaller chisels were often perforated at their rear end and worn as an ear pendant when not needed for carving.

For drilling holes in stone and bone, Maori craftsmen used a cord-driven drill with a point of flaked and chipped stone, usually argillite, quartzite or flint. The drill rotated in alternate directions as the two cords wound and unwound around the drill shaft. This motion produced a wide cratered hole that often had to be matched from the opposite side. For making lashing-holes in wood or holes for a wrist-thong in wooden weapons, the hole was cut through in a square shape using a narrow chisel driven with a mallet.

The Maori carver's mallet of wood or whalebone has a short handle and a flattened rectangular- or square-sectioned head for striking the wooden chisel handle. Even with the replacement of stone by metal tools, this form of carver's mallet has never changed. It had evolved over a long period into the form most suited for its purpose, and carvers have never felt the need to change it. Consequently his mallet is the only piece of a Maori carver's equipment that has continued unchanged from pre-European times to the present day.

Finished carvings might be left as plain wood or painted all over with *kōkōwai* (red ochre) mixed with shark-liver oil. The red ochre was found as natural deposits in clay or collected by laying fern fronds in streams where it floated in suspension. This ochre was then roasted and ground into a fine powder for mixing with oil when required. Painting the whole carving in red was by far the most common treatment but it was by no means universal.

In some areas of the country, all-over red paint was relieved with black paint, either to pick out details in carving patterns, as on East Coast treasure boxes, or to colour whole carvings, as on canoe prows and sterns in the north. Black paint was made by mixing shark oil with powdered charcoal obtained from certain resinous woods or the soot of *kauri* gum. A swamp-blackening process has been described for canoe carvings in the north, in which the carving was first soaked in a dye prepared from the bark of the *hīnau* tree, then placed in a swamp with suitable black sediment (Best 1976: 163). Most of the ancient carvings that have been recovered from swamps where they were hidden from enemy raiders have a uniform black colour, but that appears to be an accidental result of their hiding place and later treatment rather than a deliberate colour preference. A rare colour sketch of an 1840s Taranaki storehouse by Charles Heaphy shows carvings with white-painted figures against a red-ochred background (fig. 46). A mixture of oil and burnt white pipeclay produced this white paint, used on carvings for bodies, faces and details.

In some cases the surface of the wood was sized before painting with a plant sap to seal it. Paint-brushes were made with a bunch of flax fibre tied to a stick, or for finer work feathers and, later, horsehairs could be used. Large shells of the *pāua* made convenient paint-pots.

No doubt, the fish-oil component of these paints had a preservative effect on wood, but red paint in particular also had religious and ritual significance. Throughout Polynesia, red is the colour of rank and sacred value. The Maori word for red, *kura*, reflects this depth of symbolic meaning. Beyond the basic denotations of redness and glowing, the meaning extends to red feathers and cloaks ornamented with red feathers, both signs of high rank. Then, in the ancient Polynesian equation of red with value,

46 'Provision House, Otumatua Pah, Cape Egmont' by Charles Heaphy, 1840. This unique and precious view of a Taranaki raised storehouse clearly shows the interlinked sinuous figures of Taranaki-style carving emphasized with white paint against a low-relief surface-patterned background coloured with red ochre. By permission of the Alexander Turnbull Library, Wellington.

Provision House:
Otumatua Pah, Cape Egmont.

kura comes to mean precious, a treasure, a valued possession, and a chief or man of great ability. In a further expansion, *kura* includes knowledge of ritual incantations and other sacred lore, which can then become a ceremonial restriction or *tapu*. As a consequence of this powerful charge of meaning, red paint on carvings, chiefly possessions, tombs, or even a rock or post where a chief's body had rested, marked them as charged with the dangerous power of *tapu*, to be avoided by common people. Following the same logic, people of rank painted their own bodies with *kōkōwai* and oil, on special occasions even pouring the liquid paint over their head, body and clothing.

The introduction of metal tools

The change from stone to metal occurred at different times in different areas, depending on the amount of contact with European visitors. In the coastal areas this happened very early, starting with the metal obtained from Captain Cook's men and other eighteenth-century explorers such as Jean-François-Marie de Surville and Marion du Fresne (Salmond 1991) followed very soon after by the sealers and whalers. Away from the coasts, metals arrived later, in the early nineteenth century, usually as trade items brought by missionary explorers.

Maori carvers were very quick to appreciate the advantages of metal tools, although some conservative individuals no doubt clung to their trusted nephrite blades. However, even before they could obtain European-manufactured tools in any quantity, the majority of Maori woodworkers recognised the cutting properties of metal edges and began to make their own tools from whatever metal could be obtained by trade or appropriation from the new visitors.

Oral traditions of the Ngāti Tarawhai, a small Rotorua tribe famed for their wood-carving prowess, still record an incident in 1836 at the capture of Te Tumu, a fortified position of their enemies on the Bay of Plenty coast, when the Ngāti Tarawhai lost four warriors but captured four or five prisoners and seized an imported iron gate which had been incorporated in the defences of the *pā*. On first thought this seems a strangely irrelevant detail to be remembered in a tribal oral history, but the importance emerges when one begins to imagine how many carved masterpieces were probably shaped with the tools made from the iron of that humble gate.

Wood-carvers and experts trained in the ancient methods of shaping adze blades from carefully selected stones now turned their skills to metal-working in order to modify European metal forms for their own purposes. Ship's nails of copper and iron were beaten to make efficient carving chisels. Flat hoop iron from barrels could be turned into adze blades, although plane blades from a ship's carpenter's toolkit made even better adzes. Trade axes were also appreciated for rough woodworking and cutting, but in a long-established tradition of carving with adzes rather than axes, the coarse chopping movements of new metal axes never replaced the time-honoured techniques of controlled adzing. Any sort of metal knife blade was treasured for fine detailed surface patterns, while a bayonet blade could be modified into a very efficient carving tool for larger work. Nails and other small pieces of metal could be fitted directly into the old traditional pull-cord drill for faster results than the old stone drill-point.

As opportunities for trade with Europeans increased at ports and around the coasts in the 1820s and 1830s, Maori carvers began to obtain more factory-made tools which soon replaced their home-made metal cutting tools. Manufactured tools reached inland areas a little later. When Lieutenant Jones of HMS *Pandora* visited Ōhinemutu village at Rotorua in 1852 he remarked on the profusion of carvings and noted, 'They now use English carving tools, with which they make much more rapid progress than must formerly have resulted from their ruder instruments' (Jones 1970: 69). 'English carving tools' would have included the shipbuilder's metal adze or plane-blades lashed to a traditional wooden haft, the brace-and-bit, and the carpenter's hardened metal straight chisel, all of which became the basic tools of the Maori wood-carver's toolkit. He used the brace-and-bit for pierced openwork carving and also for the rapid removal of waste wood in awkward places. With the adze, figure forms were blocked out from prepared wooden slabs very quickly and much of the finer shaping could also be done by expert handling of the long-handled adze. Final details, surface decoration and tidying-up of the cuts was done with various shaped chisels added to complement the basic straight chisel.

A modern carver's toolkit now contains a wide range of chisels including round gouges, V-shaped gouges for grooves, flat-edged chisels and a cleaning chisel for clearing away waste wood left in notches and grooves. Only the carver's wood or whalebone mallet has remained unchanged.

In traditional times, the tools used by a carver acquired some of the *tapu* emanating from their owner. Nobody else would use them without proper permission. They had to be treated with respect and care, often being passed on down through his family. Oral histories that record meeting houses being built in the 1870s indicate that imported European implements used by carvers were made *tapu* in the same way as traditional Maori tools.

The act of carving

Carving was regarded as a *tapu* activity which had to be carried out under certain ritual restrictions to protect the artists, the intended users or owners, and the community at large from supernatural harm. Anything associated with common (*noa*) objects or activities had to be kept away from the work to avoid contaminating the carvings. Thus women and cooked food were not allowed where carving was in progress. Some sources suggest that sexual abstinence was observed during the period of carving. Chips and shavings should not be blown off the work by the carver, but they could be brushed or tipped away. Chips from carving should not be used as fuel for a cooking fire. According to one source (Ngata 1970: 219), carvings were turned over at night when work for the day had finished. After tobacco had been introduced, any smoking while

47 Maori carvers at work inside a house at Matapihi, Tauranga, in 1864; watercolour by H.G. Robley. These men are said to have been working on carvings for the Governor of New Zealand, Sir George Grey, becoming so engrossed with their carving that they forgot their appointment with the Governor. They work with chisel and mallet, in the posture of earlier carvers, sitting on the earthen floor of the house. By permission of the Museum of New Zealand Te Papa Tongarewa, Wellington. FA.741.

carving was prohibited, probably because of its association with food and cooking. A mistake in actual carving composition, such as a figure facing the wrong way, was also regarded as an infringement of *tapu*.

Transgression of these prohibitions could result in the failure or collapse of the building project, or even a death among the carvers or the patrons or their families, as recounted in many oral histories of famous meeting houses. With increasing European influence, some of these prohibitions lapsed but others were maintained, often depending on the attitude of the leading carver.

Any material used in art provides both opportunities and limitations. The Maori carver was limited by the shape of the prepared piece of wood, either cylindrical or a rectangular slab. He never added a figure's arms, legs or head from other pieces of timber, but always worked within the bounds of his original material. Once selected, the figure was imposed on the timber regardless of splits, knots, insect borings or other imperfections that showed up during the course of carving. Such irregularities in the timber were only very rarely incorporated as special features of the completed composition. In this respect, the Maori carver was a formalist, never making use of *objets trouvés* features.

The physical act of carving was hard work, demanding physical fitness and some strength. Development of rhythm and technique alleviated this to some degree, while the later introduction of metal tools reduced the working effort required. Under the old order, time was not an absolute abstract measure but a relative quality belonging to the activity in progress. Thus a carver simply devoted as much time as a piece of work required for its successful completion. The very high quality of most earlier carvings testifies to this availability of time and to the economic situation which enabled carving experts to devote themselves to such work.

The traditional carver followed a set order and routine of work, starting with the preparation of the slab of timber by adzing, while standing over the timber which was laid on the ground. Sometimes this preparation might be done by adzing experts who were not necessarily carving experts themselves. This adzing was done with free-swinging rhythmical strokes of the adze, often punctuated and timed by the rhythm of a traditional chant. Adzing was considered a skill in its own right, with special names

48 Arawa tribal carvers working on meeting house panels in Rotorua at about the turn of the century, using brace-and-bit and metal chisels. They work sitting on chairs beside their carvings, a stance that had become usual by this time. By permission of the Museum of New Zealand Te Papa Tongarewa, Wellington.

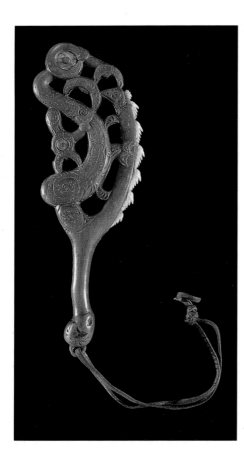

49 A shark-tooth knife, *māripi*, designed for cutting meat. The wooden frame of the knife is in the form of a *manaia* biting into and grasping the cutting edge. Surface decoration of *unaunahi* and *pūwerewere* patterns follows the curves of its body. Carved in North Auckland, possibly Hokianga style, in the late eighteenth century. BM Ethno. 1854.12–29.9. L. 24 cm (excluding thong). Grey collection.

given to different patterns of adze cuts. These patterns were judged aesthetically for their own sakes, and in the case of dugout canoe hulls were also said to improve the speed of a canoe through the water.

For larger carvings, the figure was then blocked out and a certain amount of detail cut in, still with the long-handled adze used from a standing position. Then, still with the carving lying on the ground, the carver sat cross-legged on the ground beside it and completed the details with mallet and chisel (see fig. 47). This seated working position appears in early European artists' views and in photographs taken of older carvers until about 1900. However, at about this time also, photographs of younger carvers show them working with their chisels, either standing beside their work or seated on chairs or boxes, with the carving raised to table level on trestles or saw-horses (fig. 48).

At various stages during the carving process, designs and patterns were sketched out on the wood with charcoal and later pencil, or else lightly set in with a chisel. Such sketching before carving is called *huahua*. The amount of *huahua* employed by the traditional carvers is not known but it appears to have been minimal. Most of the visionary manipulation of motifs probably took place while contemplating the piece of timber and while preparing it for carving. By the time actual carving commenced, the expert had a well-established idea of where in the timber the figure was to be located. Some experts taught their pupils by first drawing the designs on the wood for them, then gradually weaning them away from the need for too much drawing.

The period around 1900 is also the time when intricate chisel work began to replace bold deep-relief adze carving, not only on smaller articles but also on large house panels. This increase in the relative amount of chisel work required a corresponding increase in the amount of pre-carving *huahua*. In chisel work, the eye must be close to the surface and the carver loses the overall view of his composition afforded by the upright stance of adze work. He needs more lines drawn as guides to be able to follow the total composition. But an inevitable result of increased chisel work was stiff, disjointed, cramped designs with a much weakened control of the depth dimension.

Earlier Maori relief carving was primarily sculptural in conception, and carvers dislayed consummate control of the depth dimension, producing rounded sculptural forms with considerable notional depth. Spirals bulged out of the surface, hands passed through mouths from the rear, the profiles of figures met the background in various angles, and several layers of superimposed supplementary figures often overlapped each other and the main figure which supported them. But as the use of pre-carving drawing increased, so Maori relief tended to become more pictorial. Spirals were flattened, superimposed supplementary figures disappeared, and the profiles of figures met the ground surface at a more constant angle. The relative freedom of figural forms from their background matrix diminished. To compensate for this, some carvers began to experiment with innovations in pictorial composition, but overall sculptural control of the third dimension did weaken. Differences in regional styles of carving complicate this change, since some areas such as Te Arawa had earlier emphasised deep sculptural relief, while others such as Ngāti Porou and Tūhoe never did.

When the Rotorua carving school tried to revive the old skills of carving in 1928, this reliance on chisel carving with its pernicious effects was recognised as one of the main problems to be overcome. As will be seen below, this was only achieved by finding an expert trained in the old techniques of adze carving.

Form and function in Maori carving

One of the greatest strengths of Maori carving is its magnificent integration of aesthetic form and practical function. In the best traditional work, the aesthetic form is not just decoration added on later but is part of the instrumental purpose of the object. Thus the thrusting point of the *taiaha* long staff actually is the tongue of the weapon's ancestral image, striking the enemy both physically and metaphorically. Similarly, the structural framework of the shark-toothed knife is the body of the *manaia* or spiritual being whose profile head and jaws appear at the upper end (fig. 49). A man holding the handle of his canoe bailer is actually grasping the elongated nose of the ancestral face which forms the bowl of the bailer (fig. 50). The posts forming the structure of the meeting house are ancestral figures supporting the major tribal ancestor, whose body is the complete form of the meeting house. The person blowing into a *kōauau* or *nguru* flute is blowing into the lips of the ancestral face around the open end of the flute (fig. 34), and the perforated form of a stone fishing sinker takes the shape of the contorted body of a stylised ancestral figure.

Such finely integrated form and function is probably not achieved suddenly by one or two artists but is rather the result of a long period of artistic experimentation, stylisation and detailed refinement. On many

50 Canoe bailer, *tīheru*, for a large war canoe. This elegant yet functional shape is the Maori form of a widespread Pacific Ocean type of canoe bailer. Maori carvers have taken the basic Oceanic form to an extreme of stylisation and delicacy, rendering the handle as a *manaia* extending into the nose of a frontal face composed of two *manaia* heads. BM Ethno. NZ 123. L. 49 cm. Cook collection.

objects, the strategic placing of a tooth or an eye indicates how the figure is to be read. Even in some artefact forms where the figurative or meta-phorical reference is not readily apparent, the discovery of more ancient examples has occasionally revealed the figurative origins of a later abstraction. This may be the case for the archaic chevroned neck pendant, which seems to be derived from a human figure with an elongated nose and dancing arms and legs, which are repeated as chevrons along the sides of the pendant (this interpretation is suggested by an early example from Banks Peninsula; see Mead 1984: 181). While this example may suggest that the development has been from figurative to abstract, others indicate that the development has occurred in both directions, as would be expected in an art form that has been developing for about a thousand years. In the series of head combs recovered from an archaeological site at Katikati in the Bay of Plenty, a change in form can be seen from geometric to figurative and back to abstract geometric over a period of about two hundred years (Shawcross 1976).

These examples show first of all that what is and what is not figurative cannot be simply assumed by an outsider, but depends on the indigenous understanding of the image. What seems purely decorative or abstract to an outsider can be read by an indigenous insider as a very clear representation of something from the natural or supernatural world. The Maori carver's frequent use of highly simplified and stylised *manaia* figures to fill spaces or form borders is a case in point. Secondly, these examples show that the old debate about whether the language of visual forms developed from purely geometric to naturalistic or the reverse needs to be examined for each case as there are no general laws. An individual artistic genius could choose to take the development in either direction.

This debate has also occurred in studies of *kōwhaiwhai* painting and *tukutuku* latticework (Neich 1993: 32–5) based on the Maori names for specific designs, many of which refer to forms from the natural world. These names were believed to be indicative of the ultimate origin of each design, revealing the common implicit belief in the evolution of *kōwhaiwhai* and *tukutuku* design from naturalistic to geometric. In many cases, how-ever, it is now generally agreed that the names came to be applied to an existing design form because of some perceived similarity. Furthermore the particular similarity selected might be one chosen because of deeper cultural associations and connotations, rather than a simple visual simi-larity; 'correlations of ideas in the old Maori mind' as the early missionary–botanist, William Colenso, phrased it.

Design elements and rules of composition

The traditional Maori carver worked with a fairly limited vocabulary of design forms and motifs which he combined according to well-established rules of composition. By far the most important and frequent element is the human figure, either male or female or indeterminate in gender. This prominence given to the depiction of human ancestor figures is to be expected in the art of a culture that accords so much reverence to ancestors

51 Small ladle, possibly for mixing and dishing out the mixture of red ochre and shark oil used for painting the human body and carvings. The carved handle indicates that this implement is not a simple domestic tool. This higher status would be appropriate for an object associated with the *tapu* nature of red ochre. Carved in Taranaki style during the 1820s to 1830s. BM Ethno. 6858. L. 21.5 cm. Presented by A.W. Franks in 1870.

52 Portion of a war canoe thwart bearing a carved lizard, with its head in the form of a *manaia*. As omens of evil and death, lizards were depicted in carving to warn that an area or objects was *tapu*. Often carved as a pair on one thwart towards the rear of the war canoe, these lizards are said to mark the position in the canoe reserved for the *tohunga* or ritual expert. This reptile figure was carved in the mid-nineteenth century by an East Coast artist. BM Ethno. 1640. L. 51 cm.

and their ever-present power. Next in importance and frequency is the supernatural figure known as a *manaia*, which displays many of the features of a human figure portrayed in profile, sometimes combined with animal elements.

Another supernatural being which appears in more limited situations is the *marakihau*, a semi-human sea monster which sucks men and canoes down to their fate through its long tubular tongue. Real animals depicted in various degrees of stylisation are whales (fig. 45), lizards (fig. 52), fish, birds and dogs. Apart from these major figurative forms, abstract spirals of various types, almost always double in structure, are a characteristic major element of Maori carving, placed strategically among the figurative elements and often dominating the composition. On the bodies of the figurative forms and over the plain surfaces of objects, the Maori carver often added appropriate surface decoration patterns, chosen from a definite repertoire and cut into the medium in arrangements determined by the shape of the area to be covered.

A notable feature of classic Maori carving is the relative freedom of composition enjoyed by artists emancipated from the old Polynesian restriction of having to work within small demarcated design areas (Mead 1975). Provided the Maori artist understood and worked within the culturally accepted rules of artistic composition, this freedom applied to both the arrangement of major figures and their surface decoration. This enabled the classic Maori artists to elaborate a sweeping curvilinear form of art expressed on large-scale constructions, such as war canoes, storehouses, carved houses, mausolea, gateways and palisade figures. Even on small objects, such as treasure boxes, bowls, ladles (fig. 51), feeding funnels, musical instruments and fighting clubs, this freedom meant that almost every object displayed some difference, some new design touch that made it unique and individualised. Indeed, many objects from the largest war canoe and meeting house down to the smallest ear pendant or fish-hook have their own personal name, connecting them to the ancestor who gave them *mana*.

The human figure

With certain exceptions, human figures, called *tiki* in Maori carving, represent ancestors rather than gods. The exceptions are the simplified heads and occasional full figures of departmental and tribal gods carved on the top of small *tiki wānanga*, so-called 'god sticks', for the *tohunga* ritual expert

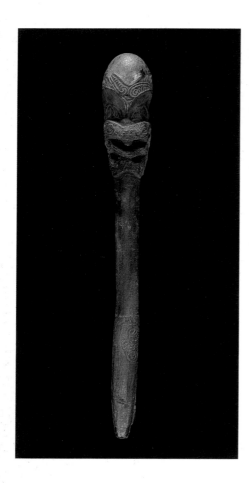

53 God stick, *tiki wānanga*, of typical simple
form, collected by the early missionary,
Rev. Richard Taylor, probably in the
Whanganui district in the 1840s. Still
bearing traces of red ochre applied during
ritual use, this was not an idol but a vehicle
for communicating with a god, in this case
Maru, who was a tribal god of the
Whanganui and Taranaki tribes. To
activate the image, it was decorated with
red parrot feathers and bound with flax
braid in a criss-cross pattern, then anointed
with red ochre in oil. BM Ethno. 1863.2–
9.6. L. 35 cm. Presented by the Rev. R.
Taylor.

to communicate with the gods and receive their commands (fig. 53). Other
possible representations of certain gods are found on door lintels (*pare*) of
important houses. Some *pare* designs relate to myths of Tāne the forest
god and his brothers separating their father Rangi, the sky god, from
their mother, Papa, the earth goddess. Other lintels are said to depict
Hinenui-te-Pō, the goddess of death and the underworld, beneath whose
legs all humankind must eventually pass. In a design symbolically comparable to a house *pare*, the stern and prow carvings of war canoes may refer
to Tangaroa, the sea god, and Tūmatauenga, the god of war.

However, the distinction between gods and deified ancestors is not
absolute in a culture where the gods and their children can all be considered as founding ancestors. So, just as the life of the living is seen as
an embodiment of the activities of the ancestors, the actions of the ancestors are seen as emulations of the processes of the gods. This emulation
is made explicit on the ridge-pole of some meeting houses, where the usual
place of Rangi and Papa as the primeval procreating parents at the beginning of the main line of genealogy is taken by representations of the eponymous ancestor of the local descent group and his wife.

The human figure in carving may be rendered either as a naturalistic
image or as a stylised one. In earlier writings on Maori art, the stylised
form has often been called 'grotesque', but since this implies a monocultu-
ral value judgement that term is not now used. On naturalistic figures,
both male and female, great attention is paid to the details of facial tattoo
especially and also to bodily tattoo (fig. 54). Naturalistic figures are more
likely to be carved as free-standing, three-dimensional sculptures, but they
also occur in relief. In some cases a naturalistic face may be combined
with a stylised body, but it is most unusual to find a stylised face on a
naturalistic body. Of course, by the very nature of art, both naturalistic
and stylised renderings are abstracted from reality and are both composed
from a system of conventionalised symbols. Nevertheless, in Maori carving
the distinction between naturalistic and stylised figures is a wide one, with
very limited merging between the two streams, sometimes seen as surface
decoration patterns on a naturalistic body. Since they are further abstracted from reality, it is the stylised carving figures that display regional and
tribal stylistic differences most clearly.

Several commentators on Maori art have tried to explain this distinction
between naturalistic and stylised figures by looking for consistency in the
type of personage represented in each. Examination of a wide sample of
carved figures soon demonstrates that claims of any such consistency are
suspect and cannot be maintained. Nevertheless, on this basis, both Mead
and Firth reached the valid interpretation that carvers have used these
two figurative choices to express different states of being. Firth (1992: 33)
describes how a naturalistic rendering represents a person from the past
in a domestic, social and political world, while a stylised figure represents
a personalised phase or aspect of mystical power and relation with the
world of spirits. Mead (1975: 178–9) sees a gradient from the naturalistic
portrait of a living person, which emphasises the human element, through

54 Naturalistic male figure
from the base of a house
interior central post,
poutokomanawa, which
supports the ridgepole. With
detailed male facial tattoo and
his hair wound up in a
topknot, this figure represents
an important ancestor of the
tribal group owning the
meeting house. His
naturalistic features, large
hands and solidly-
proportioned body show that
he belongs within a series of
similar figures carved in the
mid-nineteenth century by a
prominent school of Ngāti
Kahungunu carvers from the
central Hawkes Bay district.
BM Ethno. 1892.4–9.1.
H.85 cm.

to the stylised figure of a deified ancestor, which emphasises the supernatural spiritual aspect, and then on to the *manaia* figure and *marakihau*, which are purely spirit beings. Thus the same personage can be represented in either a naturalistic or a stylised manner, depending on whether the carver intends to emphasise the social human or the supernatural spiritual aspect of being.

Another element of the human figure that has attracted much attention is the three-fingered hand seen on many stylised and naturalistic figures. Many interpretations for this peculiarity have been advanced, most of which have been listed by Mead (1986b: 244). Some of these interpretations suggest that the origin is to be found in the deformed or mutilated hands of mythological carvers famous in a particular tribal region, while others relate each finger to an element of a set, such as the three baskets of knowledge brought back from heaven, the natural elements of earth, wind and water as represented by their relevant Maori gods, or even the Father, Son and Holy Ghost of the Christian Trinity. Obviously, the last is a post-European imposition, and many of the others also seem to be later rationalisations. What all these explanations fail to address is the fact that other numbers of fingers are just as common in Maori art, from one to five and even up to seven fingers. Many of the apparently three-fingered figures actually have a fourth digit or thumb indicated by a reversed or hooked extension of the upper finger. Most commentators now regard the choice of number of fingers to have been primarily a stylistic decision, guided by certain regional preferences and some symbolic considerations.

More recently, attention has turned to the interpretations of carving symbolism recorded by the missionary Thomas Kendall in the Bay of Islands, North Auckland, in the early 1820s (Binney 1968; 1980). In a somewhat confused report, Kendall drew attention to the symbolic message that may be communicated by the number of fingers and relative placement of hands. In Kendall's scheme, a two-fingered hand was a sign that a carving of an ancestor-god depicted him in 'a first state or before creation'. Man in this state of existence had no distinction of form or gender and was 'shut up between the thumb and little finger' of the deity, who has his three middle fingers missing. Three fingers on a carving were emblematic of creation and indicated existence and form, both for gods and humans (Binney 1980: 11). Kendall's schemes of interpretation still leave many problems unresolved but they do indicate directions for further careful readings of texts and carvings.

The *manaia*

More scholarly controversy has focused on the *manaia* figure than any other element in Maori carving (Hanson 1990), although it must be said that the argument was of more concern to European academics than to the Maori carvers, who continued to create authentic *manaia* figures in their work. H.D. Skinner writing in the 1930s and T. Barrow in the 1960s and later (Barrow 1969) were the two main proponents of the theory that

55 Unique archaic carving recovered from a swamp between Kaitaia and Ahipara in the far north. Carved to be viewed from front and rear, it is now usually considered to be from a gateway structure rather than a house lintel, but the composition of central frontal human figure and terminal *manaia*-type figures sets a precedent for later house door lintels. By comparison with similar motifs of edge-notching and chevrons on archaic personal ornaments, this carving is thought to date from about 1300–1400 AD, but it may be more recent. By permission of the Auckland Museum. 6341. w. 226 cm. Photo K. Pfeiffer.

the *manaia* was derived from a bird-headed man, pointing to such figures in the art of other Pacific cultures as supporting evidence.

Writing at the same time as Skinner, Archey (1933a; 1933b) took a more practical view and argued from internal evidence of actual carved figures that the *manaia* is derived from the human form represented in profile. However, his analysis lacked any time control – a provision which he argued was irrelevant for this type of compositional analysis. Later his theory was endorsed by McEwen (1966), who demonstrated how each type of stylised full-frontal *tiki* face has a matching *manaia* face which can be recognised as half of each frontal face, divided down the centre line. McEwen then explained how the *manaia* can be distorted or dismembered to fill any space in a composition, even sharing limbs or other body parts with neighbouring figures. This distortion can disguise the correspondence with frontal human figures, especially when avian or reptilian similarities are emphasised.

More recently, Mead (1975: 202–6) has returned to an evolutionary sequence for the derivation of the *manaia*, based on the evidence of archaic wood-carvings where there is some weak time control available. Mead began his sequence with the reptilian-like monster on the ends of the famous Kaitaia carving, which is generally regarded to be one of the oldest surviving Maori wood-carvings (fig. 55). Noting the gradual reduction of spikes to knobs and the concurrent development of a curvilinear idiom, Mead traces a progressive humanisation of the Kaitaia monster through the relief heads on the Awanui panel, then the heads on the Doubtless Bay prow, to the *manaia* on the most developed comb from Kauri Point (fig. 13), and finally to the humanised profile *manaia* of classical wood-carving (see Barrow 1969 for photos of above). As Mead realised, this progression is directly opposed to Archey's proposed derivation from human forms and also offers an alternative to the bird-man origin idea.

McEwen's matching of stylised half-face profiles with corresponding full-frontal faces reveals that what appears to be a full-frontal face in Maori art is actually a split representation composed of two profile forms, a feature of Maori tattoo and carving first described by Lévi-Strauss (1963: 256–64) following Boas's analysis of the same phenomenon in North-west Coast American Indian art (Boas 1955: 223ff). Split representation allows all the essential features of a three-dimensional animal or human to be shown clearly without perspective distortion on a flat or relief surface or on a three-dimensional form different from the natural animal form. This obviously meets the need of a 'conceptual' art anxious to represent ancestors correctly with all necessary details present. Split representation explains the deep v-shape between the brows of Maori faces, the frequently doubled nose and the convergence of lips at the centre line of the face (fig. 44). Split profile features are sometimes carried through into the delineation of the body as well. Maori carvers were well aware of these characteristics and often consciously exploited the ambiguities of split images, producing compositions that oscillate between a single figure and two facing profiles, or an apparent single figure that embraces itself.

Carvers also enjoyed a certain freedom in combining elements derived from various natural and supernatural beings. An awareness of this sophisticated and conscious playing with ambiguities in representation tends to make one wary of tight evolutionary reconstructions, which rely too strongly on a strict categorisation of the world in Western scientific terms. The concept of *manaia* may have been over-extended by students of Maori art to encompass a wide range of carving forms incorporating highly variable avian, reptilian, human and imaginary features, which then defy any unitary evolutionary explanation. Relatively naturalistic carvings of dogs, birds and lizards with *manaia* faces complicate the picture even more (fig. 52).

Shawcross (1976: 290) has made the same point with regard to the series of combs from the Kauri Point swamp, noting that in an art such as Maori carving with a high level of ambiguity between animal and human forms, it may not be feasible or valid to force an exclusively animal or human evolutionary interpretation on apparently anthropomorphic forms. Instead, when the comb seriations did not demonstrate the anticipated development of progressively more abstract forms from naturalistic prototypes, Shawcross suggested that knowledge of motifs and meanings was confined to a small group of craftsmen who were deliberately exploring the possible variations of their formal language of motifs, randomly selecting 'early' and 'late' motifs as they pleased.

Interpretation of the symbolic significance of *manaia* needs to take account of the role of birds as guardian spirits in Maori thought (Phillipps 1963), the significance of the lizard as a sign of *tapu* and the bringer of life and death, and the interaction between spirit beings and the ancestors. In describing a carving which seems to have been a storehouse *paepae* (threshold beam) with alternating frontal *tiki* figures and *manaia*, Kendall in 1823 commented that the carving seemed to represent time and the states or conditions of life through which man passes. The *manaia* figures flanking a human figure on both sides represented the sun and the moon which dictate the passage of time (Binney 1980: 19–21; 1986: 142). Obviously, the *manaia* is a motif with deep symbolic significance, perhaps too deep for simple verbal commentary. Contemporary understanding of the symbolism of the *manaia* among Maori carvers generally is that it represents a guardian spirit being, protecting the frontal *tiki* figure to which it is usually linked.

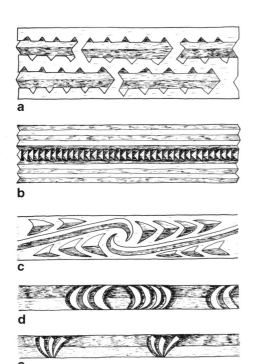

56 Surface patterns of wood carving.
a *Taratara-a-kai* **b** *Rauponga* **c** *Pākura*
d *Unaunahi* **e** *Ritorito*. Drawing R. Jewell.
After McEwen 1966.

Surface patterns

Much of the distinctive character of Maori carving is a result of the characteristic surface patterns used on the bodies of figures, on smaller objects and on architectural surfaces. In basic form, these surface patterns are either spiral or linear, although often the spirals run into the next one to produce linear effects, while the linear elements may be used in a spiral arrangement. Spirals are found in the arts of many other cultures, including some Polynesian traditions such as Marquesan. But there is no doubt that Maori artists developed spiral forms, in particular the double spiral, to an unprecedented degree, especially in later classic art. Many design elements of Maori linear decoration can be matched in other Polynesian wood-carving traditions, but Maori carvers made the great advance of freeing themselves from the old Polynesian system of working in bands and other restricted design fields (Mead 1975). This new freedom encouraged the development of curvilinear free-flowing surface decoration, often deliberately curved to fit high relief features of the new bold art forms and to suggest movement and direction.

Each of the main surface decoration patterns (fig. 56) have their own specific names, usually relating them to a form in nature such as fish scales (*unaunahi*), fern fronds (*rauponga*), shoots of young flax (*ritorito*), footprints of the swamp hen (*pākura*), and spider's web (*pūwerewere*, a spiral form of the *ritorito* motif). A common variant of the *rauponga* design in which the plain ridges suddenly curve across the central notching is called *whakarare*, which simply means distortion. The names applied to these patterns seem to be purely descriptive, with no particular symbolic associations intended. Most of these patterns are used quite freely on all sorts of carvings, but some tend to be found more frequently in certain locations, for example the use of *pākura* on the thickened edges of house thresholds, canoe sidestrakes and treasure boxes. Some patterns are more commonly associated with certain regional carving styles, for example *unaunahi* in the northern area, *pūwerewere* in western areas, and *rauponga* in the eastern and central styles.

Some patterns have passed through temporal changes which probably just reflect changing fashions. *Rauponga* on carvings from the mid-nineteenth century and later is usually standardised to three plain ridges (*raumoa*) on each side of the notched ridge (*pākati*). However, on earlier carvings the number of *raumoa* is much more variable, even on the same carving, ranging from one to seven with five being a favourite among Arawa and Tūhoe carvers.

One of the most complex patterns is named *taratara-a-kai* or *taratara-a-kae*, where *taratara* means prickly, barbed, peaked or even crooked. The difference in spelling depends on whether the name is related to food (*kai*) or to the mythological villain named Kae who stole and ate the pet whale of Tinirau (the son of Tangaroa). Kae's guilt was revealed when he was made to laugh, thereby showing his crooked teeth, *taratara*, with the flesh of the whale still caught between them. Since this pattern is mainly used on storehouses where whales are the predominant motif on the front bargeboards (i.e. in the Hauraki to eastern Bay of Plenty area), both these names make sense in linking food, whales and storehouses. The oldest manifestation of the *taratara-a-kai* pattern consists of a raised crooked line with soft notching along the edges. In later examples of Bay of Plenty *taratara-a-kai*, the raised notched line becomes sharper-edged to form a zigzag and may run parallel to a plain ridge.

Space and time in Maori carving

Most Maori carving is basically an art of relief, following the simple definition of relief as relating an image to a ground or surface. Even in those works not obviously relief, the basic concept still seems to be relief but showing various degrees of emancipation from its surface. Thus the pierced carving of canoe prows and sterns is relief made to be viewed from both sides but not from above or behind. Many figures such as palisade posts, central house-posts and gable figures are fully three-dimensional and free-standing, but their frontal aspect is clearly still intended as the most important view. This two-dimensional basis is so marked in some three-dimensional sculptures that they appear to be organised as flat designs laid on each facet of a rectangular or semi-rounded post.

As Rogers (1974: 13) has noted, reliefs can occupy a whole range of intermediary positions between the complete flatness of pictures and the full three-dimensionality of sculpture in the round. Correspondingly, the three-dimensional spatial properties attributed to relief can range anywhere between the actual three-dimensional space of sculpture in the round and the illusory space of drawing and painting. Thus in most types of relief, space is represented by a complicated mixture of both actual and notional space, depending on a fusion of pictorial and sculptural techniques and conceptions. Egyptian relief stands at one extreme where three-dimensional depth is deliberately translated into its two-dimensional planar equivalent according to a definite schema of representation.

Maori relief carving, like Egyptian, deliberately avoided representing the visual effects of perspective. But unlike Egyptian relief, Maori carvers did use some actual depth to suggest greater notional depth. Although the actual extension of depth in Maori relief is usually relatively shallow, the forms and their spatial relationships are compressed and condensed to convey an impression of greater depth than is actually present. The base plane forms a flat material surface on which the figures exist, but this plane bisects the figures longitudinally, leaving a notional volume behind the base plane. This sculptural solution gives the figures an illusion of three-dimensionality greater than one would expect from the actual depth extension available. Frequent undercutting of profiles to produce strong shadows further strengthens this illusion of volume and corporeality.

As a 'conceptual' rather than a 'perceptual' art, Maori carving did not try to represent the effects of perspective or any of the other distortions produced by viewing from one fixed point at one instant in time. Instead, the Maori carver set out to depict things 'objectively' — as he knows them to be at all times, according to the image of them in his mind — by eliminating shadows, foreshortening and any other disturbing elements. The underlying principle informing the framework of all Maori two-dimensional and three-dimensional sculpture is depiction based on frontal images (Schafer 1974). From the carver's mental standpoint, figures are always depicted as if their planes were looked at frontally. Oblique views and three-quarter profiles are avoided. The Maori carver kept to full-frontal or full-profile views or a mixture of these two within one figure, with the articulations at neck and waist.

This framework based on frontal images operates in both naturalistic and stylised Maori figures, whether human, *manaia*, *marakihau* or animal. It applies to both the principal figures of a composition and the subordinate supplementary figures that may be disposed about the main figure, although the subordinate figures usually display a much greater variety of body postures and limb articulations. The relative status of figures is indicated by differences in size and projection of relief, in direct contrast to perspective relief, in which degree of projection and relative size are used to indicate notional depth and distance from the viewer.

In accordance with this repudiation of the illusional and the phenomenal, the Maori carver did not try to render momentary impressions. Limbs, tongue and head could be shown disposed in various positions but never in the process of getting there. Activity could be shown but it was frozen, timeless. Muscles never flexed and bodies never bent with the strain. The activity was shown as an attribute of the ancestor, rather than as a particular instant in his life. Because of the depth limitation of relief, differences in placement of limbs were restricted mainly to movement in the lateral plane. The particular space about a figure was never defined, and the figure was never put into a landscape. A clear profile separated the figure from its ground, leaving it isolated without any spatial depth relationships to other figures. Thus the figure existed in ideal, timeless space.

Major ancestral figures are always shown standing upright in full frontal view. This is the direction which brings most of the figure's planes at right angles to the viewer and also clearly shows the most characteristic features of the particular ancestor. Important features such as famous weapons, items from an identifying myth, or unusual body parts were selected as essential to a particular ancestor and always shown in their most characteristic view. This often meant that natural articulations and natural proportions of the body were not followed, even in the most naturalistic figures. In some regional styles, notably Taranaki and Northland, limbs could even pass through eyes and mouths. Arms and legs could be shown in different sizes. Hands always have the palm flat with fingers extended, never with the hand clenched or the fingers in profile. Feet were turned inwards or outwards to give a profile view, but toes were often distributed along the length of the foot profile. Artefacts worn or carried by the ancestor figure are shown flat-on in their most characteristic view, never in edge profile.

This non-perspectival representation of timeless ancestors set in ideal non-specified space accords well with Maori concepts of time and the role of ancestors, continually recreating the timeless, ever-present world of the ancestors (Jackson 1972: 46). In Maori thought, time is a continuous stream or sequence of events and processes, ordered simply by their relative positions. There is no concept of an abstract time, only a relative time or a qualitative description of periods. As Johansen (1954: 172) has said about the Maori; 'He thinks history because he lives history.' Thus, 'the actions of the kinship group are not only significant as true expressions of life in the living; for the same life, the same *mana*, is active through the history of the kinship group' (Johansen 1954: 152). This means that the ancestors are still very much alive and relevant to Maori in the present. They are often spoken of in the present tense and support their descendants in present crises. Therefore, the Maori carver worked not to deny time but rather to create time as a continuous duration. He never tried to record a particular moment nor to show the effects of time and ageing on the human body: all his ancestors were stylised to a constant 'ageless' age.

Archaic carving

Very few pieces of wood-carving have survived from those several hundred years during which the ancestral Eastern Polynesian culture gradually evolved into distinctive New Zealand Maori culture. In the main, only small artefacts of stone, bone, ivory and shell have been recovered from the ground. Among such items, stone woodworking tools and bone tattoo chisels testify to the early presence of the arts of carving and body tattoo. Among early artefacts showing some artistic embellishment, the majority are pendants and necklace units, displaying the archaic features of edge notching, chevron patterns and simple human faces (Mead 1975).

These archaic features or their later derivatives are also found on the rare and precious early wood-carvings which have been preserved in swamps, especially in the far north but also in other areas. Fortunately, the old Maori practice of hiding valuable wooden items in swamps to keep them out of enemy hands has left us some notable examples of earlier art forms. Most important among these are the Kaitaia carving (fig. 55), the Awanui panel, the Doubtless Bay canoe prow and stern (Archey 1933a), the assemblage of wooden carvings from the Waitore site near Patea (Cassels 1979), and the combs from Kauri Point on Tauranga Harbour (Shawcross 1976). Unfortunately, only the latter two have been radiocarbon dated, the Waitore carvings to the fifteenth century AD and the Kauri Point combs extending from the mid-sixteenth to the mid-eighteenth centuries.

These dated collections show that the double spiral was being used in Taranaki by the fifteenth century, and by the late sixteenth or early seventeenth centuries spirals and *manaia* motifs were being carved in the Bay of Plenty. Surveying all of this material, Mead (1975) described how a strong curvilinear principle begins to be applied, and over time, notches are transformed into spikes, then into rounded knobs, before disappearing entirely in most later carvings. Interestingly, archaic rock paintings of

57 This elegant and powerful image represents the deity Uenuku, guardian of the Tainui confederation of tribes and a symbol of growth, prosperity and triumph. Originally seen as a rainbow, Uenuku is a protective and inspiring presence who continues to awe and comfort Maori people today. Uenuku, found in 1906 at Lake Ngaroto, Te Awamutu district, and identified by local elders of the Ngāti Apakura and Waikato, is a superb example of the carving style dating from the early period, between 1200 and 1500 AD. By permission of Te Awamutu District Museum. 2056. H. 267 cm. Photo N.F. Every.

the South Island, usually dated between about AD 1200 and 1500, already displayed a sophisticated cursive style (Davidson 1984: 214–15; Dunn 1972; Trotter and McCulloch 1981).

In the absence of firm datings, some carvings found in swamps may represent other intermediate stages of this transition. A remarkable fact is that some of these ancient items look like eighteenth-century carvings from eastern Polynesia. The central figure of the Kaitaia carving has been compared to the figures on a small carving collected by Captain Cook's expedition at Rurutu in the Austral Islands (Barrow 1972: 49; Kaeppler 1978: 159). A figure of Uenuku, a god symbol of the Waikato people (fig. 57), found in a local swamp has similarities to the crested carvings of Hawaii. A god stick head from Katikati in the Bay of Plenty shows correspondences with Rarotongan carvings, especially in the form of their eyes (Simmons 1985: 16).

No comprehensive explanations have been advanced for these similarities, especially in view of the apparent time gap between the New Zealand carvings and their tropical Polynesian counterparts. Perhaps the similarities are coincidental, or all these items may represent similar artistic expressions arising from the same widespread ancestral Eastern Polynesian culture. Or again, following a suggestion by Sutton (1987) they may be evidence for multiple arrivals from different areas of tropical Polynesia, even into relatively recent times, as opposed to the generally accepted theory of Maori origin from one area of Polynesia at one remote early date.

The series of combs found at Kauri Point had been purposely discarded over a period of two hundred years in a small swamp enclosure specially designated for the safe disposal of *tapu* artefacts, such as broken combs used on the *tapu* heads of chiefs. As well as documenting the changes from notches to spikes to knobs, the anthropomorphic designs on the combs provide very important evidence for the gradual replacement of earlier geometric notched square-topped designs by later knobbed round-topped forms. Some of the later round-topped forms became so stylised while still retaining their curvilinear form, that the anthropomorphic origin is no longer obvious. Combs of this later type were seen in use during Captain Cook's first visit to New Zealand in 1769 (fig. 12). By the late eighteenth century, when Captain Cook and his companions made the first full record of Maori culture and collected examples as curios, the change from a rectilinear to a curvilinear art had almost been completed. In wood-carving, tattooing, painting and personal ornaments, the curvilinear orientation was clearly dominant, although remnants of rectilinear forms did persist.

Attempts have been made (Mead 1975) to correlate the increasing predominance of boldness and curvilinearity in classic Maori art with the migration of the Awa peoples from North Auckland into the Taranaki, Bay of Plenty and Hawkes Bay regions. Faced with the need to emphasise their separate identity from the original *tangata whenua* (people of the land) inhabitants, the Awa migrants favoured a distinctive new set of art forms. In the general social reorganisation and status differentiation which followed, it is argued that the newer bold designs may have served to warn and protect commoner people from the greater *mana* and *tapu* of the powerful migrants.

The development of regional and tribal carving styles

Reference has already been made to traditional accounts of the spread of the art of carving from the north into Taranaki and the Bay of Plenty. Careful examination of actual carvings from these and other areas led Archey (1933a) and Ngata (1958, but written in 1936) to establish two main style divisions. In the north-western style area may be grouped the carvings from North Auckland, parts of the Waikato, Hauraki and Taranaki. These are characterised by an emphasis on the human figure, which is sinuously curved and rhythmically entwined, with small amounts of surface decoration and limited intervening detail between the figures of a composition. In contrast, the central and eastern style area covering the Bay of Plenty, Taupo, Whanganui, Hawkes Bay, East Coast and Poverty Bay produced carvings with more stable and static upright 'square' figures, which in many compositions become subordinate to the spirals of their surface decoration and the spirals between figures. Mainly because of the increasing predominance of the spiral in the central and eastern styles, Archey regarded these as a later development from the less-differentiated north-western styles.

Further extensive examination of carvings by Simmons (1985) has clarified the temporal differentiation between these two regional styles. He made the point that virtually all the known larger north-western carvings were executed with stone tools, while most of the central and eastern carvings are metal-tool work. Judging by this, it seems that almost none of the north-western carvers made the transition to metal tools, at least in architectural work, although there are small metal-tool carvings such as treasure boxes, weaving pegs and weapons from these areas. Various reasons have been advanced to explain why these carvers stopped work, including changes in architectural needs, epidemics, or devastating raids with the first muskets from the north in the early nineteenth century.

In the central and eastern areas, the correlation with metal-tool work is not so absolute, since a few early carvings done with stone tools have been recovered from swamps or caves. Most notable among these are the storehouse carvings from Te Kaha (Mead 1984: 204), the *poupou* (side wall panel) from Whangara said to be from Hinematioro's house (Mead 1984: 75), a storehouse threshold from Waiapu (Simmons 1985: 57), a house lintel in Te Whānau-a-Apanui style (Mead 1986b: 88) and a storehouse panel from Mokoia Island in Lake Rotorua (Mead 1984: 103). These early but undated stone-tool carvings probably reflect various stages in the development of central and eastern carving styles that were later continued and elaborated in the metal-tool era.

Clearly, the eighteenth- and very early nineteenth-century sinuous-bodied carving forms of Taranaki, North Auckland and Hauraki represent the ultimate development of this style. Already by the later eighteenth

58 Frontal *tiki* and profile *manaia* figures illustrating tribal carving styles: **a,b,c** – central and eastern 'square' styles; **d,e,f** – northern and western sinuous styles.

a Te Arawa
b Tūhoe
c Ngāti Porou
d North Auckland
e Taranaki
f Hauraki

Drawing R. Jewell. After McEwen 1966; Mead 1986b; Simmons 1985.

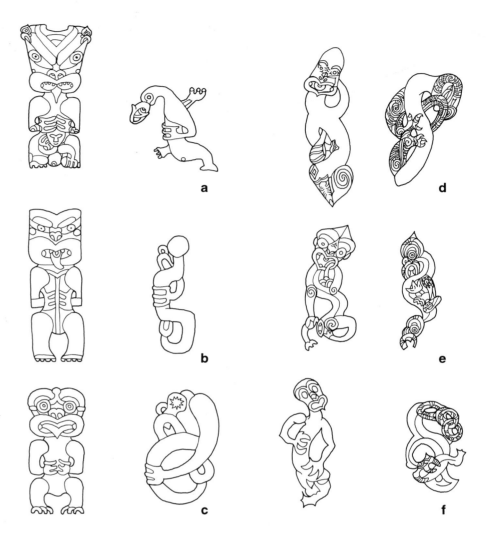

century in the central and eastern areas, a reaction to this strongly curvilinear style was producing the straight, square figures encountered there by Captain Cook. But the square-bodied styles were still relatively new when Captain Cook and later travellers introduced metal that could be used for carving tools. The artists working in the new vigorous square styles were quite willing to try these new tools, whereas their contemporaries still working in the sinuous forms of the north and west were either isolated from the trade in metal, or had little desire to experiment, or had perished in the musket wars and epidemics which soon swept the country.

A first systematic description of the main tribal styles of wood-carving was provided by McEwen (1966), based mainly on their renderings of human figures and *manaia* (fig. 58). Subsequent research into carving styles has not altered this broad scheme significantly, except to add finer details. These details indicate the complexity of developmental relationships between styles and reveal a lack of firm information regarding the art history and eventual demise of each tribal style (Mead 1986b; Simmons 1984). With his broad descriptions of many different tribal styles, Simmons

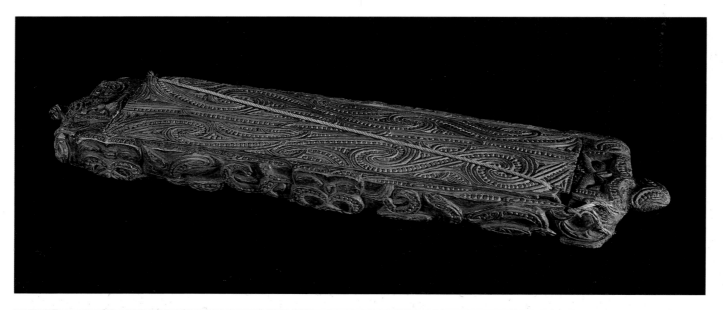

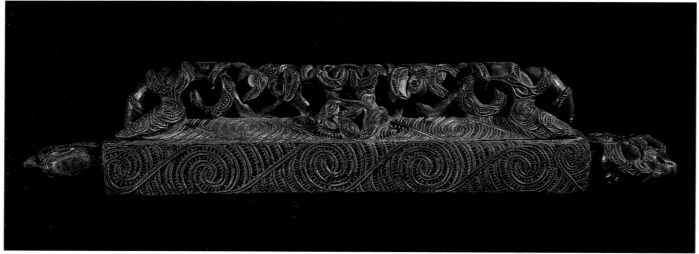

59 TOP Treasure box of the flat northern type called *papahou.* The sides and base are carved with alternating frontal and *manaia* figures arranged with their heads on the sides of the box. This box is remarkable for the boldness of its composition, producing a powerful directional flow of linked figures. Carved in Bay of Islands style during the later eighteenth century. BM Ethno. NZ 109. L. 65 cm. Cook collection.

60 Treasure box, *papahou.* The projecting handles at each end and the raised ridge on the lid are composed of openwork linked and intertwined sinuous figures in a typical Taranaki style. Probably carved in the early nineteenth century. BM Ethno. 1926.3–13.30. L. 46 cm. Presented by Sir F. Sidney Parry.

(1984; 1985) has mapped out a huge project for future students of Maori art.

Among the magnificent Maori collections of the British Museum, the fine series of treasure boxes or *wakahuia* provides valuable illustrative examples of several of the main tribal carving styles (figs 59 and 60). As with other smaller items of personal use, it seems that many individuals with varying carving skills made their own treasure boxes, usually working within the canons of their tribal style but sometimes adding their own touches. A *wakahuia* (fig. 61) collected on one of Captain Cook's expeditions and now in the British Museum has a lid uniquely painted with a *kōwhaiwhai* (abstract curvilinear) design in Poverty Bay style, the oldest surviving example of *kōwhaiwhai* painting apart from the painted paddles collected on the same voyages (Neich 1993: 59). Originally, treasure boxes were designed to be suspended from the rafter of a dwelling

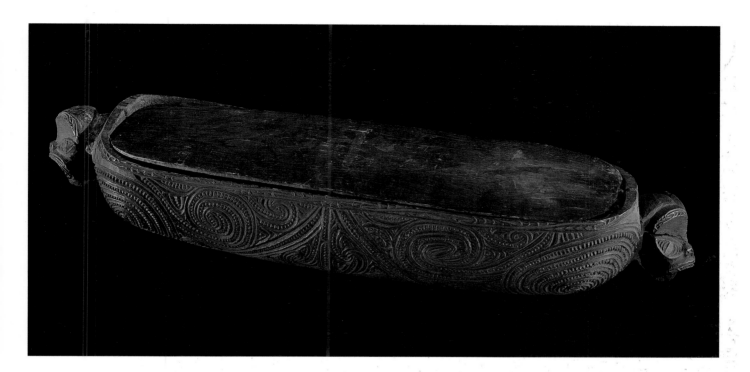

61 Treasure box, *wakahuia*, with the unique feature of a lid painted in *kōwhaiwhai* patterns. This painting is in Poverty Bay style, while the restrained *rauponga* spirals carved on the box relate to Whanganui carving style. Such a combination of styles was encountered by Captain Cook's expedition in the Queen Charlotte Sound area. Carved during the eighteenth century. BM Ethno. NZ 113. L. 59.5 cm. Cook collection.

house and therefore had as much carving on the lower surface as on the top. But as European influence increased, carvers in the central and eastern style areas of Gisborne, Rotorua and Whanganui began to experiment with flat bottoms or enlarged the terminal figures as supports to stand on a flat surface such as a table or mantelpiece.

The war canoe and its symbolism

The war canoe or *waka taua* was probably the greatest achievement of the Maori genius for melding aesthetic form with practical function. It was constructed on the basis of a single large dugout hull with separate bow, stern and side carvings, all these elements being fitted together into a sleek, efficient sea-going vessel that could be sailed and paddled for long coastal journeys. In the stormy waters of the south, two canoes might be lashed together to form a double canoe similar to those of the Pacific islands, but this was only a temporary expedient. Fishing canoes had reduced prow and stern carvings, while smaller plain dugouts were used for river and lake travel and transport. In some areas, the typical small Pacific outrigger canoe was still in use when Europeans first arrived. But for the tribal group owning a *waka taua* this was the prime focus of corporate group pride. Even the humble bailer for a war canoe was a small work of art, blending carved designs into the form of a very efficient instrument (fig. 50).

Fully decorated with fresh paint and feathers, and manned by a crew of the tribe's most vigorous tattooed warriors, a *waka taua* presented a most formidable sight. Early European visitors regularly encountered war canoes as long as around 18–21 m, and others were often larger. One that

62 War canoe sternpost, *taurapa*, following the usual prescribed composition but with the forward-facing figure confined within the margin of the front curve and reduced to an extremely stylised head and body form. Probably carved in about the mid-nineteenth century by an expert from the Bay of Plenty. BM Ethno. 1922.1–10.1. H. 210 cm. Presented by the National Art Collections Fund.

was manoeuvred alongside Captain Cook's *Endeavour* at sea as if to compare sizes was 30.5 m long. The only surviving original complete Maori war canoe, Te Toki-a-Tāpiri, now in Auckland Museum, is 25 m long and carried about one hundred warriors (Archey 1977). In the early decades of the nineteenth century, European missionaries at the Bay of Islands saw fleets of fifty to sixty canoes like this, with full crews of warriors leaving on raids against the southern tribes. Occasionally, war canoes engaged in naval battles, but their main purpose was to transport warriors around the country for hand-to-hand fighting.

Being designed for the *tapu* pursuit of warfare, the war canoe itself was also highly *tapu* at all times, but especially when in action. No women or food were ever allowed in the war canoe. Even the way for warriors to enter the canoe was ritually prescribed. As Kendall wrote, to enter a war canoe from either the stern or the prow was equivalent to a 'change of state or death' (Binney 1980: 14). Instead, the warrior had to cross the threshold of the side-strakes as a ritual entry into the body of his ancestor as represented by the canoe. The hull of the canoe was regarded as the backbone of their chief. In laments for dead chiefs, the deceased are often compared to broken canoes awash in the surf.

Whether built by local or imported experts or obtained by trade, a war canoe represented a considerable investment of group resources. When not in use, it was often unlashed and dismantled, the carved components removed, and the hull protected from the elements in a special canoe shed built at the water's edge. The hull was shaped with stone adzes from one large *tōtara* or *kauri* tree, sometimes with extra hull length added at front and rear by a large mortise-and-tenon joint. Side-strakes carved with alternating *manaia* and frontal figures increased the freeboard, and separate bow and stern pieces were carved to fit against these, all held together by flax lashings. Construction could take several years, and in its lifetime a canoe hull might be outfitted with various sets of carvings.

The composition of the stern post was very strictly prescribed (fig. 62). It consists of a *manaia* near the top holding two ribs, one of which is being bitten by the *manaia* or appears to be the *manaia*'s tongue, and another *manaia* at the lower rear. At the lower front of the stern post there is a human figure facing forward, sometimes very naturalistic or else stylised to a high degree. All of the intervening space is filled with alternating openwork spirals and small *manaia* figures. No totally consistent explanation of the symbolism of the stern post has been recorded, but hints from a description by Kendall indicate that the two ribs are the two creative principles of knowledge and life, being simultaneously attacked and defended by the *manaia* (Binney 1980: 11–12). The lines of these ribs continue along the total length of the canoe, binding the whole construction into a harmonious streamlined composition.

Two basic forms of war canoe prow are known. The most common form is often called a *pītau*; the term literally means 'openwork spiral' and this type of prow has two such spirals on its central panel. The *pītau* prow is carved from one solid piece of timber (fig. 63). At the front with its arms

63 War canoe prow of the *pītau* type, by far the most common form of prow carved during the early and middle nineteenth century. The basic form was strongly prescribed, with regional variations limited to minor stylistic carving details. This example was probably carved on the East Coast during the 1860s, not long before war canoes started to become obsolescent. Being detachable, many of the canoe carvings were obtained by collectors, while the canoe hulls were cut up to provide house carving timbers or left to rot. BM Ethno. 1895–353. L. 97 cm. Meinertzhagen collection.

trailing, an aggressive stylised figure faces in the direction of advance, parting the seas with its force. A suggestion has been made that this is Tūmatauenga, the god of war and man, forcing a path across the domain of Tangaroa, the god of the sea. An interpretation of openwork spirals like these when used on the door lintel of a house is that they represent the entry of light and knowledge into the world when Earth-mother and Sky-father were separated. The same significance may apply to their placement on the *pītau* prow. The figures carved on the *pītau* form of prow usually conform to the full frontal and full profile squared stance of the central and eastern regional carving styles, but minor figures in north-western sinuous stance may be present.

The other, much rarer form of prow, usually called a *tuere*, is similar in overall structure to the *pītau* type but in the *tuere* the front figure is reduced and the central panel of openwork carving is the most prominent component. On this central panel, the figures are highly stylised, sinuous, elongated and treated sometimes as *manaia*, sometimes as reduced human forms. *Tuere* prows from North Auckland are usually constructed from separate pieces, slotted to fit together. Behind the central panel there was a transverse splash-board, and both of these stood on a carved or plain triangular base. A carving of a naturalistic tattooed male face was often attached to the extreme lower front. In Taranaki and eastern areas of North Auckland, prows of *tuere* type are usually carved from one solid piece of timber. The Taranaki prows of this form have a naturalistic figure at the rear facing into the canoe. For surface decoration, these prows are embellished in the style appropriate for each area.

In their geographical distribution, the *tuere* prows correspond generally with the northern and western range of sinuous-bodied carving forms, while the *pītau* form covers the central and eastern style areas of static square frontal figures. Following this geographical division, the same time

64 ABOVE Central panel of a war canoe prow of *tuere* type, the finest surviving example
of this form. Although this one is carved in North Auckland, probably Hokianga, style,
tuere prows were apparently quite widespread around the northern coasts in the later
eighteenth century, judging by other examples and the illustrations of canoes seen on
Captain Cook's expeditions. While common on many small carvings from the north, the
abundance and fine quality of detailed surface decoration in *pākura* and *unaunahi*
patterns on this prow is exceptional for a carving of this size. BM Ethno. 1900.7–21.1.
w.112 cm.

65 RIGHT Two war canoe paddles. The longer paddle bears low-relief carved figures on
the blade in classic Taranaki style, with their arms and legs intertwined. It was carved

differential occurs with these two prow forms, in that the *tuere* prows are
mostly executed in stone-tool carving while the *pītau* prows enjoyed their
greatest development in the metal-tool era. However, these differences are
not absolute, in that the *pītau* form also extended over the northern and

western areas, especially following the introduction of metal tools. Conversely, later metal-tool examples of the *tuere* prow were carved in the Waikato and Rotorua areas.

One of the greatest treasures of the Maori collection in the British Museum is the central panel of a classic *tuere* war canoe prow (fig. 64). Although unprovenanced, on the basis of carving style this can be attributed certainly to North Auckland and probably to the Hokianga district. Its long sinuous figures are decorated with beautiful North Auckland *pākura* rolling spirals and the open scrolls between have northern *unaunahi*. The ethnological museums of Florence and Berlin each have a very similar *tuere* prow panel, but the *tuere* in the British Museum is the most complete and finest of these three. Unfortunately none have retained their carved base and transverse back-board, nor the separate face mask that may have been attached to the lower front. Another famous *tuere* prow in the Berlin museum does have all of these components, but this is a relatively modern example carved with metal tools by Rotorua Ngāti Tarawhai carvers in the late 1860s.

While plaited sails, such as the sole surviving example now in the British Museum (fig. 82), were used for longer distances, it was paddles that provided speed and manoeuvrability at close quarters. Although most paddles for everyday use were left plain, even these had elegantly shaped handles and terminal knobs. Paddles associated with the great war canoes were frequently carved and in earlier times also painted with geometric and scrolled designs (fig. 65). Taranaki paddles in particular often have complex contorted figures on the butt of the handle and other low-relief carving on the upper portion of the blade. Early European visitors, such as Cook and Bellingshausen along the East Coast and later at Queen Charlotte Sound and the Bay of Islands, noticed ornate paddles carved with Poverty Bay style figures at the junction of blade and handle and sometimes painted with red ochre *kōwhaiwhai* patterns on the blade. As the artist Sydney Parkinson (1773: 90) travelling on Cook's *Endeavour* remarked just a few days after first contact at Poverty Bay in October 1769: 'their paddles were curiously stained with a red colour, disposed into various strange figures; and the whole together was no contemptible workmanship.'

This painting on paddles, also in Poverty Bay style, represents the earliest expression of Maori *kōwhaiwhai* painting, much older than any known from house rafters. These carved and painted paddles must have been highly regarded for their aesthetic value to have been traded such long distances from their Poverty Bay source. A very limited number of painted paddles eventually found their way into American and European museums, including the largest group of four now in the British Museum (Neich 1993: 60–8). Painted paddles soon went out of fashion but carved paddles continued in use during the nineteenth century. When the first tourists in the 1880s began to demand smaller portable model paddles carved all over the handle and blade, carvers in Whanganui, Gisborne and especially Rotorua quickly adapted their art to supply this market.

in the later eighteenth century or very early nineteenth century. The one with painted *kōwhaiwhai* patterns on both sides of the blade was collected on Captain Cook's voyages. The red ochre painting in Poverty Bay style on this paddle represents some of the oldest surviving *kōwhaiwhai* painting. Paddles of this type were frequent in the later eighteenth century but were replaced by simpler unpainted ones in the early nineteenth century. BM Ethno. 5372, L. 229 cm, presented by W. Bragge in 1869. NZ 150, L. 179 cm, Cook collection.

66 Bone chest, *waka kōiwi*, in the form of a male figure, probably from a burial cave in North Auckland, designed to hold the bones of the deceased in a lidded cavity in the rear. Final disposition of the dead in a carved bone chest like this was mainly a North Auckland custom. The rare male gender and naturalistic face with male tattoo of this figure suggests that it may represent a particular ancestor, as distinguished from the more frequent chests of female gender with very stylised faces which may be interpreted as Hinenui-te-Pō, the goddess of death, or Hina, the moon goddess who presides over man's bones. BM Ethno. 1950 Oc.11.1. H. 92 cm.

Several museum collections, including that of the British Museum, contain elaborate models of fully carved Maori war canoes, some as long as 4 m and dating from quite early in the nineteenth century. Later and smaller canoe models were clearly made for the developing tourist trade, but the large early models are obviously of a different class. They are large enough to hold one or even two people and there are indications that they were actually paddled around on the lakes and rivers for some ritual purpose. In Maori religion, canoes are also associated with the journey made by souls back to the mythical homeland of Hawaiki, and part of the hull of a full-size canoe was sometimes set up vertically in the ground as a memorial to a dead chief. Probably, some of these miniature war canoes 3–4 m long were burial canoes never intended for water use, in which the body was exposed or in which the bones were later deposited in a burial cave. Carved burial chests made in the north to hold the bones of the dead in burial caves were often canoe-shaped with a definite keel; they shared the same name of *waka* in the form of *waka kōiwi*, meaning a canoe-shaped container intended to hold bones (fig. 66).

The practice of making these miniature war canoes was continued into the first models made in the nineteenth century expressly for gifts or trade to Europeans. One large model (fig. 67) in the British Museum was specially commissioned from Ngāti Tarawhai carvers by Rotorua Arawa chiefs to serve as their official gift to the Duke and Duchess of Cornwall and York during their New Zealand tour in 1901. At the welcome ceremony, it was presented to the royal party brimming over with extra gifts of tribal heirloom artefacts.

The storehouse and its symbolism

One of the traditional signs of a great chief was his elaborately carved raised storehouse or *pātaka*, standing across the *marae* from his house, where it could be seen from his porch. Designed to hold preserved foods, such as dried fish and flesh preserved in calabashes, as well as general storage for mats, weapons, wooden bowls, fishing gear and agricultural tools, the *pātaka* was equally important as a symbolic statement about the resources controlled by its owners. A very high percentage of the early carvings recovered from swamps are parts of storehouses such as doorways, front or rear panels, side boards or thresholds. These finds confirm that from pre-European times the storehouse was the most prominent decorated structure in a village, proclaiming the high status and command of resources exercised by the chief who owned it.

Several of the northern storehouses recorded in 1827 in the paintings of Augustus Earle were built by experts from the Bay of Plenty, captured and enslaved by the northern raiders too busy with warfare to build their own. A common theme in many traditional accounts of storehouses is that they were built with timbers cut from the war canoes of vanquished enemies. This action degrades the *mana* of the enemy by turning his *tapu* canoe into part of a store and advertises the strength of the victor. The prestige function of storehouses continued into the second half of the nineteenth

67 Model war canoe, *waka taua*, with *tuere*-type prow, probably the official gift presented to the Duke and Duchess of Cornwall and York by the Arawa people at the large Maori welcome given to the Royal party at Rotorua in 1901. Carved by Tene Waitere, a famous expert from the Ngāti Tarawhai section of Te Arawa, this model features a modern version of a *tuere* prow, showing the naturalistic head at the front. BM Ethno. Royal Loan 1902. L. 311 cm.

century, when several fine carved *pātaka* were built with modern tools and materials such as corrugated iron roofs, only becoming obsolete as the new large meeting houses of the 1870s took over this role as symbols of tribal prestige.

With a plain interior and all carvings facing outwards to the beholder, the *pātaka* was rich in symbolism. Interpretation of the construction and symbolism of earlier North Auckland and Taranaki storehouses with their complex sinuous intertwined figures is made difficult by the lack of a complete example. Charles Heaphy's coloured sketch of a Taranaki storehouse (see fig. 46) is a rare and valuable glimpse of a vanished architectural tradition, although this still leaves the doorway arrangement in doubt. The construction of ancient northern storehouses, known only from scattered finds of individual swamp carvings, is even more problematical.

More recent storehouses from the eastern and central style areas are much better known and their symbolism is more obvious, especially on those from the Bay of Plenty tribes. Prominent on each of the front bargeboards (*maihi*) is a composition of a whale or sea monster being dragged tail-first up towards the apex by small overlying figures sometimes alternating with *manaia*. The head and jaws of the whale are represented by large spirals at the lower end of the *maihi*. Although Maori people did not hunt whales until after the advent of European shore whaling, frequent whale strandings around the coasts had always provided a welcome source of fresh meat, ivory for ornaments and dense bone for hand-weapons. Above the doorway and on the two *amo* (side panels of the façade), embracing couples are often depicted, sometimes in graphic naturalistic detail with full facial tattoo. Obviously the whales and embracing couples represent the twin themes of fertility and abundance, essential for the total well-being of the tribal group. Other doorways depict a single ancestor of the tribe, as does the carved figure or *tekoteko* projecting from the apex of the bargeboards.

In addition to this direct symbolism, alternating frontal and *manaia* figures across the frontal *paepae* (threshold beam) and sometimes along the side panels, evoke a deeper symbolism of spiritual guardians, the passage of time, and thresholds between states of existence (Binney 1980: 19; Jackson 1972: 65–8). An annotated drawing by Thomas Kendall of a storehouse doorway describes a North Auckland tribal origin deity named Nukutawhiti in the 'first state of existence', that of undifferentiated potential. This

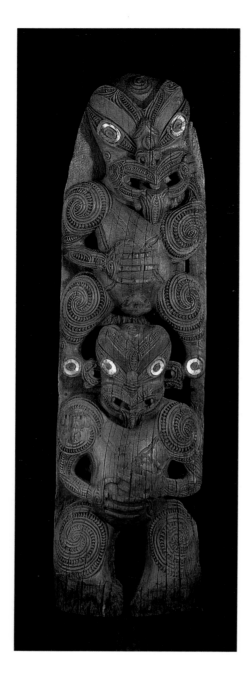

68 Front side post, *amo*, from a meeting house which was carved with metal tools in the Poverty Bay district in the 1840s or 1850s. Each stylised figure in bold high-relief with *raupongo* patterns represents a particular named ancestor of the tribal group owning the house. Rongowhakaata and Te Aitanga-a-Māhaki tribal carvers from this district were leaders in the early development of the modern meeting house concept. BM Ethno. 1894.7–16.1. H.152 cm. Sudeley collection.

gives substance to other scattered hints of a coherent Maori cosmos conceived in terms of three states of existence (Binney 1980). The first is a primal state of undifferentiated matter, the second is life in this world and the third is the afterworld following death. The dangerous passages between these states of existence are marked by thresholds which have to be negotiated with the aid of *tapu* rituals. Such carvings as storehouse doorways and *paepae*, canoe side-strakes, and meeting house door lintels articulate the symbolic structure of these thresholds and warn people to treat them with respect.

The meeting house and its symbolism

By the second half of the nineteenth century and continuing until the present, a medium to large meeting house (*wharenui, whare rūnanga, whare whakairo*) standing on a separate *marae* area had become the most important architectural feature of every Maori settlement. Some of these houses are uncarved, but most have carvings and other artistic embellishments on the front and interior. They are used for funerals, religious and political meetings and for entertaining visitors, but no members of the local community live in them permanently. By the 1870s, the meeting house had completely replaced the war canoe and the storehouse as the focus of local group pride and prestige (fig. 68).

Archaeologists have been able to reconstruct the plans of several large houses which have features found in post-European meeting houses. However, the extent to which these early structures functioned like a nineteenth-century meeting house is uncertain. They were probably the dwelling houses of chiefs while also serving other community functions of hospitality and meetings. Such large houses were not a constant element of every settlement.

Observations made by European visitors in the late eighteenth and early nineteenth centuries show a continuation of this settlement pattern, with rare large carved houses (about 10 m long) and a range of very small to medium-sized dwelling houses (up to about 5 m long) (Prickett 1982). Probably the most famous of these early large decorated houses was the one seen by Cook and his men at Tolaga Bay in 1770, which although unfinished was 10 m long and had all the interior timbers carved with figures. Its purpose remained a mystery to the European observers.

Included among the small to medium range of community houses was the private house of the chief of each settlement in which the foreign guests were usually accommodated. Most of these were so small and the single doorway so low that the visitors had to crawl on hands and knees to enter; then during the night the house became so hot and stuffy they could not remain inside. These smaller houses frequently had a carved lintel over the door and a carved figure at the base of a central interior post. There were no large completely decorated houses specifically set aside for political meetings, religious services, funerals, or for the entertainment of visitors.

However, by the 1830s European travellers noticed some communities beginning to build larger (about 14 m long), completely carved houses which, although still considered to be owned by a chief, were built expressly for the reception and accommodation of visitors. These visitors included travelling parties of chiefs and their retainers, European officials, and Maori and European missionaries. The need to accommodate the crowds that gathered to hear the new Christian message led to the rapid spread of local village churches, built to the same design as traditional houses but usually without carvings. These in turn stimulated further construction of larger visitors' houses (*whare manuhiri*). Construction of visitors' houses continued through the 1860s and led directly on to the standard meeting house with its complex of functions, now considered as the property of the local community.

Symbolically, the meeting house was still identified with the body of the chief and his ancestors. Names given to meeting houses usually refer to a particular ancestor and frequently describe the house as his or her bosom or seat of affections. In speeches given on the *marae* in front of the house it is addressed as a living person. Much of the symbolism of the war canoe was transferred to the meeting house. In the same way that the hull of the war canoe had been regarded as the backbone of the chief, so the ridge-pole of the meeting house became his ancestor's backbone. This ridge-pole backbone is also equated with the genealogy of the tribal ancestors listed in a single unbroken descent line beginning with the founding eponymous ancestor, whose representation appears as the carved *koruru* or *tekoteko* at the apex of the bargeboards.

Further expression of the importance of ancestral descent in defining the identity of the group owning the meeting house was recognised by naming the carved figures in the house as important ancestors. Some of these were identified by showing characteristic attributes or incidents from myth and legend, but even as early as 1842 the names of individual ancestors were inscribed on their bodies in the alphabetical script taught by missionary schooling. The whole house became a genealogical plan of the ancestry of the tribe, linked together by the rafters painted with *kōwhai-whai* scroll patterns symbolising the eternal life spirit flowing along the descent lines. As a composite symbol of the sacred body of the main chiefly ancestor and enclosing representations of tribal ancestral origins, the meeting house itself became a highly *tapu* object. Anything *noa* or common, such as cooked food, that may defile this *tapu* is not allowed to be taken on to the porch or into the house.

To some extent, the meeting house serves as a model of the Maori cosmos. The front or porch of the house is associated with the mythological world of the past, since it faces out towards the ancestral homeland of Hawaiki across the ocean. Hawaiki is the source of *mana* and power, the source of human life and the home of the dead to which their spirits will return. The rear or interior of the house is associated with the present and future world of this land and its forests, where the living find their livelihood.

The idea that a carved threshold can signal changes between states of existence, which applies to the war canoe, the storehouse and the chief's house, was elaborated in the full complement of meeting house carvings. The *paepae* (threshold) across the front of the porch and the *pare* (lintel) over the door and window are carved with comparable compositions of alternating full-frontal *tiki* and profile *manaia* figures that signify a dangerous threshold (Jackson 1972).

In symbolic terms, the *pare* is the most important carving in a meeting house, marking the passage between two states of existence or between the domains of different gods. The *marae* outside is often referred to as the domain of Tūmatauenga, the god of war, reflecting the hostilities of debate on the *marae*, in contrast to the interior of the meeting house which is the domain of Rongo, the god of agriculture and peaceful pursuits, who calms the people and ensures peace within the intimacy of the house. This threshold is a dangerous place where one should not linger. Modern practice for people entering the meeting house is to remove shoes before crossing this threshold, for practical reasons of cleanliness but also as a recognition of the passage between different domains.

Door lintel compositions can be grouped into two main types, although there are numerous variations on these themes. One type consists of a central full-frontal figure, usually female, in squatting posture and hands on body, with a *manaia* figure at each end always facing outwards, and interstitial minor figures or vestigial loops and spirals between (fig. 69). The other type has two, or more often three, full-frontal upright figures, usually male with their arms upraised, standing on a transverse base and separated by large prominent pierced spirals (fig. 70). Depending on certain details, the first type with its central female figure is usually interpreted as Papa or Mother Earth giving birth to the main gods, or Hinenui-te-Pō, the goddess of death, defeating Māui's attempt to gain immortality for man, or in more general terms as referring to the ability of female genitalia to remove *tapu* power from visitors entering the house, thereby protecting the local community.

As suggested by Thomas Kendall's information, the second type of *pare* with two or three upright, usually male, figures may be seen as a representation of Tāne and his brother gods pushing their primal parents of Earth and Sky apart by standing on the base, which symbolises Papa or Earth, thereby allowing light in the form of the pierced spirals into this world (Binney 1980: 21). Although by no means absolute, there does tend to be a time differential between these two types of *pare*, with the first type slightly earlier than the second, if subjective judgements of age can be trusted. Or perhaps the difference is to be understood by reference to regional styles, in that the second type is more common in the Bay of Plenty and East Coast, which also happen to be those areas where carving survived throughout the nineteenth century.

These conceptions of cosmology translated down to the human level in the model of the meeting house regulate the behaviour of living people within the house. Longitudinally across the house there is an opposition

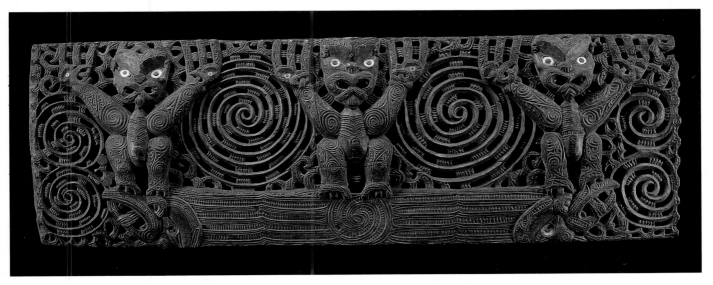

69 Door lintel, *pare*, from a small house of the 1800–1820 period, carved in Poverty Bay Rongowhakaata style. Large outward-facing terminal female *manaia* figures flank a central frontal human figure which is probably female although a small face mask replaces the genitals. The delicate surface patterns consist of plain double spirals with sets of angular *unaunahi* at intervals. BM Ethno. 1854.12–29.89. w.98 cm. Grey collection.

70 Door lintel, *pare*, for a meeting house. Probably carved in the Whakatane district of the Bay of Plenty by a Ngāti Awa carver working in the later 1840s. Three male figures stand on a *manaia*-headed base representing Papatuanuku, the Earth Mother, with their arms upraised to allow openwork spirals of light and knowledge into this world. BM Ethno. 1854.12–29.90. w.131.5 cm. Grey collection.

between the side with the window, which is the *tapu* side associated with men, visitors and death, and the side with the door, which is the *noa* or common side associated with women, hosts and life. With its associations with the ancestral homeland, Hawaiki, the front of the house is sacred and senior as opposed to the rear which is more common and junior in status. These symbolic orientations function to maintain social hierarchy and ritual status among the hosts and their visitors inside the house during meetings and while sleeping overnight. Thus the place of honour on the *tapu* side occupied by the highest-ranking visitor is the position at the front below the window, also the position closest to Hawaiki. Similarly on the host's side of the house, their chief occupies the position opposite, at the front and close to the door.

In the early 1870s as the New Zealand Wars came to a close, those tribes who had been involved on both sides entered a period of intense religious and political realignment. New large meeting houses up to 30 m long were built in many parts of the country to accommodate all the tribal meetings and to express the historical identity of their owners (fig. 71). By this time war canoes were becoming obsolete and many were cut up to provide timber for the new meeting houses. Group identity defined by genealogical descent continued to be a major organisational principle in the design of these houses, but this was now supplemented by a new ideology of group identity defined by the specific history experienced by the owners in post-European times. This new expression of identity was needed to deal with finer political and religious distinctions between groups, distinctions that had not existed in the indigenous Maori world. Innovative religious and political symbols of multicolour painting on carvings, new patterns in *tukutuku* latticework panels, and new geometric designs painted on rafters and other surfaces developed at this time to signal these distinctions.

Group identity defined by history became especially relevant for the Ringatu millenialist church founded by Te Kooti in the final years of the wars (Binney 1995). Drawing its members from various tribal groupings in the eastern Bay of Plenty and the East Coast, Ringatu services are held not in separate church buildings but in the meeting houses of the Church's adherents. In meeting houses designed and supervised by Te Kooti himself or built for him and his followers in the 1870s and 1880s, the ideology of group identity defined by history stimulated the development of a new form of figurative painting which told these new narrative histories in visual form (Neich 1993). In some of these houses, paintings of ancestors and historical characters completely replaced carved figures (fig. 72). Combining elements from *kōwhaiwhai* painting, carved figure forms and introduced European naturalistic art, Maori figurative painting lasted only for a short period between the 1870s and 1920s before a government-sponsored orthodoxy led to a return to traditional wood-carving. However, during this short burst of creativity, Maori figurative painting radiated rapidly into several distinctive styles and laid the foundation for the later development of modern Maori art.

71 LEFT Interior side wall panel, *poupou*, from a large meeting house called Tumoana-kotore which stood at Mamaku *marae* in Hicks Bay, East Cape. It was carved in the 1860s by experts from the local Ngāti Porou tribe, although this panel may be a later addition to the original carvings as shown by the rather unorthodox naturalistic animals beside the ancestor figure. The height of this panel reflects the increasing size of later meeting houses. BM Ethno. 1922.5–12.1. H. 262 cm. Presented by Sir C. Hercules Read.

72 RIGHT Painted ancestor figure, flanked by *tukutuku* panels, in Te Poho-ō-Rukupō meeting house, Manutuke, near Gisborne, Poverty Bay. Built and decorated by the Ngāti Kaipoho *hapū* of the Rongowhakaata tribe in 1887, this house was officially opened at a large three-day political meeting which discussed the relative merits of the Church of England, Mormonism and the Maori Ringatu church founded by Te Kooti. All of the ancestor figures in this house are painted in a restrained sophisticated style based on carved figure forms rendered in *kōwhaiwhai* painting motifs. Published by courtesy of Darcy Ria, Manutuke. Photo R. Neich.

Schools, carvers and patrons

From an economic base of fishing, hunting, horticulture and trade in specialised items, traditional Maori society supported quite a wide range of part-time specialists and some almost full-time experts. Prominent among these experts were the wood-carvers, especially in those tribes which gained a reputation for developing this skill. Famous expert carvers were in great demand, often travelling widely among distant tribes to build and carve their war canoes, storehouses and meeting houses. Specialist skills were usually handed down by some formal teaching and practical apprenticeship within family lines, so that certain family and sub-tribal groups became renowned for their artistic abilities. Wood-carving was considered a suitable activity for men of noble birth and therefore, apart from these recognised experts, most higher-ranking men were quite proficient in wood-carving and stone-working, shaping their own weapons, personal ornaments and treasure boxes in their spare time. Many of these smaller personal items became treasured family and tribal heirlooms, gaining in value and *mana* from the prestige of the ancestors who had owned them.

Payment and recognition for expert services in building and carving canoes and houses was given in food, hospitality and valuables such as fine woven cloaks, nephrite weapons and ornaments. In early European times, these valuables were very quickly replaced by blankets, guns and ammunition, followed soon after by cash payments. Patrons and clients of expert carvers had to be people of substance, able to marshall the considerable resources required for major carving projects. The conspicuous success of a carving project reflected and enhanced the *mana* of chiefs and leaders and their reputation as persons of consequence. For many meeting houses, the names of the carvers were not always remembered, but the name of the local chief who initiated the project lives on through the stories told about the house. In a classic statement of the prestige function of carvings serving to validate the status of a chief, Te Pokiha Taranui, the paramount chief of Ngāti Pikiao at Rotorua, introduced himself to a sitting of the Maori Land Court in 1882 thus:

At one time I was the owner of a very large canoe called Te Arawa twelve fathoms long. There are three large houses now standing at Mourea. One is called Te Awanui, another called Manuhuia and another one recently built called Te Takinga. At Te Taheke there are two large houses standing – one is called Rangitihi, [the other] Tutea and my carved house at Maketu is called Kawatapuarangi and I have a carved pataka called Tahuakatere. I have a fishing net about half a mile long. I want to show the court what an industrious and wise man I am. Although the claimant presumes to be my equal in rank, my resources are far beyond his, so I leave the court to judge whether these are the signs of a common individual or a great chief.

(Rotorua Minute Book 4: 161–2)

Momentous and rapid changes occurred in Maori society and its art during the eventful years of the nineteenth century. In the lives of the carvers who pursued their art through that century, these changes presented huge challenges and new possibilities. For the reasons discussed, most of the western and northern tribal styles that had been vigorous in the later years of the eighteenth century failed to make the transition into metal-tool work, and by the early decades of the nineteenth century they had become extinct. In the central and eastern areas where metal tools opened up new possibilities, the changes were so rapid that some individual carvers made the transition from war canoe builder to meeting house builder to tourist art producer in one lifetime.

Half-way through the century as meeting houses became the major focus of the wood-carver's art, a few exceptional individuals emerged who were able to articulate virtually new styles of meeting house carving for their respective tribes. Among the Rongowhakaata of Poverty Bay, Raharuhi Rukupō who carved the house Te Hau-ki-Tūranga in 1842 was undoubtedly one of the first and most innovative of these individuals (Kernot 1984). His other carving projects included the war canoe Te Toki-a-Tāpiri and the first church at Manutuke near Gisborne. Natanahira Te Keteiwi of Te Aitanga-a-Mahāki tribe in Poverty Bay was probably another artistic innovator with his work on Te Poho-ō-Rawiri house in 1849 (Neich 1993: 80). Among Te Arawa of Rotorua, the names of Te Amo-ā-Tai and Wero Taroi of Ngāti Tarawhai and Pūwhakaoho of Ngāti Pikiao are remembered along with others for their role in establishing Arawa meeting house carving styles during the 1850s and 1860s. Among the Ngāti Porou of the East Coast, Tāmati Ngakaho and Hone Taahu worked with several others during the 1870s and 1880s in the formulation of another distinctive meeting house style (McEwen 1947). Tūhoe carvers of the Urewera region such as Te Whenuanui and Kokouri, and carvers from the Ngāti Awa of Whakatane, led by Wēpiha Apanui who worked on houses in the 1870s and 1880s, accomplished similar artistic revolutions for their tribes (Mead 1986b).

With the great surge in meeting house building that followed the end of the wars and the development of the Ringatu Church, major tribal schools of carving flourished on the foundations created by these innovators. Carvers from these major schools built houses all over the North Island, often for other tribes who had lost their own carving styles before 1830. As a result of this importation of carvers, many houses built during this period display the style of their imported carvers instead of the local style. Te Arawa and Ngāti Porou carvers were the most active of these itinerant carvers. Over a hundred meeting houses carved by men from these major schools in the later nineteenth and early twentieth centuries are still in use around the country.

A totally new patronage for Maori carving appeared with the development of Maori tourist art in the 1870s and 1880s, especially in the Rotorua, Gisborne and Whanganui districts (Mead 1976; Neich 1983: 254; 1990). In these areas large concentrations of Maori populations with relatively intact cultures met the stimulus of European interest in Maori carvings as curios. Many famous names among carvers became involved in the production of replica weapons, paddles, treasure boxes, carved bowls, and models of canoes and houses for sale to anonymous tourists. At the same time, local Maori were buying and commissioning the same items for their own use in ceremonies and for gifts to distinguished visitors. Consequently, the dividing line between tourist art and Maori ceremonial art of the later nineteenth century is not always easy to determine. Rotorua had always continued as one of the most vigorous centres of surviving traditional carving and it also emerged as the premier tourist centre of the country. Arawa carvers in Rotorua soon came to dominate the tourist art trade, and the Arawa tribal carving style became generally accepted as the standard national Maori carving style.

Maori carving in modern times

Within thirty years, the creative house-carving impetus of the post-Land War years and the stimulus of Ringatu house building had waned. By around 1900 the Maori population was at its lowest ebb numerically and economically, with many people living in substandard housing and unable to support the building of new meeting houses. Without any call for their skills, experienced carvers turned to other means of livelihood and lost their desire to pass on their skills. By the 1920s the tradition of Maori wood-carving was in a sorry state. Sir Apirana Ngata, the senior Maori parliamentarian of the time, realised how serious this situation was for the survival of the art. As he explained: 'In the second decade of this century the bald position was that outside the Arawa tribe there were only two experienced carvers, one in the Urewera country and the other among the Ngāti Porou of the East Coast' (Ngata 1940: 321).

Hone Ngatoto, the last Ngāti Porou carver, died soon after completing St Mary's Memorial Church at Tikitiki in 1926. This event spurred Ngata to establish the School of Maori Arts and Crafts by an Act of Parliament later in the same year. The school commenced in 1928 at Rotorua, chosen as the centre for the school because it was now the only place where the old carving skills survived. Six Arawa carvers mainly from Ngāti Whakaue were employed as the first tutors at the school, but some were very reluctant to teach the students from other tribal areas. And because all were exclusively chisel carvers, they could not achieve the moulded flowing lines of the old adzing experts. Ngata was not satisfied and so in the summer of 1929–30 he encouraged Pine Taiapa, one of the first students, to search for an expert in the old art of adze carving.

After much seeking, Taiapa found Eramiha Kapua living at Te Teko in January 1930. Eramiha, then an active fifty-five year-old farmer and leader in the Ringatu Church, had been trained in the ancient Ngāti Tarawhai carving tradition as an expert with the long-handled adze. Taiapa persuaded Eramiha to come and teach adzing and carving at the Rotorua School. There the students found Eramiha to be a strict carver of the old tradition who knew all the *tapu* observances concerning wood-carving. He never blew his wood chips away, did not smoke while carving, and would not allow women near carving in progress. However, Eramiha reasoned that since his students could never know the *tapu* rituals exactly, they would be safer to keep clear of *tapu* entirely. Therefore, with the appropriate rituals, Eramiha removed all *tapu* from the work of the School and taught the students all that he knew about adzing and carving techniques.

Pine Taiapa became the master carver of the School, and by the time of his death in 1972 he had worked on almost one hundred meeting houses. The School closed during World War II, when most of the students enlisted in the New Zealand Army, but it was revived as the New Zealand

73 Multi-media mural combining carving, painting and *tukutuku*, illustrating the Maori myth of the separation of Rangi and Papa, Heaven and Earth, by their children including Tāne, the forest god, who stood on his hands and finally pushed them apart with his feet. Designed and executed by a group of people working under the direction of Cliff Whiting, this mural was completed in March 1976. By permission of the National Library of New Zealand, Wellington.

Maori Arts and Crafts Institute in 1965 with Pine's younger brother, Hone Taiapa, as the senior carver. Several carvers graduate each year from the Institute after training in meeting house carving and the production of smaller items for sale to visitors. While the influence of the Rotorua School and the Institute has been generally conservative by virtue of its emphasis on traditional skills, some graduates have continued on from this sound basis to produce bold innovative work. Prominent among these are Tuti Tukaokao with his murals and Lyonel Grant (fig. 120) with his bronze-castings and the new meeting house carved under his direction for Waiariki Polytechnic at Rotorua.

Another, more diffuse group of modern Maori artists, working in a contemporary idiom with various media including carving, painting and *tukutuku*, has emerged from a background of European academic art training in the 1950s and 1960s. Many of them worked as special art advisory teachers in schools before gaining a name as individual artists in their own right. These included Sandy Adsett, John Bevan Ford (fig. 119), Para Matchitt, Selwyn Muru and Cliff Whiting (fig. 124). While concerned with their own individual expression, these artists have also initiated and led community-based co-operative art projects such as new artistically innovative meeting houses and multimedia murals in *marae* dining halls. Cliff Whiting and Para Matchitt developed art styles and techniques especially suited for non-specialists working on *marae* group art projects, following in the footsteps of Ngata and Pine Taiapa who realised that community art projects offered a powerful tool for the revitalisation of small Maori communities (fig. 73).

Nowadays, many younger Maori artists, both men and women, are active in the traditional arts and the contemporary scene, producing art for their communities and for the national and international art world. Large numbers of others enjoy producing art for their own satisfaction, turning to the museum collections for guidance and inspiration as they carve their musical instruments or shape their bone pendants into new forms. From a long proud history, Maori art looks forward to an exciting creative future.

5
THE FIBRE ARTS
Mick Pendergrast

Introduction

When the Polynesian ancestors of the Maori arrived in Aotearoa they found a country abundant with birds, lakes and rivers rich with eels, coastlines thick with shellfish, and oceans and estuaries teeming with fish. Finding food was not difficult; however, protection from the elements – for a people accustomed to the warmth of the tropics – must have been a priority. These early settlers were used to light garments made from barkcloth, and they brought with them the plant from which the cloth was made, the paper mulberry (*Broussonetia papyrifera*). However, it did not thrive in the cool climate, and search for a substitute began. Some plants were similar to those of the tropical homeland, so similar in fact that the settlers gave them the same names, although they soon discovered most such plants failed to provide the properties they had hoped for. The solution was found in a plant native to New Zealand which came to be known as New Zealand flax and the material *par excellence* of Maori fibrework in general and of cloak-making in particular.

Fibre arts are predominantly women's arts. Among them the most prestigious is the art of making cloaks. Fine cloaks are the most splendid and highly valued examples of this art. They were worn by men of high status, and the finest of them were given personal names and ranked with the greatest treasures of the land – the great war canoe Te Toki-a-Tāpiri, now in the Auckland Museum, was once exchanged for a fabulous cloak known as Karamaene. Cloaks have always played a very significant role in Maori culture and have continued to hold their position of importance to the present day.

Apart from making cloaks, women were also responsible for the production of more utilitarian objects, such as plaited mats, baskets and other fibre objects. Men were also fibre experts, but they directed their expertise towards survival activities for which they were responsible, notably canoe- and house-building, and hunting and fishing. In all these, as in other aspects of the traditional life style, cordage and binding techniques were of major importance.

Traditional clothing – which included belts and sandals – consisted essentially of waist-mats and cloaks, ranging from simple functional rain capes to the important prestige garments mentioned above. Everyday dress was simple, providing protection from the elements and freedom of movement, and for women the modest cover considered appropriate. Both men and women wore garments of the same material and construction. These consisted of a woven foundation of flax fibre with tags made from short lengths of leaf, spread across the surface to form a rain-shedding thatch. Two of these garments were worn, one around the waist and the other around the shoulders. Although this was the usual protection from cold and rain, it was often dispensed with (fig. 74); Captain Cook wrote:

but this is not common especialy with the men who hardly wear any thing about their middles observing no sort of decency in that respect . . . The women on the other hand always wear something round their Middle, generaly a short thrum'd

74 The everyday costume of men and women consisted of two garments, one worn around the shoulders and the other around the waist. However, one was often discarded, and men threw off both when engaged in strenuous activities. By permission of the British Library. Add.MS. 19954 f.80, drawing no. 116. [Untitled, unsigned; from a collection of watercolours and drawings illustrating New Zealand 1848–53.]

Matt which reaches as low as their knees; sometimes indeed I have seen them with only a bunch of grass or Plants before ty'd on with a peice of fine plating made of sweet sented grass; they likewise wear a peice of cloth over their shoulders as the Men do, this generaly of the thrum'd kind. (Beaglehole, 1955: 280)

The 'peice of fine plating' described is the *tū*, a woman's belt of multiple cords, and the 'thrum'd cloth' is the rain cape, the simplest and probably the oldest type of Maori garment.

The most prestigious garment at the end of the eighteenth century was the dog-skin cloak (*kahu kurī*), which was closely woven, with narrow strips of dog skin with hair covering the outer surface. There were also cloaks, made solely of flax fibre which were very tightly woven, heavy and plain (*pukupuku*). Some had decorative twined borders in two colours, but the finer ones had coloured borders woven in a more complex technique known as *tāniko*.

Patterned *tāniko* borders at the sides and bottom were the main decorative element of the *kaitaka* cloak, which replaced the dog-skin cloak as the most prestigious garment in the early nineteenth century. Apart from the *tāniko*, these cloaks were plain; their beauty derived from the perfection of the weaving and the glossy appearance of the soft pliable fibre.

The importance of the *kaitaka* cloaks declined around the 1830s in favour of another type of garment, *korowai*, in which the body of the cloak is decorated with loosely hanging black cords. This basic decoration of black cords could be further augmented with red wool pompoms or coloured wool panels. This type of cloak was the most versatile and lent itself to a great deal of experimentation in the application of decorative elements and their combinations. Perhaps this experimentation was partly responsible for the sudden emergence, and the subsequent never-wavering popularity, of feather cloaks (*kahu huruhuru*), rarely mentioned by early writers but appearing with increasing frequency towards the end of the nineteenth and the beginning of the twentieth centuries.

During the first half of the twentieth century Maori culture was at a low ebb. A severe influenza epidemic, two world wars, economic depression, displacement and urbanisation of large parts of the Maori population all took their toll – traditional arts and crafts, including the art of cloak-making, went into a decline. Around the 1960s, however, the tide turned. Maori culture regained its strength, and the traditional arts and crafts their vitality. Today the fibre arts flower again and the contemporary Maori cloak is an eclectic creation incorporating a number of decorative art elements from earlier styles. Once it was a symbol of local prestige, today it is a proud emblem of national Maori identity.

Materials

New Zealand flax must have attracted attention early – its long, narrow and easily split leaves had obvious potential to a people accustomed to binding and plaiting with strips of leaf and vine. Eventually flax was to become the main fibre source for clothing and many other purposes. There are two species: *Phormium tenax*, called *harakeke*, the most widely used, and *Phormium cookianum*, a smaller plant often found growing on dry cliffs and known as *wharariki* or mountain flax. The latter, much less important as a fibre source, is used occasionally for special purposes. *Harakeke*, however, has maintained its importance in Maori craftwork to the present day. Strips of flax leaf are still used to make baskets, floor mats and the decorative *tukutuku* wall panels which line the interiors of carved houses.

There are many varieties of *harakeke*. Thus some leaves may be too hard and stiff to use for fine work, most do not contain large quantities of fibre, and the fibre itself varies in length, fineness and softness. There must have been considerable trial and error before the settlers were able to identify plants with useful properties and to develop a satisfactory method of extracting the fibre. These problems were eventually overcome but probably over a long period of time.

The flax fibre (*muka*) became the raw material for clothing, fishing lines and cordage, used in bindings and lashings for canoes, houses, chisels and adzes and on all kinds of artefacts, from the most sacred ritual objects to fighting weapons and everyday utensils. Flax was always close at hand for temporary tying and binding during ordinary day-to-day activities. The missionary William Colenso records Maori astonishment on hearing that there was no *harakeke* in England with such comments as 'How is it possible to live there without it,' and 'I would not dwell in such a land as that' (Colenso 1892: 464).

As the settlers became more familiar with the properties of flax, they began to select and name individual varieties that were suitable for special purposes. Leaves that provide unusually long strips are suitable for making floor mats. Shorter strong strips are required for harvesting and gathering

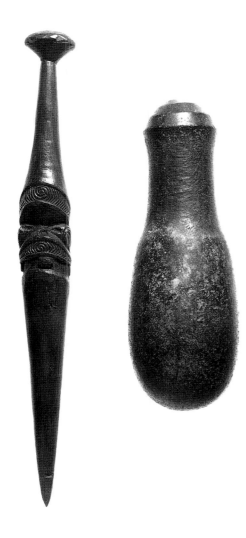

75 Carved wood weaving peg collected on Captain Cook's voyages, and stone beater for pounding flax fibre. BM Ethno. NZ 68, L. 40.5 cm, Cook collection; 1895–875, L. 25.5 cm, Meinertzhagen collection.

baskets. Strips that are both long and strong are necessary for fishing nets and traps. The fine silky fibre extracted from special varieties of *harakeke* is the raw material for most items of Maori clothing. A series of spectacular garments was to evolve over the following centuries, particular types of cloaks requiring fibre with specific qualities. Plants with specially valued properties were propagated and cultivated near the settlements. This collective knowledge of the plants and methods of preparing them for weaving has been handed down and continues to be used by contemporary Maori artists and craftspeople today.

Early Pākehā (European) visitors were quick to recognise the commercial possibilities of the fine, soft flax fibre. They called it New Zealand flax in hope that it would prove a viable competitor for linen flax. A demand quickly developed, and entire Maori communities became involved in separating the fibre for export. During the 1820s it became New Zealand's main export but never quite lived up to the original expectations, being mainly made into ropes to be used as ships' rigging. Gradually exports diminished, and efforts to discover other profitable use for the fibre have been unsuccessful. Even though from the second half of the nineteenth century machines have been developed for the extraction of the fibre, none can produce fibre of a quality equal to that produced by Maori craftspeople using the ancient method.

After the leaves have been carefully selected and harvested, the edges and hard midribs are removed and discarded. The two remaining strips of leaf are split into strips 1 cm wide. Next a transverse cut is made with a sharp knife across the dull underside of each strip, cutting through about half of the thickness, but leaving the inner fibre and the upper side undamaged. The strip is then turned over so that the cut side faces down. A mussel shell is placed over the cut and held firmly. The strip is drawn under the shell towards the tip of the leaf. This action peels off the underside of the leaf, leaving the fibre and upper epidermis. The strip is then turned around and the other end treated in the same manner. The peeled-off lower surface is discarded. The remaining fibre is then lightly scraped again to remove the upper cuticle. This scraped and cleaned fibre is known as *muka*. It is soaked in water before drying and then rolled on the thigh into plied cords. These are hanked and soaked again before being pounded with a stone beater, *patu muka* (see fig. 75), to soften them and finally rubbed between the hands to further soften and clean the fibre. These processes may be repeated until the fibre is soft, white and crinkly. It is then ready for weaving.

Flax, although the most important, is not the only material used in Maori fibre arts. The leaves of *kiekie* (*Freycinetia baueriana*), a rambling climber related to the pandanus plants of tropical Polynesia, are split in strips and boiled for a short time to make them whiter, then combined with black-dyed strips to work patterns on mats, baskets and *tukutuku* panels. The fibre, which can be extracted after soaking the leaves in water for several weeks, is used in certain types of rain capes. The bright yellow leaves of *pīngao* (*Desmoschoenus spiralis*), a sand-binding sedge that grows near the seashore, are also used in baskets, mats and decorative wall panels; less often they are added to the thatch on rain capes.

The New Zealand cabbage tree (*Cordyline australis*), known in Britain as the Torbay palm, is known by various Maori tribal groups as *tī kāuka* and *whanake*. The fibre can be separated after soaking in water for several weeks and is used for the thatch on coarse rain capes. It is stronger and longer lasting than flax fibre, and suitable for braiding ropes and strong cordage. The related mountain cabbage tree, *tōī* (*Cordyline indivisa*), provides a very strong fibre used to make an important type of black-dyed warrior's cape.

Other plants have also been used but to a lesser extent. A few rain capes in museum collections incorporate additional species in the thatch, but their usage appears to be restricted to certain areas and may never have been common.

Dyes

The traditional colours used in Maori weaving are black, red/brown and yellow; the undyed fibre provides a fourth choice.

The most widely used colour is a permanent black. The fibre is first soaked in a mordant made from crushed and soaked bark, preferably from the *hīnau* tree (*Elaeocarpus dentatus*). These trees are less common today and a range of other barks and leaves may be used instead. The flax fibre is then dried and later soaked in, or rubbed with, a dense black swamp sediment known as *paru*. A deposit of *paru* is highly prized. It may have ritual prohibitions to protect it and its location be kept secret within a family. Although the dyed fibre is a beautiful deep black, the acid content of the *paru* (and perhaps the bark in the mordant) causes the fibre to deteriorate over time. In the traditional life-style this was not of particular importance since a garment would be replaced when it became tattered and dirty, but today there is a desire within Maori families to protect old family pieces, and in museum collections there is a particular concern for the preservation of the black-dyed areas of ancient garments. Many are so fragile that they cannot be moved without damage. For this reason old cloaks in collections cannot always be displayed.

To provide the red/brown range of colours, bark is collected from the *tānekaha* tree (*Phyllocladus trichomanoides*) and pounded before being boiled. The fibre is then placed in the boiling dye until the colour takes (fig. 76), when it is removed and rolled in hot ashes to fix the colour. Yellow is less popular and in the past was not used in all areas of New Zealand. The dye is obtained by boiling bark from the trunk and roots of a group of *Coprosoma* species.

Today synthetic dyes are used by many craftspeople, especially for baskets and mats, because they are easily accessible and comparatively easy to use. Moreover, some workers do not have access to *hīnau* bark or black *paru*, and others are concerned for the conservation of the dye-producing trees, which are damaged and may eventually be killed by the continuous removal of bark.

76 Preparing the red/brown *tānekaha* bark dye at an Auckland University workshop. The stones, which have been heated for several hours in the fire, are being transferred to the wooden bowls containing the pounded bark and water. The long tongs manipulated by tutor Dante Bonica are necessary because of the intense heat. As the stones cool, they are removed and immediately replaced with fresh hot ones and the water is kept boiling until the desired colour is obtained. In today's situation many young Maori no longer live in the ancestral tribal areas and many search for traditional knowledge through other teaching institutions. Photo M. Lander 1995.

Techniques

A common Maori fibre technique is the cross-stitching used on decorative *tukutuku* panels in meeting houses, where they are placed on walls between carved wood panels (see figs 38, 72, 129). The crossed stitches are worked on a lattice consisting of horizontal wooden slats and vertically placed reeds, stems of *toetoe* (*Cortaderia* spp.), the latter now often replaced by stems of the exotic pampas.

A range of plying, braiding and netting techniques were used to make fishing lines, nets and traps, bird snares, cordage and binding. The Maori were expert at fishing and their nets impressed early visitors by both their size and success. Cruise wrote: 'Our seine . . . was contemptible when compared with those of the New Zealanders. Theirs are made of a very strong kind of weed; they are immensely large, and they are hauled remarkably slow but with great success' (Cruise 1823: 317).

Two techniques, however, have always held a special place in Maori fibre work. They are plaiting, known to the Maori as *raranga*, and used in the construction of mats and baskets, and *whatu*, the twining or 'finger-weaving' method used for the manufacture of clothing, in particular *whatu kākahu* or cloak-weaving.

Raranga (plaiting)

Throughout Polynesia, and in fact the whole Pacific area, plaiting is the most widespread craft. Baskets and mats are produced in huge numbers for many purposes. The basic techniques were brought to New Zealand from tropical Polynesia by the forebears of the Maori, who instead of strips of coconut and pandanus leaf used strips of flax and *kiekie*. For plaiting, the strips of leaf are laid diagonally (fig. 77a–d) and not divided into wefts

77 *Raranga* (plaiting techniques). **a** Close checkerwork: the strips pass over one, then under one; they are placed close together. **b** Open checkerwork: the strips pass over one, then under one; there are open gaps between them. **c** Close twilled twos: the strips pass over two, then under two; they are placed close together. **d** Plaited patterns are created by varying the length of the strokes. **e** Open, three-directional plaiting: the strips are laid in three directions and there are open gaps between them. Drawing M. Pendergrast.

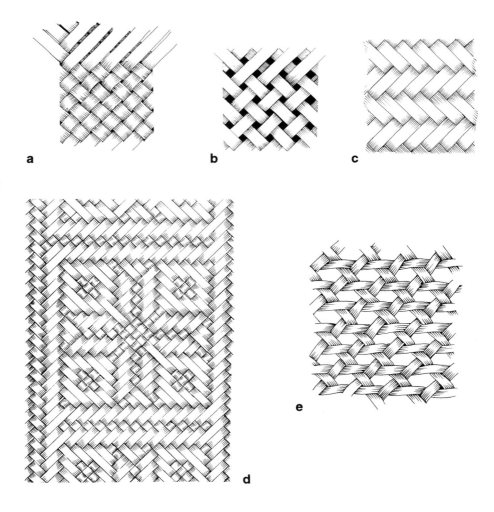

and warps as in weaving and twining. Using this technique a great variety of objects is produced.

MATS *Whāriki* is the general term used by the Maori to describe a wide range of specialised mats – in the past, the lower floor-covering of strewn rush or dried fern was also described as *whāriki* – but the mats most likely to be seen today are the patterned ones used in the carved meeting house (fig. 78). They are spread on the floor when guests are expected, and the mattresses and bedding for the visitors are laid out on them. They are treated with great respect by both the hosts and visitors. When spread in a private home, family and guests alike remove their footwear before walking on them. Similar mats, less common today, were made for rougher floor coverings, for covering food in the earth oven and for other purposes.

Fine mats with close plaiting are made from prepared, usually boiled, strips of flax or *kiekie*. The boiling causes the strips to shrink, but no further shrinking takes place when they are plaited into a basket or mat, and so the weave remains close (see fig. 77a,c,d). Some strips are dyed black and contrasted against the paler undyed strips; strips of yellow *pīngao* may also be included. The strips are not long enough to reach from one side of the mat to the other, so the mats are worked in panels, usually between three and five in number, which are joined together as the work proceeds. The dyed strips used to form the patterns are laid out in diagonal bands among the undyed warps at the commencement.

BASKETS The *kete* or basket (fig. 79) is the other plaited piece which remains in common use. Basketry was already a highly developed craft in tropical Polynesia, but adaptions were made in New Zealand to suit local requirements and materials. Baskets are still frequently made although in much smaller numbers than in the past. Work baskets for gathering cultivated and wild food were once produced in large numbers, especially when the crops were maturing or fish were due to school. Each set of baskets was kept for one purpose only. In some families these traditions are still practised and no one would consider carrying any other food in a basket intended for shellfish. Shortly before the commencement of the harvest or beginning of a fishing season it was the job of older women of the family carefully to check the baskets and replace those no longer serviceable.

A specialised basket was developed for gathering the sweet potato at harvest time. Careful winter storage was a necessity, and crops were lifted in autumn and carried nearer to the village to be stored in underground pits. Each load was carried individually in a basket made from untreated flax. As the untreated strips of flax dry, they become very hard and curl slightly so that the underside of the strip becomes concave with two sharp edges. Should one of these have scratched the surface or otherwise dam-

78 Plaited mats, *whāriki*, are still made to cover the floor of the meeting house when guests are expected. This example, of strips of flax leaf, was made by Biddy Konui of Turangi in 1994 for the British Museum. The pattern which is known as 'Kauaengarara, the jaw of the dragon', is one that has been handed down in the family of the artist. The main area of the mat is usually plaited in twilled twos (fig. 77c) and the patterns are created by varying the length of the strokes of the working strips. BM Ethno. 1994 Oc.4. Photo K. Pfeiffer.

79 Mrs Huraee and Miri, the wife of Hone Ratema, displaying a *kete whakairo* with a complex spiral pattern. Both women were from Lake Rotoiti and photographed by William Hammond at Ruato, Lake Rotoiti in 1901. By permission of the Auckland Museum.

aged a tuber, the entire contents of the store pit would have been threatened with rot. For this reason such baskets were made with the convex shiny upper surface of the strips of leaf on the inside, the reverse of the normal construction, so that the tubers would not be damaged. (New varieties of the sweet potato grown today do not require such careful handling or storage.)

Loads were carried in different manner by men and women: women, and slaves, carried loads on their back slung in a flax carrying-strap (one of the objects for which mountain flax was used), while warriors and men of chiefly rank carried the load on one shoulder. Handles were not required but baskets were made with small loops arranged around the rim so that it then could be laced closed and carried without fear of losing any of the contents. Shrinkage caused by the drying of the raw flax created an open plait (see fig. 77b) with spaces between the weave which allowed loose soil from the tubers to drop through.

Special baskets for gathering shellfish and diving for seafood are also plaited from untreated flax. The open plait resulting from the shrinkage allows water to escape when diving, and sand to be washed free from shellfish gathered on the beach. The basket is tied around the waist and worn as an apron, leaving the hands free; the loops around the rim allow the top to be closed with a draw-cord.

Many other kinds of basket were made for special purposes. A simple dish-shaped type is still used for serving food on important occasions. Other baskets were used as wringers to squeeze out juices from berries or pounded bark. In more recent times a simple basket made to fit over a calf's head prevented it from drinking from the house-cow until after milking.

Today Maori baskets continue to change their form to suit new functions. Most prestigious is the *kete whakairo* (figs 80, 81), a basket with a plaited pattern very similar (and sometimes identical) to those used on

80 Traditional Maori baskets, *kete*, seldom have handles since they were normally carried on the shoulder or back. The loops around the rim allow the basket to be laced closed so that objects will not be dropped. A fine *kete whakairo*, patterned basket, such as this would be used for storing or carrying important personal possessions. It was collected by the missionary William Colenso, probably between 1852 and 1899. BM Ethno. 1960 Oc.11.5. w.81.5 cm.

81 Contemporary patterned baskets, *kete whakairo*, and one *kete muka*: left, two baskets of *kiekie*, made by Christina Hurihia Wirihana; top right, basket of flax, made by M. Murray; bottom right, basket of *kiekie*, made by Eva Anderson; centre, basket of flax with *taniko* and feathers, made by Erenora Puketapu Hetet. BM Ethno. 1993 Oc.3.70, w. 38 cm; 1993 Oc.3.71, w. 26 cm; 1995 Oc.5.2, w. 29 cm; 1991 Oc.2.1, w. 34.5.cm; 1994 Oc.4.98, w. 23 cm.

mats. Such baskets were formerly used for storing and carrying valuable objects such as cloaks. Now they are used by women, and sometimes by men, to carry personal items. Special care is taken of the *kete whakairo* out of respect for the knowledge and skill required to produce it, and because of its relationship with the artist, relative or loved one who made it; and perhaps also as a mark of pride in cultural identity.

CANOE SAILS Plaited triangular sails were once used on long coastal canoe journeys. The only one to have survived is in the British Museum (fig. 82). It is made from thirteen plaited panels joined together in the same manner as floormats. The surface is plaited in check (fig. 77a) from narrow strips of flax, with zigzag bands of three-directional open plaiting (fig. 77e), a technique unusual in New Zealand. It is not known if this

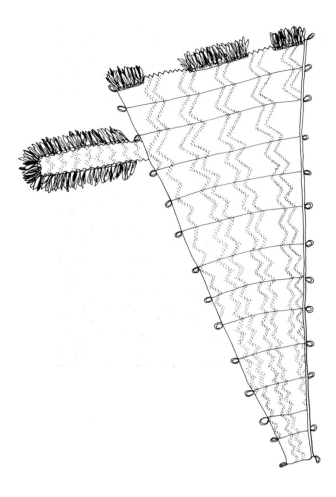

82 The only traditional sail to survive. It is plaited in thirteen panels joined together as the work progresses, in the same manner as floor mats. BM Ethno. NZ 147. L. 435 cm. Drawing R. Jewell.

openwork serves a function in allowing some wind to escape or if it is purely decorative. Along the top edge and around the 'tail' are fringes of dark-coloured feathers. The quill of each has been carefully cut transversely (fig. 84a) and alternate sections separated on each side (fig. 84b). This breaks the rigidity of the feather and allows it to move freely in the wind.

TĀTUA (MEN'S BELTS) Plaited and woven belts (fig. 83) known as *tātua* (and often regarded as war belts) were worn by men. In some areas, Cook notes, this belt was part of minimal dress, 'to which was generaly fasten'd a small string which they tye round the Prepuce. In this manner I have seen hundreds of them come off to and on board the Ship but they generaly had their proper cloathing in the boat along with them to put on if it rain'd etc' (Beaglehole 1955: 280). At other times a belt was worn around the waist to hold clothing in place. Both plaited and woven types of belt are worked in a rectangle, which is folded in longitudinally from top and bottom and then folded in half, making a band with an opening along the upper edge. Small objects could be carried inside. The free ends

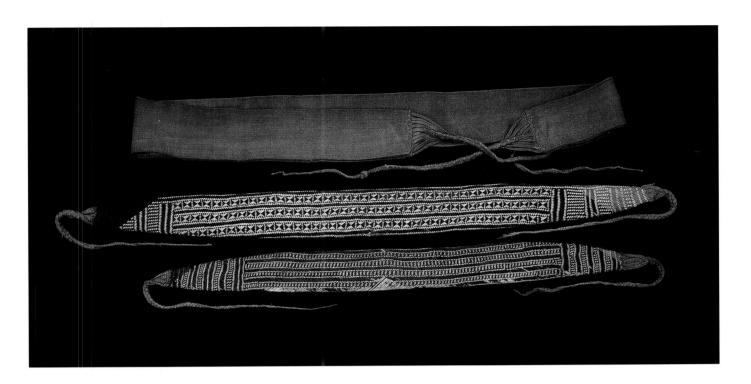

84 Feathers attached along the top of the canoe sail and around the 'tail' have been specially prepared. **a**. The quill of each has been cut transversely at intervals. **b**. Each feather has then been split along the centre to allow it to flutter in the wind. Drawing M. Pendergrast.

83 Maori men wore belts known as *tātua*. They are open at the top so that objects can be carried within. The wide woven belt (top) is from the contact period – it was collected on Captain Cook's voyages – but the type soon became obsolete. The smaller plaited belts (below) were also in use at the time of contact and continued to be made and used for at least another sixty years. BM Ethno, top to bottom: NZ 131, L. 340 cm, Cook collection; 1854.12–29.98, L. 222 cm, Grey collection; NZ 129, L. 199 cm.

of the working strips are not cut off but are hidden inside the fold, making the band thicker. A braided cord was attached to each end as a tie for securing it around the waist. Flax and/or *kiekie*, with some strips dyed black, and yellow *pīngao*, were used so that patterns similar to those on mats and baskets could be worked.

PĀRAERAE (FOOTWEAR) Plaited sandals were made to protect feet on unusually rough or thorny ground and for crossing passes in snow-bound mountains. The most hard-wearing were made from cabbage tree leaves but flax was also used.

KĀKAHU RARANGA (PLAITED GARMENTS) Plaited cloaks were made, but it is not known whether they were common for very few have survived in collections. There is one in the Canterbury Museum in Christchurch, New Zealand (Te Rangihīroa 1950: pl. 9. It is described there as

Moriori, the term used at the time of publication to refer to the early Maori settlers, but later applied only to the inhabitants of the Chatham Islands). It is plaited in six panels in the same way as a floor mat, but at the joins the ends of the strips are utilised to create a thatch which covers the outer surface. The British Museum and the Ethnographical Museum of Sweden (Ryden 1963: Figs 33–4) hold examples similar to the Christ-church specimen. The British Museum also holds a dress cloak plaited in panels, which in this case are arranged vertically (fig. 85). At the joins and around the edges are fringes of single-ply rolled flax fibre cords combined with cylindrical rolls of dried flax leaf strips (the latter now mostly missing). This garment may be unique.

Whatu kākahu (cloak-weaving)

Cloak-weaving is the most respected women's art. No loom is used and so the technique has sometimes been described as finger-weaving. There are no tools other than the upright weaving sticks (*turuturu*, fig. 75), which support the work at each side (fig. 86). For larger cloaks two pairs of sticks are required, the second pair being used to keep the work off the ground. A foundation of vertical warps is set up between the pegs and the wefts are twined across them from left to right. Working the wefts across the warps in this way makes it possible to describe the technique as weaving in spite of there being no loom. Because the work continues downwards, with each row being placed beneath the previous one, it has sometimes been described as 'downward weaving' (loom weaving normally works upwards and away from the weaver). Traditionally the weaver sat on the ground with the working edge kept at a suitable height. Contemporary

85 Plaited garments, *kākahu raranga*, are very rare in museum collections and apparently not described by early visitors. They may have always been uncommon. The dress cloak pictured is made in four vertical panels, with decorative fringes added at the joins and edges. A note in the Museum register describes it as 'Middle dress of a NZ chief, given to J. Everett by Mr White, a missionary' (possibly Francis White, who arrived in New Zealand in 1835 and died in 1877). BM Ethno. 1921.10–14.18. w.125 cm.

86 A *kaitaka* cloak in the process of manufacture. If the drawing is correct, the garment is unusual in that it has been commenced with the *tāniko* border which will form the lower edge on the completed garment. By permission of the British Library. Add. MS 19954 f.59, drawing no. 69. C. Heaphy, 'A Half-caste girl making a kaitaka' [from collection of watercolours and drawings illustrating New Zealand 1848–53].

weavers use a chair, with the work placed on a higher frame within comfortable reach.

Most cloaks are worked upside-down, with the commencement at the lower edge which is suspended between the weaving sticks. The weaving continues downwards to finish at what will eventually become the upper edge of the garment. After completion the garment is simply turned up the other way. This method is used for rain capes, cloaks with black tags (the *korowai-kārure* group) and feather cloaks. As the tags or feathers are added they are attached pointing upwards leaving the working edge clear for the next weft. However, the fine cloaks of the contact period (the *kaitaka*, *kahu kurī* and *pukupuku*) all commence at the upper edge and are worked downwards towards the lower edge. An exception is the *paepaeroa* of the *kaitaka* class of cloaks which has vertical wefts.

Towards the end of the nineteenth century small twined bags appeared in response to tourist demand. They are woven from flax fibre, and occasionally from the 'lacebark' (*Hoheria* sp.). The weaving is done in the

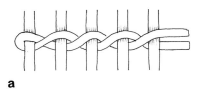

a

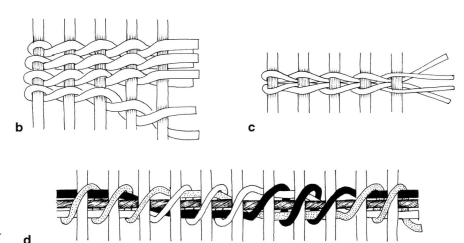

b

c

d

87 Maori cloak-weaving techniques, *whatu kākahu*. **a** Single-pair twining: the weft consists of two (a pair) of threads. **b** Close single-pair twining: each weft is placed close to and touching the previous one. **c** Double-pair twining: each weft consists of four (two pairs) of threads. **d** *Tāniko* weaving: besides the flexible coloured wefts an additional straight thread is carried behind. Drawing M. Pendergrast.

same way as cloaks, and often includes a patterned band of *tāniko*. A method of creating openwork patterns by diverting selected warps, which apparently developed at this time, has since been applied to cloaks. The late development of this is acknowledged, but today *kete muka* (fibre bags) are considered by Maori a legitimate part of traditional fibre art (fig. 181).

WHATU AHO PĀTAHI (SINGLE-PAIR TWINING) The simplest of the methods used in cloak-weaving is single-pair twining, a technique that is or has been used almost everywhere in the world. To the Maori it is known as *whatu aho pātahi*. Each weft consists of two (a single pair) of threads (fig. 87a). One of these passes behind each warp and the other in front of it, before they are twisted together, firmly enclosing the warp between them. The weaver then moves on to the next and subsequent warps and encloses them in the same manner. At the end of each row the weft is knotted off and the next weft commenced at the left-hand side at an interval below the previous weft. Its most common use among the Maori was on quickly-made rain capes and occasionally on finer garments. (This technique was also employed, using stiffer materials, on a range of fishing traps.)

PUKUPUKU (COMPACTED SINGLE-PAIR TWINING) *Pukupuku* is a form of single-pair twining in which each weft is placed close to and touching the previous row (fig. 87b).

WHATU AHO RUA (DOUBLE-PAIR TWINING) Double-pair twining or *whatu aho rua*, the technique most used for cloak-making, is more difficult to manipulate. Again the weaving begins at the left-hand side, but in this case four threads (a double pair) are carried for each weft, two passing behind and two in front of each warp (fig. 87c). Between each weft there is a space ranging from 5 mm on the finest cloaks to 20 mm or more in more open weaving.

TĀNIKO The most complex technique, in which more colours can be introduced, is known as *tāniko*. It is used to create patterns for decorative borders on cloaks. The surface of *tāniko* weaving appears identical to that of single-pair twining, except for the coloured patterns (Te Rangihīroa 1926: 79). In the case of *tāniko*, an additional straight foundation cord is carried as part of the weft, and the coloured weft threads wrap around it (fig. 87d). During the weaving process the straight weft is regularly pulled to keep the work straight. For the weaver, manipulation of the threads is similar to that of single-pair twining, the difference being that the working weft threads pass around the passive straight weft thread as well as the warps. *Tāniko* is usually placed on the lower and side borders on fine cloaks. When it appears at the top of a cloak in a photograph or painting, the garment has usually been rearranged by the photographer or artist. *Tāniko* has often been considered unique to the Maori, but recent research (Fraser 1989: 98) has described examples from peoples of the American Northwest Coast and also from Africa.

For all the above twining techniques the work is slow and tedious but the weavers become very dexterous and work with surprising speed, carefully arranging each twist in its correct position to keep the work straight, and pulling firmly on each twist to make sure that the work cannot loosen. In spite of the speed at which an expert works, a weaver expects to take about nine months to complete a modern cloak. Early *kaitaka* cloaks are said to have taken two years or more to finish.

ORNAMENTATION Over the years, ornamentation on cloaks has changed. At the contact period it was minimal and sometimes completely absent (fig. 88), the artist relying entirely on the perfection of the weaving and the colour of the flax fibre to attain a special effect. The finely woven

88 Some superior cloaks from the contact period are entirely undecorated, as is this example which shows a complete mastery of the weaving technique. Others have minor ornamentation such as dog's hair, feather or a rectangle of coloured single-pair twining placed at the lower corners. BM Ethno. Q82 Oc.700. W.170 cm.

89 Rain capes can be quite small, just large enough to keep rain off the shoulders. These would have been used for travelling, fishing or hunting in cold, wet weather. BM Ethno. +4348. w.120 cm. Presented by J. Edge Partington in 1889.

tāniko borders from this time have continued to provide inspiration for later styles to the present day.

The thick rain-shedding thatch of the rain cape (fig. 89) serves its purpose admirably. The tags are woven into the cape to lie flat against the surface so that water drains directly downwards. Elements of colour, or the arrangement of different materials in patterns, provide a decorative element which remains functional. In other examples, particularly after the introduction of coloured wool, bright borders were added, nonfunctional and purely decorative.

Cloaks decorated with short cords or tags, the *korowai-kārure* group of garments (figs 104–106), have technical similarities with the rain cape and may be a direct development of them, but now the tags have become purely decorative, adding beauty and interest to the surface. They are woven into the cloth in a manner similar to that used on the rain capes but are attached so that they hang gracefully away from the surface.

The decoration called *paheke*, used especially on the *korowai* class of cloaks, consists of coloured panels and borders of running cords and loops of coloured wool or flax fibre (figs 90 and 91g, h and i). It often appears to have been embroidered on to the cloth after the weaving has been completed, but this is not the case. It is planned within the original concept for the garment and worked in during the weaving. The prospect of new and brighter colours when wool became available led to an explosion of experimentation, and by the 1840s coloured wool had become a fully integrated element in the design and weaving of the classic *korowai*.

On the garments made in the last hundred and fifty years feathers have been the most prestigious ornamentation. They are attached to the *kau-*

91 OPPOSITE Attachment techniques. **a** For rain capes of the simplest type, no warps are used but bundles of roughly prepared fibre are treated as warps and twined together, and in subsequent rows similar bundles are added to form the thatch. **b** Alternatively, the warps may be prepared beforehand and the tags attached during the weaving of the cloth. **c-d** On related garments a popular tag was the *pokinikini*, similar to those used on modern *piupiu*. **e-f** Rain capes are related to feather cloaks and *korowai*, and the cords and feathers are attached in a similar manner. **g-i** Examples of the type of decoration known as *paheke*. The coloured threads are woven into the weft as the weaving progresses. Note: The attachments are shown in the position they take when the cloak is worn. To see their position during weaving, the drawing should be viewed upside down. Drawing M. Pendergrast.

90 *Korowai* cloaks with black *huka* cord tags appear to have become popular and quickly developed at the same time as coloured wool became available. The woollen *paheke* decoration on the lower border of this example is typical. BM Ethno. Q82 Oc.701.

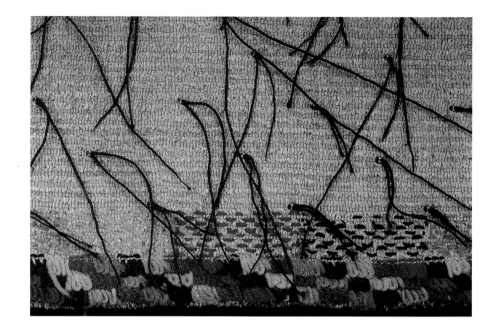

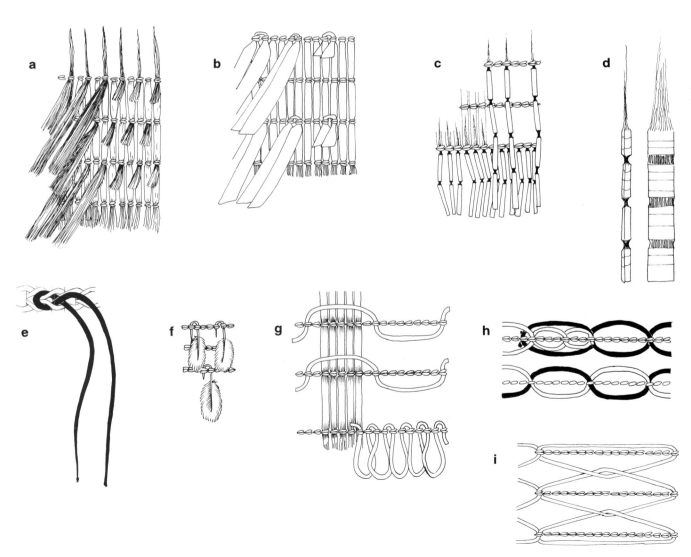

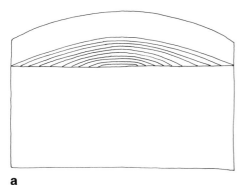

a

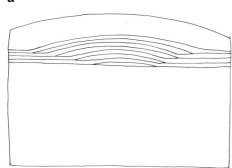

b

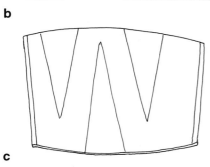

c

92 To allow the garment to fit closely and snugly, insets of additional short wefts are included. On cloaks with horizontal wefts these occur at the shoulders and buttocks, and may be grouped together, **a**. The first short weft is made at the centre and each subsequent weft is longer than the previous one. In an alternative arrangement short wefts are interpolated between full-length warps, **b**. The number of short wefts is decided by the artist. There are usually two groups of short wefts, one placed to accomodate the shoulders and the other for the buttocks. However, some garments may have up to five groups of short wefts. These make the cloak more concave, clinging to the body, but may also help the cloak to drape more gracefully. On *paepaeroa* garments with vertical wefts, wedge-shaped inserts of short wefts widened towards the top and bottom of the cloak, **c**. Drawing M. Pendergrast.

papa, the body of the cloak, in a manner very similar to that in which tags are attached to the rain capes and *korowai* cloaks (fig. 91b and f).

SHAPING Distinct from ornamentation, but dramatically altering the appearance of the cloak when it is worn, is the introduction of shaping. This is brought about by weaving in groups of short wefts or *aho poka* (fig. 92a–c). These allow the cloak to follow the curves of the body, providing additional warmth and causing the garment to hang gracefully.

Types of cloaks and capes
Rain capes (para) and related prestige garments

The basic rain cape (see fig. 89), woven in single-pair twining with thick warps and a thatch of long strips of leaf, can be made in a comparatively short time. It is, however, very efficient at turning the rain 'for which they are certainly not ill adapted as every strip of leaf becomes in that case a kind of Guttar which serves to conduct the rain down and hinder it from soaking through the cloath beneath' (Banks in Beaglehole 1963 II: 14).

Temporary rain capes, with roughly prepared materials, thick warps and widely spaced wefts in single-pair twining, were apparently not attractive enough to tempt collectors, and are not represented in museum collections. Those that survive are rather more carefully made, the wefts closer together and the warps better prepared. There is usually quite marked shaping in the shoulders so that the cloak fits well and is not pulled down the back by its wet weight. Often there is a design element, sometimes quite spectacular, in the selection and arrangement of the materials for the thatch.

The thatch is made of strips of flax, cabbage tree or *kiekie* leaves, or alternately cabbage tree or *kiekie* fibre. It may be prepared so that each tag of leaf is at the end of a length of fibre which is then treated as a warp. This makes it unnecessary to make specially prepared warps (see fig. 91a). Alternatively, the warps may be prepared beforehand and the tags attached as weaving progresses (see fig. 91b).

The *kahu tōī* is a special type of rain cape, black and shiny, worn by warriors of chiefly class. It is made from the fibre of *tōī*, the rarer mountain cabbage tree. The fibre which is extracted after a long process of steeping in water, is used for both weft and warp and is coarse, hard and very long-lasting. Dyeing is done after the weaving is complete, when the entire garment is pushed down and left for some time in a black mud dye.

Other cloaks of the general type are large (fig. 93). Sometimes they are finely made and incorporate such elements as collars and borders of wool, not suitable for shedding water. These should be regarded as prestige cloaks. The upper garment worn by Moana (fig. 94) is covered with *pokini-kini* tags – the strips of flax leaf which have rolled into hard cylinders separated by black-dyed fibre; these would not be efficient at shedding water and are purely decorative. Although these garments have been

93 ABOVE Horomona of Ruato, Lake Rotoiti, wearing a large rain cloak. Early writers described people squatting and sleeping wrapped in large rain cloaks, when it was necessary for them to camp out in the rain. William Hammond photograph. By permission of the Auckland Museum.

94 ABOVE RIGHT Illustration by George French Angas. The upper garment worn by Moana (standing) is covered with *pokinikini* tags like those on modern *piupiu*. Beneath is an attractive *korowai-ngore* with black-dyed flax fibre cords and coloured wool *paheke* and pompoms. Rawiri (sitting) also wears a *korowai-ngore*. Both men were of Ngāti Whātua of Orakei, Auckland. The artist described the two on another occasion wearing 'the costume of English gentlemen . . . riding furiously along the road mounted on spirited horses, and gaily dressed in blue coats with bright buttons.' By permission of the South Australian Museum. Reproduced in Angas 1972: Pl.16.

described as rain cloaks for rough use, they are in fact dress cloaks of social importance and prestige.

It is assumed that the simple functional rain cape was the original and earliest form of cloak made in New Zealand and that the other styles of cloak developed from it. However, the simple form did not disappear as new types emerged, but continued to fulfil a useful role throughout the nineteenth century. In a few remote areas it survived until the 1920s, when it was finally overtaken by the commercial raincoat. Recently there has been a renewal of interest in traditional rain capes, especially among young men, some of whom are also involved in the revival of canoe voyaging and see rain capes as an appropriate masculine attire for the crew.

Pukupuku ('war cloaks') and *kahu kurī* (dog-skin cloaks)

Among fine cloaks in use at the time of European contact is a group of garments woven in compacted single-pair twining, each weft being close to and touching the previous row (fig. 87b). A huge amount of labour and expertise was expended on these cloaks, both the technique and the garment being known as *pukupuku* (Te Rangihīroa 1926: 74). When they were completed they were very valuable and worn only by the most distinguished men. Banks described the cloth as 'coarse as our coarsest can-

95 Some of the most important cloaks of the contact period were woven in compacted single-pair twining. Decoration was usually restrained, often a single band of *tāniko* at the lower border, and even the *tāniko* patterns showed a controlled simplicity when compared with later designs. Strips of dog's hair were often attached to the lower edge or the lower corners. BM Ethno. Q82 Oc.691.

vass and ten times stronger but much like it in the lying of the threads' (Beaglehole 1963 II: 15). *Pukupuku* have been described as war cloaks and are said to have been heavy enough to provide protection from club and spear thrusts. Their great weight must have restricted a warrior's freedom of movement. Possibly they were worn by commanders directing operations from a distance.

Within this group there is what appears to be another class, comprising cloaks in which the close single-pair twining is very fine, and which may be either completely undecorated or have a *tāniko* border at the bottom (fig. 95). The *tāniko* on some of these cloaks is complex and not well understood. It seems that some wefts were twisted in reverse, altering the texture of the surface by raising or lowering some areas to give an embossed effect to parts of the pattern (fig. 96). On other examples an additional meandering weft appears to have been introduced. These raised

96 Some early fine *tāniko* has raised or lowered surfaces, giving an embossed effect on black areas. BM Ethno. 1927.3–7.20. Presented by Mrs J.E. Birch and collected by Alfred Clay 1867–77.

or lowered patterns are normally in black on a black ground and are so restrained that contemporary students often fail to notice them. Some of these garments have strips of dog skin or small rectangles of patterned single-pair twining at the lower corners. Others have bundles of dog hair along the lower edge. They show no evidence of European influence, such as the use of wool, and all appear to be from the late eighteenth century, collected by Cook or other early European visitors. A number of these remarkable garments are held in the British Museum and other museums around the world, and it is strange that they appear not so far to have been described as a separate group.

The most prestigious of all garments of the contact period was the *kahu kurī* or dog-skin cloak (fig. 97). Banks wrote 'the great pride of their dress seems to consist in dogs fur, which they use so sparingly that to avoid waste they cut into long strips and sew them at a distance from each other upon their Cloth, varying often the coulours prettily enough. When first we saw these dresses we took them for the skins of Bears' (Beaglehole 1963 II: 15). The *kahu kurī* is woven as a *pukupuku* cloak, in compacted single-pair twining. Usually a narrow border of two-colour patterns is worked on each side edge. These are woven in single-pair twining. It was a comparatively simple matter to introduce the additional colour, since the single-pair wefts were already in place. All that was required was to replace one of the pair with a contrasting coloured thread. It is possible that this is the origin of full *tāniko* and in fact, very occasionally, *tāniko* has been used for these borders.

The weaving of the body of the cloak was done by women. The outer surface was worked by two men, who covered it with vertically arranged narrow strips of dog skin with the hair attached. One man sat on each side of the suspended garment and they passed a bone needle back and forth through the weaving. Presumably this represented a continuation of men's responsibility for killing and skinning the dog and preparing the rawhide.

The dog-skin strips are arranged in patterns using the natural colours of the hair, and it was from the arrangement of the colours that the Maori divided *kahu kurī* into named sub-groups.

The *māhiti* is a garment woven in close single-pair twining, often with a *tāniko* pattern as the lower border and the surface decorated with bundles of long hair selected from the tails of dogs. Another type is not woven but consists of a number of dog skins sewn together.

The Polynesian dog (*kurī*) was introduced to New Zealand by the forebears of the Maori and was regarded as a valuable property of chiefs. Its hair was so fine and soft that it could well be described as fur. Important as the *kurī* was for its skin and fur, it was also used for hunting flightless birds, and its flesh was regarded as a delicacy. The arrival of Europeans with other breeds of dogs resulted in the *kurī* being bred out. Their hair became coarse and their cultural importance was lost; the *kahu kurī* were never made again.

Men's belts (*tātua*) were also made using the twining technique. They

97 The chief Te Rangihaeata, wearing a dog-skin cloak over a classic *kaitaka* with *tāniko* border. By permission of the British Library. Add. MS 19954 f.60, drawing no. 70. C.D. Barraud, 'Rangihaeata' [from collection of watercolours and drawings illustrating New Zealand 1848–53].

98 *Kaitaka* from the contact period are large prestigious garments. Sometimes two-colour patterns in single-pair twining at the lowers corners are the only ornamentation. This may be an earlier form of the classic *kaitaka* illustrated in fig. 99. BM Ethno. NZ 135. Cook collection.

99 On the classic *kaitaka* the glow of the plain surface is highlighted by fine *tāniko* borders (see detail above), narrower on the side edges and wide at the bottom. BM Ethno. 1938.10–1.79. w.211 cm. Presented by Miss E.K.B. Lister and collected by the donor's father about 1842.

were woven as a rectangle and then folded three times, in the same way as the plaited belts, making three thicknesses of this thick cloth. An important example in the British Museum (see fig. 83) is finely woven and pigmented with *kōkōwai* or red ochre; it is unusually wide and long. The reason for the width and thickness of this belt is not known. It obviously protected the stomach and kidney areas as did the extra thickness added to the plaited specimens; but whether protection from the cold or weapon thrusts was intended we can only surmise.

Kaitaka

The other important group of prestige cloaks from the time of European

contact is the *kaitaka*. These garments were woven in spaced double-pair twining (a space is left between each weft), and decoration is sparse and sometimes absent. Dog skin or hair may be attached to the lower corners or edge, or a small rectangle of pattern, woven in single-pair twining in two colours, may be placed at the lower corners (fig. 98). These may be an early form of the classic *kaitaka* which was already in vogue at the same time. The 'classic *kaitaka*' is a large garment relying for its beauty on the perfection of its weaving and the type and quality of the flax fibre used. Banks commented that this type of cloak was 'sometimes stripd and always very pretty, for the threads that compose it are prepard so as to shine almost as much as silk' (Beaglehole 1963 II: 15). There is no ornamentation to conceal the body of the cloak. Beating and rolling the fibre destroy the lustre, and for this type of cloak these processes were omitted. Only unbeaten fibre was used for both weft and warp, and the weaving was very fine. When completed, the cloth glowed with a golden sheen.

On classic *kaitaka* this effect is complemented by refined *tāniko* borders on each side and a wider one at the lower edge (fig. 99). During the weaving the warps on which the *tāniko* will later be woven are attached to each side edge, and after the body of the cloak has been completed the

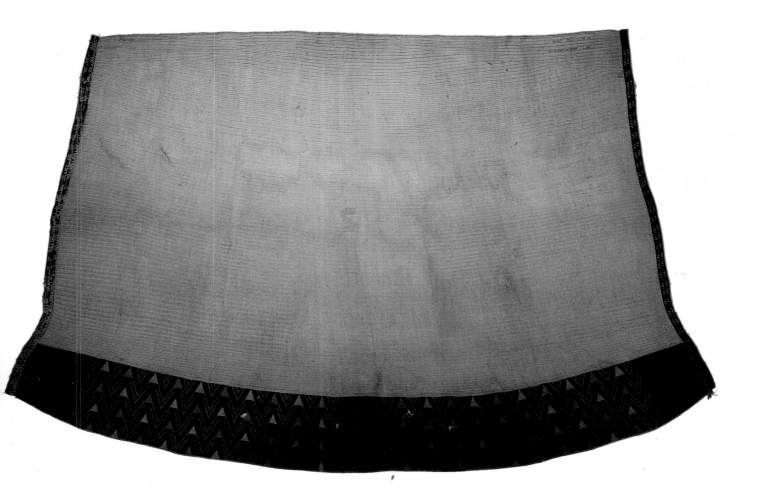

100 The rare *huaki* belongs to the *kaitaka* class of cloaks, but is distinguished by double rows of *tāniko* borders. The upper band of *tāniko* and the goat hair (a substitute for dog's hair) on this cloak have been added later. BM Ethno. Q82 Oc.718. w.127.5 cm.

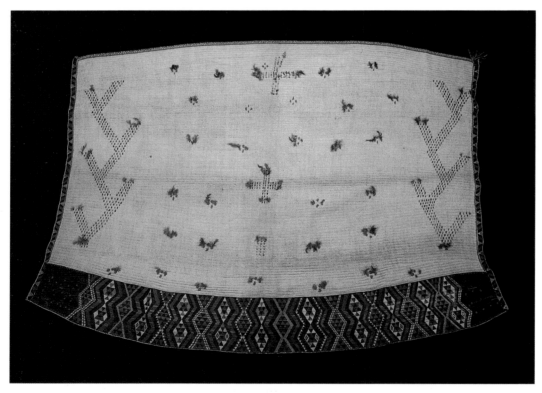

101 The enthusiasm for coloured wool led to the demise of the restraint usually exhibited in traditional *kaitaka*. Eventually the garment became obsolete, and attention was focused on the quickly developing *korowai*. BM Ethno. 1854.12–29.133. w.206 cm. Grey collection.

Paratene maioha.

102 Paratene Maioha, a chief of Ngāti
Mahuta, is wearing a large dramatic cloak
ornamented with bundles of dog's hair. It is
a finely woven garment described by the
artist George French Angas as *parawai*, a
synonym for *kaitaka*, and from the South
Island. Angas 1847: pl. 35.

tāniko patterns are woven on to these threads. The embossed 'black on
black' *tāniko* patterns also appear on *kaitaka*. The beauty of the garment
relies on contrast between the attractive dark *tāniko* patterns and the perfect workmanship and golden glow of the specially selected fibre of the
body of the cloak. The remarkable restraint of these garments creates a
simple elegance that has never been surpassed.

Kaitaka are divided by Maori into sub-groups, all beautifully woven,
nearly always in double-pair twining and without surface decoration.
When the wefts are placed horizontally (fig. 99) the garment is known as
pātea; on the *paepaeroa* the wefts are vertical (fig. 98). For the *pātea* the
commencement is at the upper edge and the work continues downwards
to finish with the *tāniko* at the lower edge. If there are to be side borders,
the warps on to which the *tāniko* will be woven are added during the
weaving of the body. The *tāniko* will be worked on to these warps after
the rest of the garment has been completed. On the *paepaeroa* the vertical
wefts are achieved by suspending the work with one side edge uppermost.
This is the commencement, and the weaving continues downwards to
finish at the opposite side edge. The entire garment is woven in this position, and only after it has been completed is it turned to its correct position
(fig. 98). Coloured bands may be formed by placing groups of dyed warps
among the uncoloured ones. Therefore on the *pātea*, which has horizontal
wefts, the bands will be vertical, those on the *paepaeroa*, with vertical wefts,
the bands will be horizontal (fig. 98).

The rare *huaki* cloak is a *kaitaka* with two, very occasionally three, borders at the lower edge and usually two on the side borders (fig. 100).
Another uncommon and valuable type of *kaitaka* has tassels of glossy white
hair taken from the tails of *kurī* arranged across the surface of the garment
during manufacture (fig. 102), in a manner similar to the close single-pair
twined *māhiti* cloaks.

During the early part of the nineteenth century the *kaitaka* became the
most important garment, taking the place of the dog-skin cloak. When
wool became available, experiments were made by introducing it into the
tāniko borders. Later small motifs were added to the main surface (fig.
101) and sometimes extended over the entire area. Perhaps it was the
emerging delight in working with colour that led to the decline of interest
in the *kaitaka* and the transference of experimentation to the less formal
korowai, which permitted more freedom with its quickly changing and
developing form. *Kaitaka* were no longer produced after about 1840.

Korowai and related cloaks

A class of cloak stained red with *kōkōwai* (red ochre), and with decorative
string cords, was in fashion at the time of European contact in the late
eighteenth century (fig. 103). They were seen by Cook and his men and
recorded by his artists. All of those held in museums around the world
were collected by early visitors. Since then similar garments and fragments
have been found in caves. They are woven in double-pair twining and the
fabric is quite thick, its main function apparently being to provide warmth.

103 Cloaks with undyed cords, which were stained entirely red with red ochre, *kōkōwai*, appear to be the forerunners of the *korowai* with black tags. BM Ethno. Q82 Oc.712.

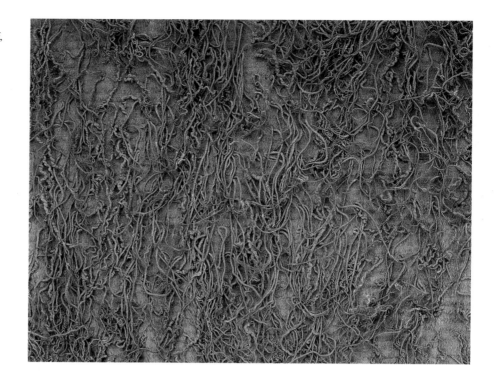

104 The classic *korowai* is identified by its black cord tags. For a long period in the nineteenth century it was the most commonly made garment. The tags are attached in a manner that will cause them to hang away from the surface of the garment. The woman is identified as M. Brenner of Thames. William Hammond photograph, 1906. By permission of the Auckland Museum.

Attached to the outer surface are single-ply, two-ply or three-ply cords, usually a combination of all three. The whole cloak is coloured red with ochre, sometimes by rubbing it on to the cloth and sometimes by steeping the garment in an infusion of ochre and water. At that time red ochre was also used for painting the face and body.

This type of cloak with its string tags appears to be the forerunner of the better known 'classic *korowai*' (fig. 104), a distinctive white garment with the outer surface decorated with hanging cords of two-ply, rolled flax-fibre cords, usually dyed black. The special magic of the *korowai* lies in the method used to attach the cords during manufacture. Each cord is caught at its middle and secured into the weft in a manner similar to that used for rain capes. In this case, however, it is arranged in a way that forces the semi-stiff tightly-rolled cords to stand out, away from the surface of the cloak (fig. 91e). As the wearer moves, so do the tags, giving the garment an apparent life of its own. Later, woollen tags were tried but were found to cling to the surface and so were eventually rejected.

At the upper edge of the *korowai* is a thick collar made of the same rolled black cords. Down each side are narrower borders of black cords, and at the bottom a black fringe is attached by a single weft which is added after the completion of the body of the cloak. The tags are arranged in rows, horizontally, vertically or diagonally, and at each end of the black collar is a fringe of undyed fibre formed from the ends of the warps.

The *korowai* is at the centre of a group of related garments including the *kārure* and *ngore* discussed below, none of which were recorded by Cook but which appeared early in the nineteenth century. From about 1830 to 1870 they were extremely popular, were produced in large numbers and became the dominant style. They are closely related to rain capes and probably developed from them. Like rain capes, the *korowai* group all commence at the bottom edge and are worked upside down. However, the fibre for *korowai* is carefully prepared for softness: washed in water, rolled into two-ply cords and then beaten with a stone beater (fig. 75). This process is repeated until the cords become soft to the touch, more like wool in appearance and probably warmer. It also makes them whiter. These cords become the vertical warps. The threads for the weft are finer and are not beaten. The three characteristics of softness, whiteness and rolled and beaten warps separate this group from the silky golden lustre which was the priority for the unrolled and unbeaten warps of the *kaitaka* class.

The *kārure* (fig. 105) is very similar to the *korowai* and decorated in the same manner, but in this case the peculiar hanging black cords are three-ply and are rolled in reverse so that they have the appearance of becoming unravelled. On the *ngore* the decoration takes the form of pompoms, usually of red wool, attached into the weaving. Sometimes the red pompoms are combined with black cords and the resulting hybrid garment is known as a *korowai-ngore* (fig. 106). Similarly, the combination of two-ply back cords of the *korowai* with the unravelling three-ply *kārure* cords produces the *korowai-kārure*. *Paheke* patterns of running cords and loops of coloured wool are most commonly seen on the *korowai* group of garments.

Kahu huruhuru (feather cloaks)

Feather cloaks are rarely mentioned by visitors during the first half of the nineteenth century and do not appear in the works of visiting artists of the period. Richard A. Cruise, visiting New Zealand in 1820, says 'Wheety, who was now a very important personage, laid aside his European clothes, and putting on his emu-feathered mat [See Note 14], seated himself upon the deck to receive his countrymen' (Cruise 1823: 211). In the Note 14 he adds 'a mat ornamented with them, is the most costly dress a chief can wear' (Cruise 1823: 318) but makes no other comment. (The feathers may have been kiwi feathers, although emu feathers did appear on cloaks in the second half of the nineteenth century.)

At the end of the eighteenth century Captain Cook recorded seeing a woman wearing an apron of red feathers. He also collected a feather cloak, now in the Pitt-Rivers Museum, Oxford (Roth 1979: 89). The feathers on it have since been destroyed by insects and their colour cannot be ascertained. However the quills of the feathers which are still in position show that they were knotted together on to a cord and the cord was later attached to the garment.

On another garment woven in compacted single-pair twining, collected by Cook and now in the Museum für Völkerkunde, Vienna (Kaeppler 1978: 173), the feathers are sparse and widely spaced in small bundles, inter-

105 The *kārure* is closely related to the *korowai*. The only difference is that the black cords with which it is decorated are rolled to look as though they are unravelling. The cords as well as the cloak are known as *kārure*. The photograph was taken at Ōhinemutu, Rotorua, by William Hammond, *c.* 1903. By permission of the Auckland Museum.

106 Tamahiki Te Rewiti wearing a *korowai-ngore* which combines the black cords of the *korowai* with the pompoms of the *ngore*. The style was popular during the 1840s. Seated is his uncle, Te Kawau, wearing a large rain cloak. Angas 1847: Pl.56b.

107 For almost a hundred and fifty years the feather cloak or *kahu huruhuru* has been widely admired by both Maori and Pākehā. The young woman on the left wears a *kahu kiwi* (kiwi feather cloak) and her friend a *kahu huruhuru* (feather cloak) over a *korowai* with bands of black or coloured warps. The women have not been identified. A.J. Iles photograph. By permission of the Auckland Museum.

108 The *kahu huruhuru* or feather cloak, at least in the form it is known today, appeared quite suddenly in the middle of the nineteenth century. The feathers are added individually or in small bunches of two or three caught into the weft during weaving. BM Ethno. 1913.6–12.1. Presented by C.H. Waterlow.

spersed with bundles of dog hair and strips of skin. All of these have been woven in so that they stand upright.

The English artist George French Angas, who visited New Zealand in 1844, took a special interest in traditional clothing. Although he noted that the Maori, and particularly the women and girls, had almost completely adopted European clothing by that time, he left an exceptional record depicting at least 150 traditional garments being worn. Not once does a *kahu huruhuru* appear; nor are they mentioned in his writings.

In other written records there is rare mention of tufts of feathers and bird skins. The descriptions do not give the impression of vivid colour and did not excite the visitors sufficiently to bring forth the superlatives elicited by the feather cloaks of the twentieth century. After a description of clothing in general, and in particular the enthusiastic response to the *kahu kurī* and *kaitaka* quoted above, Banks simply remarks 'Some there were who had these dresses ornamented with feathers and one who had an intire dress of the red feathers of Parrots, but these were not common' (Beaglehole 1963 II: 15). Elsewhere he refers to the use of 'the skins of divers birds' (Beaglehole 1963 II: 5).

The oldest feather garment in Auckland Museum (No. 1491) is one from the Sir George Grey Collection. The surface is entirely covered with tail feathers from the *tūī* (*Prosthemadera novaeseelandiae*), but the feathers have

109 Today the most prestigious cloak is the *kahu kiwi* which is entirely covered with kiwi feathers. The example illustrated here has a wide border of blue *tūī* feathers and white feathers from the native pigeon, *kererū*. BM Ethno. NZ 134. w.165 cm.

been twined together on to cords (Pendergrast 1987: 113) and these have then been sewn on to the surface of the cloak, which is a rectangular piece of coarse commercial cloth, backed with barkcloth, probably of Eastern Polynesian origin.

Fabulous *kahu kura*, cloaks of red feathers, appear in oral traditions throughout Polynesia associated with gods, culture heroes and famous ancestors, but there appear to be no feather cloaks in museum collections that are firmly dated to before the 1850s. The scarcity of clear descriptions and fully documented specimens from before that time make this type of cloak something of a mystery. The type of feather cloaks we are now familiar with seems to have appeared quite suddenly in the middle of the nineteenth century and from then on was recorded with increasing frequency (fig. 107).

These *kahu huruhuru* of the later period are woven upside down with the commencement at the lower edge. The feathers are attached singly (fig. 91f) or in small bundles, and woven into the weft on every second or third row in a manner similar to the attachment of tags on rain capes. They quickly became the prestige garment *par excellence* and have maintained that status to the present day (figs 108 and 109).

Contemporary cloaks

Maori clothing has been strongly influenced by the outside world ever since contact with the first European explorers. Commercial cloth, carried on the ships as trade goods, was eagerly sought and immediately became part of popular attire. Items of clothing obtained through trade with the officers and crews of the ships were proudly displayed by the fortunate recipients. The first attraction was the bright colour and novelty, but the garments were not always worn as their makers had intended. Shirts and trousers were found to be restricting to movement and were worn around the neck or waist for display. Later, woollen blankets were in great demand when the warmth they provided was realised. Soon items of imported clothing were regularly worn for both warmth and amusement, with traditional cloaks sometimes worn over them on important occasions.

The speed at which this acceptance took place cannot easily be assessed. It depended to a large extent on locality, for people with access to ships, and later to traders and settlers, were able to trade much more easily than those from more remote areas. Missionaries and European women introduced new concepts of modesty, which were enforced as much as possible in the vicinity of mission stations, so they were able to report the 'advances' made by their work and presence. Artists and photographers, on the other hand, often wished to record the 'noble savage' and encouraged their models to pose in traditional garments. Some went to the extent of buying suitable cloaks to dress their subjects in, so it is common to find a number of images by the same photographer in which all the subjects are wearing the same set of garments. This influence continued well into the twentieth century, when the painter Charles Goldie continued to provide cloaks for his clients to pose in.

This dressing of models in traditional garments has resulted in a record of a remarkable range of styles, some of which may have otherwise been forgotten. However, when using them for research it should be remembered that the artists were not above re-draping cloaks, turning them upside down and dressing pretty young women in the garments reserved for chiefs of high standing.

For 150 years and more, Maori people have dressed in Western clothing, with traditional garments sometimes worn over them to express identity, pride, or *mana* and sometimes protest. The great size of some of the old cloaks is no longer necessary for warmth or modesty, and modern ones are normally much smaller. They may be worn by the Maori recipient of honours, on receiving academic recognition or when welcoming a respected visitor or dignitary. Some are reserved to cover the coffin at the funeral of a deceased family member.

Cloaks are still designed and woven with great care and attention to detail. The work is suspended on a more substantial frame than the traditional weaving sticks, but the weaving technique is identical to that of the past, the wefts being painstakingly twisted with the fingers (fig. 110). When candlewick and other manufactured materials are used today, it is usually not from preference but because the weaver concerned does not have access to the necessary flax varieties or plant dyes. Brightly coloured wool is no longer seen, and there is a strong reversion to traditional fibre, dyes and colours whenever possible.

Since the first collections and records of Maori costume were made there has been a continuous evolution of styles. Changes have probably always occurred, but the process was undoubtedly hastened by the arrival of the first Europeans and subsequent missionaries and settlers with alien ideas and attitudes, who brought with them new, brightly coloured materials.

110 Modern cloaks are still woven in the ancient tradition. Puti Hineaupounamu Rare is seen here working on a flax fibre garment with ornamentation of black cords, feathers and openwork. Photo G. Hanley, 1990.

From the first exchanges, pieces of cloth became desirable, especially if they were red. Woollen comforters were soon being unpicked, the wool unravelled and then re-rolled to be integrated into *tāniko* patterns on *kaitaka*. Small experimental motifs in colour began to appear on the main surface of the *kaitaka*, and soon *paheke* patterns and pompoms were spread across the entire garment. This bright decoration detracted so much from the plain golden surface that it became redundant and the *kaitaka* ceased to be. Experimentation with wool was then transferred to the less formal *korowai*, which was for a time converted into a garment of many colours. It became the most popular cloak made during the period *c.* 1830–1850.

Thereafter, the *korowai* style appears to have split into two distinct streams. One group expressed a new conservatism by using completely traditional materials but occasionally adding *tāniko* or feathers. The other group worked with non-traditional materials, the warps of the cloth being of undyed wool or candlewick, with cotton or linen wefts, and feathers often included. This group continued the exploration of *paheke* decoration in bright colours. Occasionally there were attempts at producing naturalistic motifs using the twined *paheke* method and rare experimentation in needle embroidery (fig. 111). These last unusual and inventive deviations are quite rare and are perhaps related to a similar movement in painted figurative art, which was explored in decorated meeting houses of the period.

From *c.* 1850 feather borders were commonly introduced onto the *korowai*, and cloaks completely covered with feathers appeared quite suddenly. By the end of the century they were in great demand and have continued to be so to the present day. The combination of different styles that has been taking place since contact has accelerated in the last fifty years, and most recent cloaks include elements taken from more than one earlier style.

Contemporary cloaks are finely woven in double-pair twining, using rolled and beaten flax-fibre cords for the warps (fig. 110). Another variety of flax often provides fibre considered more suitable for the wefts. A single garment may be decorated with elements from many of the earlier types:

111 At the end of the nineteenth and beginning of the twentieth centuries the cloak weavers experimented with non-traditional colours and materials. Although the weaving and general form are in the traditional style, the materials are all exotic. The naturalistic interpretation of the flower is a major departure from the norm although it is worked in the traditional *paheke* style. The rainbow (?) has been embroidered with a needle. BM Ethno. Q82 Oc.709.

112 Diggeress Rangihuatahi Te Kanawa of the Kinohaku sub-tribe of Ngāti Maniapoto, Oparure, Te Kuiti, wearing a flax cloak with *pūkeko* feathers and a *tāniko* border, which she made for the British Museum in 1993–4. BM Ethno. 1994 Oc.4.87.

bands of *tāniko* and undecorated areas inherited from the *kaitaka*; black-dyed rolled fibre cords from the *korowai* and *kārure*; coloured *paheke* motifs, now of dyed flax-fibre; borders and/or blocks of feathers from the *kahu huruhuru*, and areas of openwork which appeared in the second half of the nineteenth century on small woven baskets made for sale to Europeans.

Most native birds are now threatened by loss of habitat and introduced predators, and so the feathers are generally from introduced species such as the domestic fowl and pheasant. Newly made cloaks normally remain within the family of the artist and on important occasions are worn by male or female relatives across the shoulders and over standard contemporary Western dress.

Modern cloaks show a very strong link with the past and can be viewed as a continuation of the fashion changes that have been evolving for at least two hundred years (figs 112, 126). However, as well as these traditional weavers, a new group of weavers and artists are actively exploring and extending the borders of the fibre tradition. The techniques, materials and forms of the past are reinterpreted to create works in tune with the late twentieth century and international art movements. Exhibitions of contemporary Maori art frequently include traditional fibre pieces alongside more contemporary interpretations which often take the form of wall hangings or sculpture.

Contemporary performance costume is a twentieth-century development using the *piupiu* skirt of *pokinikini* tags as the basic element. To this has been added a bodice for women, head-bands, and sometimes cloaks, weapons and ornaments. These are commonly made using non-traditional techniques and materials, and they are influenced by contemporary fashions and interpretations of the past.

Maori fibre work has survived as an active and developing part of contemporary life in Aotearoa. The finest work is viewed as art rather than craft and is much admired by Pākehā as well as Maori, the names of the most prominent artists being well known to both races. *Kete* are still to be seen on the *marae* and elsewhere, used and valued by both Maori and Pākehā. Cloaks are still seen on special occasions on the shoulders of an elder. Both *kete* and *kākahu* are viewed as *taonga* or cultural treasures.

6

THE MAORI COLLECTIONS IN THE BRITISH MUSEUM

D. C. Starzecka

Ethnography in the British Museum

The British Museum is the oldest national, public, secular museum in Britain. It was founded in 1753 and owes its existence to the collecting zeal and encyclopaedic interests of one man, Sir Hans Sloane. Sloane's personal collection, purchased for the nation in 1753 with funds from a national lottery, formed the basis of the Museum's collections along with the Cottonian Library and the Harleian manuscripts.

The history of the Ethnographic collections in the British Museum goes back to its very foundations, for among the original Sloane collection there were 350 ethnographical objects (Fagg 1970:19) from different parts of the world (except Oceania which, of course, was almost totally unknown at that time). In spite of that, throughout the greater part of their existence the ethnographic collections were the Cinderella of the British Museum's antiquities. This is reflected in the numerous administrative shifts of the collections from one department to another and in the fact that the Department of Ethnography acquired an independent identity only after World War II.

Although its formal independence came so late, Ethnography has always been popular with the general public. Objects collected during Captain Cook's three voyages of exploration between 1768 and 1780 were displayed in the 'South Sea Room', drawing crowds of the curious. They are specifically mentioned in the *Synopsis of the contents of the British Museum* (1808) as forming 'now one of the most conspicuous parts of the Museum' (p.xxiv). The Museum was obviously popular, for further on there is a mention of 'the curiosity of the multitudes, who incessantly resort to it in quest of amusements'. In the 1880s A.W. Franks, Keeper of the Department of Medieval and British Antiquities and Ethnography, predicted that after the removal of the natural history collections Ethnography would be the greatest attraction to visitors. The truth of this statement was partly confirmed twenty years later, when 'the Ethnographical collections were next in popular interest to the Egyptian mummies' (Miller 1973:317). Between the wars 'the Ethnographical collection remained one of the most popular sections of the Museum' (Miller 1973:341).

However, the senior staff of the Museum, brought up in the classical tradition of the eighteenth century, did not care much for the ethnographic collections. During discussions in 1859–60 about the planned removal of the natural history collections to a new site, a sizeable body of opinion firmly believed that it was Ethnography which should go. Nevertheless, when a final decision was made, Ethnography remained with other, more august, antiquities in the British Museum. By the time the natural history collections were moved to South Kensington, Ethnography already had a champion on the Museum staff in the person of the Keeper of the Department of British and Medieval Antiquities and Ethnography himself, Augustus Wollaston Franks.

His initial interests were those of a prehistorian and medievalist, and his interest in ethnography developed later. It was largely thanks to him that in 1865 the Museum acquired the largest private ethnographic collection in existence at the time, formed by Henry Christy, a prosperous textile-manufacturer who became interested in collecting during his business travels. When Christy died in 1865, his collection consisted of about 30,000 objects, among them about 1,000 ethnographic ones (King 1997). In his will he instructed his Trustees to offer it, and a sum of money to maintain it, to an existing institution or to create a new one to house it. One of these Trustees was Franks and there is no doubt that it is owing to Franks's good offices that the collection was offered to the British Museum. Franks's role in the development of the ethnographic collections in the British Museum cannot be overemphasised. His generosity and personal fortune allowed him to buy for the Museum what he considered desirable. Through his wide social and professional contacts he could influence collectors and induce them to present objects or to sell them on favourable terms; and he maintained good relations with museums overseas and arranged exchanges and reciprocal gifts of duplicates. When he joined the Museum in 1851 the ethnographic collections numbered 3,758 objects; when he retired as Keeper in 1896, they totalled 38,048 (King 1997), including well over 8,000 pieces which he personally gave to the Museum, among them 222 Maori objects (M. Downing, pers.com.).

The steady, and in the second half of the nineteenth century greatly increased, growth of the collections caused some problems. Exhibition space has been a perennial problem in the Museum and Ethnography was especially afflicted by it. When the Christy collection was acquired, it had to remain at Christy's house at Victoria Street in central London because the Museum did not have sufficient space to accommodate it until the natural history specimens were removed. However, by 1883 it had been transferred to the British Museum and in 1886 new ethnographic displays were opened to the public in the long gallery over the King's Library, once occupied by the bird and shell collections. They stayed there, except for the war years when the collections were evacuated to safe sites in the country, until the late 1960s when the Trustees decided that Ethnography would be transferred temporarily to outstations. Exhibitions went to the Museum of Mankind near Piccadilly, and the reserve collections to a specially acquired building at Orsman Road in East London.

The Maori collections in the British Museum

The British Museum's Maori collections are probably the finest outside New Zealand but they are comparatively small, numbering about 3,000 items, and uneven in scope and nature. They are particularly strong in late eighteenth and nineteenth century material and, like other ethnographic collections in the Museum, they are connected with Britain's colonial history. Collections were made by travellers, colonial administrators, military and naval men, missionaries and amateur collectors and scholars, and not infrequently they were sold or presented to the Museum by the collector's relatives or descendants. Inevitably, such collections vary greatly for they reflect the collectors' personal tastes and interests, the perceived value of objects, their portability or simply chance. Not surprisingly, therefore, the Museum has, for example, large collections of beautifully carved treasure boxes and flutes, and of nephrite *tiki*, all small portable objects, which must have been particularly attractive to the collectors; the fish-hook collection, extensive and in an excellent state of preservation, has been often admired by visiting New Zealand scholars. On the other hand, large objects are few and ordinary domestic implements are also poorly represented.

In the early stages, when Ethnography had a lowly status within the Museum, the overwhelming majority of Maori objects were acquired as gifts: before 1865, 207 objects were presented and 32 purchased; from 1866 onwards the balance is about equal. This increase in the number of purchases is undoubtedly the result of Franks's policy, helped by the readily-available Christy fund which made such acquisitions possible. It also has to do with the changed status of anthropology which was coming of age as a scientific discipline in its own right, though still closely connected with prehistory. Ethnographic objects were used to throw light on and to draw parallels with European prehistoric finds, and the material cultures of exotic peoples were neatly arranged within the evolutionary scheme of the time.

All this was reflected in museum exhibitions. The early mishmash of 'artificial curiosities' – when it did not matter whether a 'South Sea object' was from Tahiti or New Zealand – was replaced in the mid-nineteenth century by a more systematic organisation of displays. In 1849 'labels and names were extensively attached to objects, which have made them more interesting and instructive', and two years later this practice became a well-established system (Braunholtz 1938:5). For a long time, though, the exhibitions seemed to display an extreme case of Victorian *horror vacui*, with glass cabinets crammed full almost to bursting point. This state of affairs persisted until after World War II, when the number of ethnographic objects on display was reduced from about 200,000 to a mere 13,000 (Miller 1973:356). Even so, judged by the contemporary standards the design was not particularly impressive (fig. 114). The change came with the move of the collections to the Museum of Mankind, where a new exhibition policy was adopted, concentrating on temporary displays devoted to one culture or a particular theme. Inevitably, this removed large sections of the collections from view. Individual Maori objects have been exhibited at various times but only once were a small number of them put together into a distinct display – in 1990, as a commemoration of the 150th anniversary of the signing of the Treaty of Waitangi (fig. 115).

In view of the acquisition policy of the nineteenth century, it is no surprise that documentation of the Maori collections is poor or even non-existent. The basic documentation is to be found in the registers, as the British Museum catalogues are known, and the system according to which they are organised is not straightforward. Different numbering systems

113 The oldest surviving example of a Maori kite. Wood framework covered with cotton cloth, haliotis-shell eyes. BM Ethno. 1843.7–10.11. w.265 cm. Presented by Mr Reed and brought from the Bay of Plenty by Capt. Manning.

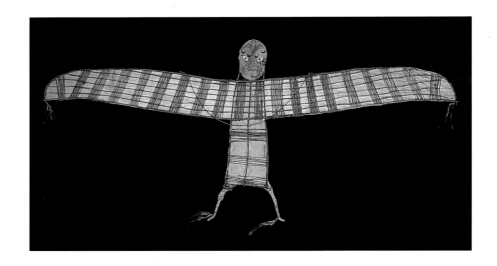

were used at different times, and some material was registered decades after its acquisition, by which time the original documentation may have been lost or forgotten. At present, all essential information about the collections is easily accessible on the computer. The computerisation of the collections, begun in the 1980s, has been completed, and from 1991 all acquisitions have been registered directly on the computer.

The earliest Maori material in the Museum comes from Captain Cook's three voyages of exploration of 1768–71, 1772–75 and 1776–80. The first entry for it in the Museum records was made on 18 October 1771: 'A curious collection of weapons, utensils, and manufactures of various sorts, sent from Hota Hita [Tahiti] and other newly discovered islands in the South Seas, and from New Zealand made by Captain Cook: from the Lords

114 A case displaying Polynesian and Maori material in the old Ethnography gallery in the British Museum in 1963. Photo D.J. Lee.

115 Maori display, marking the 150th anniversary of the signing of the Treaty of Waitangi, in the Museum of Mankind in 1990.

of the Admiralty'. Between 1771 and 1780 there are six other, similar, records of gifts originating from the voyages and presented by Cook himself, Joseph Banks (a collector and naturalist on the first voyage), the Admiralty and various officers and expedition members. All these records are equally general and for none is there a list or a catalogue specifying what precisely was given at the time. The objects were catalogued much later, at the end of the nineteenth century, in a numerical sequence with a self-explanatory prefix NZ, by James Edge Partington, a well-known authority on Pacific cultures who worked for many years at the Museum on a voluntary basis. As far as it can be established at present (for detailed discussion of the Cook voyages collections, see Kaeppler 1978), there are twenty-eight Maori objects in the collections, for which there is either very strong circumstantial or documentary (including pictorial records of the voyages) evidence supporting their Cook provenance (Kaeppler 1978; Simmons, n.d.). Twenty-four of these have NZ numbers and are eighteenth century acquisitions; the remaining four came later. Among the objects in the NZ series there are probably some others – apart from the twenty-four mentioned above – which may have been collected on Cook's voyages, some of which have been suggested as such on the basis of style (Simmons, n.d.; M. Pendergrast, pers. com.) This series may also include two donations of 1777 (the date testifies to their Cook voyage provenance) by Thomas Pell and Charles Smith, which cannot be identified today. Further research may eventually throw more light on the Cook material.

From the time of the Cook collections until 1854 the Museum acquired a relatively small amount of Maori material, most of it as individual objects, some of which were mentioned in various editions of the *Synopsis*. The 47th edition (1844:10) mentions the only kite in the Museum collections, 1843.7–10.11 (fig. 113), presented by Mr Reed (or Read) and collected by Capt. Manning: 'Over the door leading to the passage is a New Zealand kite, from Plenty Bay'. Eight years later the 59th edition points out two objects (1847.11–28.1 and 1847.8–27.24) deserving attention: 'Coat of Eh Puni [Honiana Te Puni, Te Ati Awa chief], a chief of the Pa

116 Nephrite pendant with flax cord and bone toggle, given by the Ngāpuhi chief Titore to Captain Sadler in the 1830s. BM Ethno. 1896–925. L. of figure 8.5 cm. Presented by A.W. Franks.

of Ki Warra [Kaiwharawhara, near Wellington], entirely made of native flax ... Above this case is the prow [incorrect: it is a stern] of the canoe of the celebrated New Zealand chief, Heki [Hone Heke Pokai, Ngāpuhi chief]. Presented by Captain Sir Everard Home, Bart.RN'.

In 1854 one of the most important Maori collections was presented to the Museum, consisting of well over a hundred objects and including gifts presented to Sir George Grey, Governor of New Zealand, during his first tour of duty there, between 1845 and 1854 (1854.12–29.), some of these named pieces of great *mana* and historical importance (Davis 1855). Before Grey gave his collection to the Museum he had sought to clarify its legal status and wrote to the Colonial Office for instructions. The reply, dated 12 June 1854, was unequivocal: 'I am directed by the Duke of Newcastle ... to acquaint you that considering the peculiar nature of their presents his Grace feels no difficulty in authorising you to retain them' (PRO CO 406/14 f.67v). The gifts were thus legally Grey's, to dispose of as he wished and, he gave them to the national Museum.

In 1855 a number of Maori objects entered the Museum in a large ethnographic collection from Haslar Hospital Museum, presented by the Admiralty. Haslar is a Royal Naval hospital near Portsmouth, and the objects then in the museum had been collected by men serving in the Royal Navy. Another museum which also disposed of its ethnographical collections a decade later was the Royal United Services Institution Museum in Whitehall. Many of its ethnographic objects found their way into the Christy collection. Unfortunately, documentation for all this material is poor. The same is true of over seventy objects from the Rev. William Sparrow Simpson, an amateur scholar and collector, and a recognised authority on stone implements (Sparrow Simpson 1899:36) who also had a good eye for ethnographic objects of high quality. His material was acquired by purchase in 1875, as gifts prior to that, and in 1895 via Franks.

In 1878 a small number of Maori objects (1878.11–1.) came to the Museum within a collection purchased from Major General Augustus Meyrick, significant for its early date for most of it was formed by Sir Samuel Meyrick before 1827 (King 1981:37). In 1892 five carved storehouse boards (1892.12–11.) were purchased from Alfred Fowler, a member of a well-known Leeds firm manufacturing steam-engines (V. Johnstone, pers.com.). He travelled extensively abroad on business (Davis 1951:232) and did some collecting in the process. Offering the boards to the Museum, he wrote: 'The boards you have I bought from a Maori's whare about 20 miles from Rotorua but the name of the place I cannot recollect. I saw them in situ & the owner only sold them because he had fallen on evil days' (BM MLA Corr. A.Fowler 3.12.1892). Two years later another small collection of architectural carvings (1894.7–16.) was purchased, from Lady Ada Sudeley (figs 44, 68). The carvings were collected in New Zealand, probably between 1850 and 1873 (BM Ethno. Corr. Sir Lyonel Tollemache 18.4.1996) by the Hon. Algernon Tollemache, Lady Sudeley's uncle. In the Museum's list of 'Purchases Recommended' the Sudeley purchase is annotated: 'from a pah in the Bay of Plenty'.

117 Contemporary artists may use non-traditional materials and forms, and yet produce objects which are unmistakably Maori: two pots and a pottery globe made by Manos Nathan. Left to right: 1994 Oc.4.85, D. 14 cm; 1994 Oc.4.84, D. 13 cm; 1994 Oc.4.86, D. 8 cm.

In 1895 the Museum purchased its largest single Maori collection from Miss Gertrude Ellen Meinertzhagen. It consists of over 600 items, many of them stone implements and it includes also other Pacific material. It was formed by Frederick Huth Meinertzhagen between 1866 and 1881. He emigrated to New Zealand in 1866 and two years later acquired a lease of Waimarama station in the Hawkes Bay area where he went into the sheep-breeding business. It seems, however, that business affairs were conducted mainly by his partners and Meinertzhagen devoted himself to the more gentle pursuits of ornithology, conchology and Maori artefact collecting (Grant 1977). In the 1870s he corresponded with Julius von Haast of the Canterbury Museum in Christchurch with whom he exchanged specimens (Turnbull Library MSP-37 fold. 119). He visited the Chatham Islands where he did some collecting (Skinner 1974:24). Precisely how he formed his collection – apart from simply picking up some archaeological finds – is not clear. He probably bought objects or possibly received some as presents. He had an adopted Maori son, Tame Turoa te Rangihauturu, and the fact that he 'had been permitted to take a high-born son of the tribe in adoption . . . must surely indicate that he was held in esteem by the local people' (Grant 1977:79). In 1881 he returned to England where on their arrival his wife, two of his five daughters and the adopted son died of scarlet fever, a tragedy from which he never recovered and which seems to have put an end to his collecting activities.

In 1896 two small and interesting collections were acquired. In the collection presented by William Strutt (1896.11–19.) there is a carved stone pounder, probably ceremonial (fig. 8). Strutt was a Paris-trained artist who emigrated to Australia and in the years 1855–56 lived in New Zealand, near New Plymouth. In his autobiography (Mitchell Library. Ms 867/3) he describes how, during a walk, he stumbled on a stone which, after scraping off some of the dirt, he saw was carved, but about which he never managed to find any information. The other collection consists

118 Makereti, also known as Maggie Papakura, Mrs R. Staples-Brown, a Maori scholar and author of *The Old-time Maori*, with her sister Bella and Tatiana Hiini, photographed in Sydney in 1910, in front of the raised storehouse, *pataka*, carved by Tene Waitere. The storehouse is now in the British Museum. BM Ethno. 1933.7–8.1. Presented by Mrs George Todd. Photo by permission of the Pitt Rivers Museum, University of Oxford. Makereti Papers, Box IX, Green Album, p.3.

of four objects given by Titore, a Ngāpuhi chief, to F.W. Sadler, Captain of HMS *Buffalo* which sailed regularly between Sydney and the Bay of Islands in the 1830s, and includes the well known nephrite pendant combining the features of the *tiki* and the *hei matau* (fig. 116).

In 1908 a collection of fifty, mostly Oceanic and including twenty-two Maori, objects was bought from Miss E.S. Budden who wrote 'they were collected by George Fife? [French] Angas I think, and given to my father some years ago' (BM MLA Corr. E.S. Budden 8.3.1908). Angas was a well-known naturalist and artist, author of several published volumes of illustrations of life in South Africa, Australia and New Zealand, some of which are reproduced in this book. The name 'Budden' appears in Angas's letter to William Hogarth, his London publisher, in which he asks Hogarth to send him some drawings 'through Messrs Bell, Budden & Co, 2 Jeffrey Square, St Mary Axe.'(Tregenza 1980:21). Bell, Budden & Co were his father's London agents who handled all the Angas wool sales (Tregenza 1980:22; Angas senior was one of the founders of the South Australia colony) so the Angas provenance of the collection is confirmed.

In 1890 the London Missionary Society placed on loan at the Museum a very large and important Polynesian collection (purchased by the Museum in 1911) which included not only many famous and frequently reproduced Polynesian carvings, but also some Maori objects. Some of these may have been collected during the tour of the Pacific mission stations by a deputation consisting of Daniel Tyerman and George Bennet in 1821–29 (one of the registration slips is annotated 'July 1824 Geo. Bennet'). Although New Zealand was not in the sphere of the LMS influence, the deputation stopped in Whangaroa Bay for a few days in July 1824 on their way to Australia. Describing these few days, the Journal of the travels concentrates mainly on a confrontation which developed when some Maori came on board, but it also mentions trade: 'The commerce in various articles, on both sides, went pretty well for some time ... Up to this time we had been in friendly intercourse with the chiefs, rubbing noses, and purchasing their personal ornaments and other curiosities ...' (Montgomery 1831:132). Indeed, some of the LMS pieces have been dated to the late eighteenth and early nineteenth centuries (R. Neich, pers. com.; Simmons, n.d.) but others are later and must have been obtained from other, as yet unidentified, sources.

In the collection (1921.10–14.) purchased by the Museum in 1921 from the Yorkshire Philosophical Society Museum there are twenty-five Maori objects. Some of them were acquired quite early, for example, in 1824 the puppet (1921.10–14.2; fig. 31) collected by Capt. Fred Vernon RN, and in 1844 the ceremonial adze (1921.10–14.4) from the Rev. John Blackburn (BM Ethno. Eth.Doc. 1912). In 1927 Mrs M. Reid presented a collection of seven Maori objects collected by her father, Capt. John Proctor Luce, of HMS *Esk* which was involved in the 1860s wars on the East Coast. In his Journal he mentions his acquisitions. In November 1865: 'Our friends the Waiapu natives came forward & gave us a war dance ... My old friend Wekiuopi came out strong making a vigorous speech with much energy &

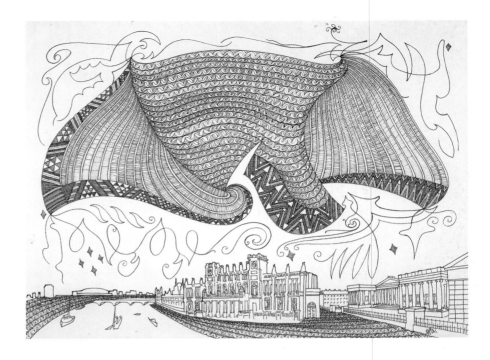

119 '*Te Hono ki Ranana* – The Connection with London', an acknowledgment of the Museum of Mankind, the British Museum and the Maori collections of which they are guardian. Pigmented ink drawing by John Bevan Ford, 1993, executed to mark the planned Maori exhibition in the British Museum. The hallmark of John Bevan Ford's drawings has been the precious chiefly cloak symbolising the chiefs' *mana* which extends to the land below and, in this case, envelops the British Museum. BM Ethno. Library. 57×76 cm.

having a Flax cloak over his shoulders all covered with feathers & holding in his hand a handsome Taiaha, a war club, which on finishing his speech he gave to McLean who afterwards kindly handed it over to me' (RAI MS 280:5). The *taiaha* in questions is probably our 1927.11–19.7. On 10 November in Poverty Bay: 'Capt Fairchild [who was also involved in obtaining the house Te Hau-ki-Tūranga (fig. 38) for the Wellington Museum; Brown 1996:14] gave me four specimens of native carving, he has a large quantity on board which was taken at Opotiki. Some of the Wanganui natives are fighting on our side in the Bay of Plenty. These carving are their loot & they are sending them to Wanganui to their tribe' (RAI MS 280:5). This, incidentally, illustrates nicely one of the ways in which objects travelled from one area to another and also the universality of war plunder. The following day Capt. Luce notes with satifaction: 'Had the Maori carvings cleaned up & they promise to look well' (RAI MS 280:5). One more of Capt. Luce's carvings joined the collection much later, in 1950, a houseboard presented by his grandson, Mr J.A. Reid (1950 Oc.6.1).

In 1933 Mrs George Todd presented a large model of a Maori storehouse (1933.7–8.1). During the 1970s inventory this storehouse could not be located but a number of house carvings without any history were found and given new numbers. Eventually these carvings were identified as forming a complete storehouse, undoubtedly Mrs Todd's gift, and the work of Tene Waitere, a well-known carver from Rotorua (R. Neich pers. com.). It was carved in 1910 for a model Maori village erected in Clontarf, Sydney, under the leadership of the famous Rotorua tourist guide and Maori scholar, Maggie Papakura (fig. 118). The village was then shipped to London for the Coronation of George V in 1911 (Dennan 1968:51–53).

120 Male wood figure carved for the British Museum by Lyonel Grant of Rotorua. The form of the figure is traditional, but surface embellishments reflect contemporary interests. It also expresses the Maori's link with, and attachment to the land. BM Ethno. 1994 Oc.4.117. H. 2.64 m.

It was set up first at the Festival of Empire exhibition in Crystal Palace and then it was moved to White City, to the Coronation exhibition (R. Neich, N. Te Awekotuku pers.com.) where it and Maori performances were 'by far the most popular and unusual attraction' (Greenhalgh 1988:93). How the storehouse came to be in Mrs Todd's possession, still has to be established – no information about her has as yet been found in the Museum's archives.

In 1944 one of the most important and largest private ethnographic collections formed in this century was presented to the Museum by the collector's wife, Mrs H. Beasley. Harry Geoffrey Beasley was a wealthy brewery-owner and an enthusiastic collector of ethnographica from all over the world, with his own private museum, the Cranmore Ethnological Museum, in Chislehurst, Kent. Although he collected widely, his main interest was in Pacific material. After his death in 1939 his wife kept many pieces (eventually sold at auction) but the bulk of the collection was offered to several museums in Britain, the British Museum having first choice.

Ten years later some Maori material came to the Museum with the Wellcome Historical Medical Museum collection (1954 Oc.6.), and the 1960 transfer from the Royal Botanic Gardens at Kew also included a small number of Maori objects (1960 Oc.11.). In 1993 and 1994, partly in anticipation of the planned Maori exhibition and partly in pursuance of the Departmental policy of collecting contemporary material, two field collections were made in New Zealand, totalling over seventy items (figs 81, 112, 117, 119, 120, 121). Most of these were bought directly, or commissioned, from the artists; some were purchased from Maori art galleries.

Apart from these general collections, the Museum has acquired at various times more specialised collections of stone implements and archaeological material. These include: the 1876 gift of specimens from New Zealand and the Chatham Islands from Sir James Hector on behalf of the Colonial Museum of New Zealand; a Chatham Islands collection purchased in 1898 from W.J.William; and an archaeological series, mainly fish-hooks, presented in 1937 by Dr H.D. Skinner of the University Museum, Dunedin. These gifts testify to well-established contacts between the British Museum and museums in New Zealand, begun by Franks and continued by his successors.

A special category of objects in the Museum's collections comprises Royal Loans. These are objects presented to members of the Royal Family on various occasions and placed by them on loan at the Museum. They are not part of the Museum's own collection, can be withdrawn at any time and, although recorded, are not given Museum registration numbers. The first such loan, and the largest, was deposited in 1902 by the Prince and Princess of Wales. These were gifts presented to them during their visit to New Zealand in 1901 as the Duke and Duchess of Cornwall and York. For some strange reason some items in this loan were given Museum numbers with the prefix TRH (Their Royal Highnesses) while others were not. It seems that only smaller objects, twenty-seven of them Maori ones, mainly nephrite ornaments and clubs, were so numbered and of these only fourteen are today in the Museum's collections. But the loan included other objects, too, although there is no list of items lent and none could be found in the Royal Archives (BM Ethno. Corr. Royal Archives 7.2.1996). The British Museum's 1903 *Guide to the Exhibition Rooms*, after describing the case containing 'weapons and ornaments' of this loan, goes on: 'models of houses, canoes, etc., deposited at the same time, will be seen in Case G. . .'. For two of these there is clear evidence that they are part of the same loan: a model storehouse carved by Jacob Heberley (Neich 1991:92–93) and a model canoe carved by Tene Waitere (R.Neich pers.com; fig. 67). The storehouse has a plaque stating: 'Presented by the women of the City & suburbs of Wellington N.Z. to H.R.H. The Duchess of Cornwall & York on the occasion of the visit of H.R.H. to Wellington', and the circumstances of the presentation of the two gifts are described in detail in the official account of the visit (Loughnan 1902: 106, 183–5).The Duke recorded the presentation of gifts in his diary: 'June 15th, Grand Hotel, Rotorua, N.Z. . . . At 9.30 we all went to the race course, where all the Maoris were assembled, over 4000. On our arrival they placed cloaks on May's & my shoulders & Huia feathers in our hats, which we wore all the time. Then there were dances, songs of welcome & poi dances (women) began, each tribe at a time. As each dance was finished the tribe presented us with beautiful presents, which were piled up in a heap in front of us, they consisted of greenstone Meres, whalebone Meres, whalebone paddles, carved sticks, feather cloaks innumerable, mats & other cloaks, also reed kilts. May & I then walked round, passing through the lines of Maoris, we were photographed with them. Major Fox the old Chief [Te Pokiha Taranui, the paramount chief of Ngāti Pikiao, whose impressive introduction to a sitting of the Land Court is quoted on p. 110] gave us a model of a war canoe. (Royal Archives. Diary of King George v; quoted by the gracious permission of Her Majesty The Queen). There is evidence that some of the cloaks presented were included in the the loan, for the Museum has a collection of thirty-three cloaks which have been traditionally known as 'Royal Loan' of unknown date. Stylistically, these cloaks are congruent with the date of the visit (M.Pendergrast, pers. com.) and there are several letters in the Departmental correspondence in which references are made to the cloaks given or lent to the Museum by the Prince of Wales (BM Ethno. Corr. Lady M.Dalrymple 17.11.1927, NZ Government Office London 16.8.1932, Mrs E.Carey Hill 13.9.1933). This circumstantial evidence is confirmed by the recently discovered documents in the Museum's archives. In 1907 thirty-seven Maori objects 'from the collection lent by H.R.H. the Prince of Wales' were transferred to the Imperial Institute [now the Commonwealth Institute] 'by desire of the Prince' (BM Ethno. Eth.Doc.1947). Among them were sixteen cloaks and thirteen numbered TRH pieces, precisely those which are missing from the Museum's TRH collection. Today only five of these TRH-labelled objects are still in the Commonwealth Institute, for in 1926 there was a great re-assignment of the Royal Presents lodged with the Institute, 'prompted by instructions given by

121 Nephrite hook pendant carved by Clem Mellish of Havelock, Marlborough, and presented by the carver and his wife Pimia to the British Museum. BM Ethno. 1994 Oc.4.92. L. of hook 7.5 cm.

the Queen after a visit to the Institute' (Birgit Dohrendorf, Commonwealth Institute, letter 22.7.1997, in BM Ethno. Eth.Doc.1947) – some were retained at the Institute, some were dispatched to other museums, and others were returned to Buckingham Palace.

There is still much work to be done on the identification of all the component pieces of this loan. All the gifts presented during that visit were exhibited in the Imperial Institute in 1902 and a catalogue published. Descriptions of the individual items in it, however, are so general (Imperial Institute 1902) that only some of them can be clearly identified at present.

In 1905 a puppet was placed on loan by the Prince of Wales (later George v), possibly yet another gift from the 1901 visit, and in 1938 King George vi lent a *taiaha*, annotated on the Windsor Castle list of items lent 'Brought by the Maori Chiefs, 28th July, 1884' (BM Ethno Eth.Doc.1915). It is possible that the club was brought by the deputation led by the Maori King, Tawhiao, who came to England in 1884 to petition Queen Victoria. They were not granted an audience with the Queen but on 22 July they did see the Colonial Secretary Lord Derby. The club may have been presented on this occasion but no record has been found of it either in the Royal Archives or the Public Record Office. King Tawhiao's visit received considerable coverage in the press, including his visit to the British Museum: 'The mummies at the British Museum seem to have impressed our latest regal visitor, the Maori King, more than any other London sight. He went to the Museum on Monday, chiefly to see these relics of old Egypt, but on entering the department he was literally appalled. He clung to his attendant's arm, and shrunk from the ancient figures as if they were ghosts . . .' (*The Graphic*, 5 July 1884, p.7). It is doubtful whether King Tawhiao did want to see the mummies in particular but his reaction, which to his English hosts was faintly amusing and incomprehensible, is perfectly understandable in the context of Maori veneration for ancestors and their remains. The English must have seemed an uncivilised lot to the Maori King to treat ancestors in such an unseemly manner.

The latest Royal Loan entered the collections in 1990 and consists of three gifts presented to the Queen during her visit to New Zealand in that year for the celebrations of the 150th anniversary of the Treaty of Waitangi: a wood carving by Rangi Hetet, a flax wall hanging by Diggeress Te Kanawa, and a nephrite *tiki* in a carved wood box by Arthur Morten.

What has been described above is but a rough outline of the British Museum's Maori collections, for it is impossible to do them any measure of justice in a short article. This task will be fulfilled by a catalogue, planned to appear in a few years' time, which will describe in detail all the Maori material in the Museum. Meanwhile, this brief sketch may give some impression of the nature and highlights of these collections.

7

CONTEMPORARY MAORI ART: FACT OR FICTION

Robert Jahnke

The history of New Zealand art has tended to be a European construction (Docking 1971, Cape 1979, Brown and Keith 1982, Pound 1985), a legacy of which has been Maori exclusion, unless the work created appeared to move beyond the use of Maori pattern. Despite this legacy, the first generation of 'contemporary' Maori artists organised their own art forums to give voice and expression to their vision (Davis 1976: 28–9, Mane-Wheoki 1997: 61–5, Ihimaera 1996: 31–5). The 1990s have witnessed an unprecedented infiltration of Maori into art galleries while their work has been exposed in print. Nevertheless, a Eurocentric bias continues in recent publications about New Zealand art (Pound 1985, Brown 1995, 1996, Dunn 1996) and many of the pioneering contributors to 'contemporary Maori art' continue to be marginalised. Only the recent publication *Mataora: The Living Face* (Ihimaera 1996), designed, written and edited by Maori, presents a view of the current state of Maori art. However, this view is conditioned by a syncretic transformation of the 'traditional' model. Works by artists like Tuti Tukaokao and Lyonel Grant have been selectively chosen to promote examples which demonstrate an advance beyond the 'traditional'.

The term 'contemporary Maori art' continues to be used when speaking of current developments in art, and to distinguish between 'contemporary' (here synonymous with 'modern') and 'traditional' developments. Herein lies a contradiction, since art defined as 'traditional' is also created today. In coining the phrase 'contemporary', Maori participate in the elitist game of reinforcing a hierarchical structure that promotes the new (novel, innovative) over the old (traditional, hackneyed). Equally, Maori perpetuate the anthropological dislocation of culture into past and present. Maori art did not cease when the Europeans arrived, nor when Maori appropriated images from Pākehā at the turn of the century. Nor has it ceased today as Maori attempt to re-configure the multiple visual stimuli and sophisticated technology at their disposal. Current practice by Maori is characterised by its diversity. To accommodate this dynamic it is vital to substitute the term 'traditional' with 'customary'. Apart from the fact that 'customary' is less susceptible to a chronological stasis, its use within discourse related to the Treaty of Waitangi is an added endorsement for its acceptance (Durie 1995 XIII: 1–19). Maori art may thus be perceived as art that ranges across a continuum of customary and non-customary practice. This chapter charts the relationships between a selected number of artists whose work reflects this continuum.

Tangata Whenua

Te Whenua, Te Whenua Engari 'The land, the placenta
Kaore he Tūrangawaewae.   but nowhere to stand.'

This saying formed the title of a 1987 painting by Robyn Kahukiwa (fig. 122), whose works are a visual expression of Maori cultural values. They

122 *Te Whenua, Te Whenua, Engari Kaore He Tūrangawaewae* ('The land, the placenta, but nowhere to stand'). Alkyd paint on loose canvas. Collection of Auckland City Art Gallery. By permission of the Auckland City Art Gallery and R. Kahukiwa (Ngāti Porou, Te Aitanga-a-Hauiti, Ngāti Hau, Ngāta Konohi, Te Whānau-ā-Ruataupare). Photo Auckland City Art Gallery.

also record her protest against a legacy of colonial subjugation of Maori under British sovereignty. The images which populate her canvas are strategically composed to reveal the surrendering of land and subordination of culture under the tricolour banner of colonialism as it encroaches on the blood-red field of ancestors. These ancestors appear sectioned and quartered beneath the red cross of assent to partnership in the Treaty of Waitangi. But why does the blood-red cross loom so ominously?

Dr Ngahuia Te Awekotuku eloquently expresses the importance of land for Maori while endorsing the sentiments evident in Kahukiwa's painting:

Papatuanuku is the Earth Mother, combining all elements of the planet; her immediate form is *whenua*, the land. Continuing the organic metaphor, *whenua* is also the word for the placenta, which is promptly buried with simple ritual after birth. The practice is still observed today, even in cities; thus the word itself reflects the relationship between people and the land, clearly stated in the concept of *tangata whenua*. (Te Awekotuku 1991; see p.33, this volume)

In her earlier development as a painter Kahukiwa interpreted *whenua* as 'landscape' and later as personifications of Papatuanuku and of the mountain Hikurangi. Kahukiwa's changing perception of *whenua* charts her growing awareness of customary principles for the representation of land and its cultural significance as inseparable from the notion of being. In her journey of discovery Kahukiwa has acknowledged and endorsed her genealogical ties to the tribal groups of Te Whānau-ā-Ruataupare, Te Aitanga-a-Hauiti, Ngāti Hau and Ngāti Konohi. The most powerful and central image in her work emanates from her ancestress Te Ao Mihia, whose carved figure graces the wall of the Te Whānau-ā-Ruataupare meeting house, Te Hono-ki-Rarotonga, at Tokomaru Bay. Te Ao Mihia, sister of Ruataupare, was remembered for her humility and kindness. According to Iritana Haig (1997: pers. comm.), Te Ao Mihia is still seen to weep at the passing of Maori of significant stature. The image of Te

Ao Mihia suckling her young has been an inspirational model for Kahukiwa and has appeared in multiple guises as Kahukiwa paints the plight of women and children dislocated from their villages. She reappears as Kahukiwa protests against the failure of successive governments to honour the principle of a shared nation as promised in the Treaty of Waitangi (see Hakiwai, pp 60–62 this volume). In rendering her figures without literal references to the land, Kahukiwa employs the customary practice of conceptualising the land as *tangata* and *tangata whenua* as Papatuanuku. Papatuanuku, Earth Mother, and Ranginui, Sky Father, are conceived by Maori as genealogically linked to humankind and therefore an intimate part of their being.

Without *kōrero* you have nothing

While Kahukiwa visualises her intimate relationship with the land in paint, Pakariki Harrison articulates his intimate association with it within the tradition of the carved meeting house (figs 123, 129). The walls of these houses continue to be lined with ancestral images whose existence as descendants of the land is expressed through a cosmological sequence which unites ancestors with deities in a genealogical continuum. The life blood of these ancestors, whose deeds include the discovery of new lands, and the naming of mountains, rivers, lakes and oceans, pulses through Aotearoa New Zealand.

Ko Hikurangi te maunga Ko Waiapu te awa Ko Ngāti Porou te iwi.
'Hikurangi is the mountain, Waiapu is the river, Ngāti Porou are the people.'

This proverb appeared in a 1985 painting of Kahukiwa as an endorsement of her tribal connections within the East Coast region of the North Island. It is a proverb that is often cited in oratory to make people aware of their tribe and it links Harrison to Kahukiwa as descendants of Porourangi. This proverb also springs to mind when one encounters ancestors from Ngāti Porou within meeting houses around the country.

Harrison contends that 'Without the *kōrero* you have nothing to carve. Without the *kōrero* you have nothing to learn. Without it you have nothing to understand' (cited in Winitana 1994:14). Indeed *kōrero* is paramount in the meeting house Tane-nui-a-rangi (figs 123, 129) which was carved under Harrison's direction for the University of Auckland *marae*. Opened in 1988, this house was created as a house of learning. 'Canoe builders, navigators and discoverers' are aligned along one side of the house while the 'priests, the keepers of knowledge and the maintainers of ritual' (New Zealand Dept. of Internal Affairs 1990: 24) are aligned along the other. An ancestor from Rarotonga appears as a 'navigator', thereby reinforcing the genealogical links beyond the shores of New Zealand into the Pacific Ocean and, by implication, farther beyond, into Hawaiki. Historically, the establishment of a cosmological order was regulated by a genealogical continuum within the structure of the meeting house as a statement of the *whānau, hāpu* or *iwi* world view, which was never static but always culturally malleable. As Neich has observed, 'Group identity defined by

123 Interior of Tane-nui-a-Rangi with rafters painted in shades of blue and grey. Auckland University *marae*, Auckland. Published by courtesy of Photographic Archive, Department of Anthropology, University of Auckland and Pakariki Harrison (Ngāti Porou). Photo M. Lander.

genealogical descent continued to be a major organisational principle in the design of these houses, but this was now supplemented by a new ideology of group identity defined by the specific history experienced by the owners in post-European times' (see p.108, this volume). A genealogical imperative remained visible even though the art forms within the meeting houses at the turn of the nineteenth century were subject to a syncretic representation of new narrative histories, in which European conventions of naturalism were fused with the strict frontal and profile tradition of Maori to express a post-European history. This amalgamation of alternative art conventions revealed subtle shifts in the spatial articulation of narratives within the interior of the house both longitudinally and laterally. Nevertheless, an overall integrity was retained in the interrelationship between ancestors, descendants and even Pākehā whose presence influenced the Maori world view. This was exemplified in the retention of a largely non-figurative visual vocabulary on rafters inside the meeting house, while the porch area was subject to a more liberal inclusion of 'exotic' imagery.

In contrast with Robyn Kahukiwa's gradual acceptance of a customary conceptual vocabulary, artists at the turn of the century often substituted images of plants for carved or painted ancestors. Although patently incongruous when compared with more conventional ways of genealogical representation, these departures from convention merely represent a creative fusion of Maori and European iconography. Plants - native, exotic or hybrid specimens - enter the visual vocabulary as representations of hope and despair. As blossoming plants, these images presage a new Eden under the protection of the new messiah in the person of the nineteenth-century prophet Te Kooti Rikirangi; as hybrid plants, they record the power of the transplanted culture; as products of the land, plants emerge as a metaphor for the union of Maori and Papatuanuku, the Earth Mother.

The cosmological continuum

A Maori cosmological paradigm remains relevant for Maori artists today. In simple terms it links the ancestors of the house to deities while reinforcing the passage through time and space of Maori from life to death. Thus, descendants are connected through their ancestors to Tāne, god of the forests. The son who separated his parents Ranginui and Papatuanuku, he is also the harbinger of light and knowledge, and the creator of humankind through Hine-ahuone, the earth-formed woman. An incestuous relationship with his daughter Hine-titama foreshadowed the mortal destiny of humankind, symbolized in Hine-titama the dawn maiden's becoming Hinenui-te-Pō the maiden of the great night. This change charts the transition of Maori from Te Ao Mārama (life in this world) to Te Pō (life in the world of night).

The articulation of this cosmological sequence begins in the porch area of the meeting house with the ridgepole figures of Ranginui and Papatuanuku. The internal front wall post symbolises Tāne. The side wall panels, on which ancestors may be carved or painted, are linked through the rafters to the ridgepole which runs longitudinally through the house linking the front post of Tāne to the back post of Hinenui-te-Pō at the rear. This genealogical sequence reinforces the inseparability of Maori from their deities while endorsing the holistic union of Maori with the universe through Papatuanuku.

Tane-nui-a-rangi, a house of learning, extends this basic paradigm to encompass a broader cosmological/genealogical narrative, which features Maori deities alongside ancestors to acknowledge 'origins and charters for human behaviour and ritual pertaining to war, taking revenge, building of canoes and houses and other social practices' (New Zealand Dept. of Internal Affairs 1990: 24). There is also a retention of the general principle of a temporal order, with the distant past at the front and a more recent past towards the rear. It is an order that is also observed in the placement of progenitor figures above their descendants on the vertical posts.

The incorporation of the hull of a canoe into the ridgepole of Ihenga, a meeting house carved by Lyonel Grant in 1996, carries the symbolism associated with the canoe into the meeting house (Simmons, 1985: 24–7, Neich, this volume pp 98–9). Like the interior of the house, the hull of the canoe is viewed as the body of an ancestor (New Zealand Dept. of Internal Affairs 1990: 24, Neich, this volume p. 105). This innovative syn-

124 *Maumahara* ('Lest we forget'), multi-media commemorative structure for *Te Hokowhitu ā Tūmatauenga* (The Māori Battalion). Designed and executed by Cliff Whiting (Te Whānau-a-Apanui) and completed in 1990 for the National Archives of New Zealand, Wellington. By courtesy of the National Archives and C. Whiting. Photo National Archives of New Zealand.

thesis of canoe and house symbolism finds its ultimate expression in the 1990 commemorative tribute to the Maori Battalion by Cliff Whiting.

More than any other Maori artist, Whiting extends the cosmological continuum of the meeting house beyond the marae. In his multimedia mural of *Te Wehenga o Rangi raua ko Papa* ('The Separation of Rangi and Papa') Whiting offers a synthesis of the arts of the meeting house in an innovative rendering of the Maori genesis narrative. According to customary iconography, the sons of Ranginui and Papatuanuku are identified by the implements which they hold (see fig. 73). Thus Tūmatauenga, the god of war, clutches a short club while Haumiatiketike holds a digging implement used for gathering fern root, and the fern root, an offspring of the god, is shown between his legs. In a similar manner other deities are represented according to their roles or as participants in the separation of Ranginui and Papatuanuku.

Tūmatauenga once again features in Whiting's commemorative structure *Maumahara* (fig. 124) for the Maori Battalion. In this example, Tūmatauenga assumes the form of a canoe figurehead at the gable of a house structure. Here the symbolisms of the war canoe and the meeting house have merged. Tāne, as the central white figure of the world of light, and Hinenui-te-Pō, as the black figure of the world of night, sustain the customary notion of the cosmological significance of colour. According to this notion, black symbolises Te Pō, white Te Ao Mārama, and the colour red stands for 'the mixing of the two bloods from Rangi and Papa that produced red ochre or kokowai' (Whiting cited in Neich 1993: vii). The fusion of colour symbolism and the customary iconography of two paramount structures in customary Maori art offers an intensely poignant tribute to *Te Hokowhitu ā Tūmatauenga*, the Maori warriors of Tūmatauenga, who fell in battle during World War II.

Iwi narratives

Brett Graham has emerged as a young Maori sculptor in whose work indigenous narratives are an important component. At first glance, the threads that link the work of Whiting and Graham are not apparent, but beneath the seeming economy of Graham's sculpture there beats a Maori pulse. Consistent with the artist's practice, works are arranged in a narrative sequence to complement passages of texts drawn from indigenous sources. A saying by Pōtatau, the first Maori King, provided the textual rationale for Graham's 1995 exhibition:

Kotahi te kohao o te ngira e kahuna ai te miro ma, te miro pango, te miro whero.
'There is but one eye of the needle through which the white and the black and the red threads must pass'.

According to James Ritchie, the academic, historian and Tainui spokesman:

When Pōtatau used the image of the three [coloured threads] there is no doubt that he was contrasting the brilliant light of day (white) with the mystical original night (black) between which humanity (the red) rises, has its being and then rests. (Ritchie 1995: 58)

Graham's use of colour, like Whiting's, is grounded within a customary paradigm. In this instance it is an endorsement of the allusions to birth, life and continuity articulated by Pōtatau. Ritchie suggests that, together with posts as markers and monuments, allusions to male and female sexual organs emerge as common threads. Discussing Graham's sculpture *Te Kohao o Te Ngira* ('The Eye of the Needle') (fig. 125), he says:

The eye of the needle is transformed into a dark, lovely elongated oval, a vaginal shape ... whose deep mysterious interior descends in step-like fashion ... The vaginal image is a powerful one. It stands at the threshold between day and night, the entrance to the eternal warmth and security of the original *po*, the embracing enveloping night of all possibility, containing all experience, the night of everything. Hine-nui-te-po stands astride the horizon at evening and through her Rangi enters the enveloping night. (Ritchie 1995: 60)

At one level, Ritchie's interpretation of Graham's work reinforces the importance of customary narratives and visual templates for the artist. It

125 *Te Kohao o te Ngira*
('The eye of the needle')
One of five works by Brett
Graham (Ngāti Koroki
Kahukura) in 1995 for a
solo exhibition at the Artis
Gallery in Parnell,
Auckland. Private collection.
By courtesy of B. Graham.
Photo Michael Roth.

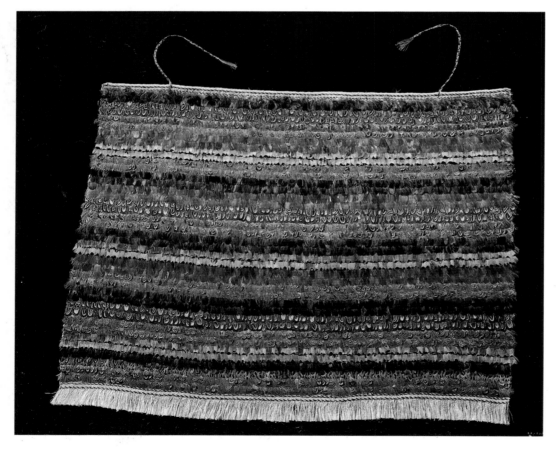

126 *Kahuhuruhuru* by Dame
Rangimarie Hetet (Ngāti
Maniapoto). Published by
courtesy of Te Hetet
Whānau and the Waikato
Museum and Art Gallery.
Photo Museum of New
Zealand Te Papa
Tongarewa, B. 024256.

127 *Marama Taiohaoha* ('Shining light') created in 1995 by Heni Kerekere (Ngāti Porou, Te Whānau-a-Apanui, Ngāti Kahungunu). By courtesy of the Dowse Art Museum and H. Kerekere. Photo Julia Brooke-White.

also demonstrates how related concepts can be realised in dramatically different ways while retaining connections grounded in customary narrative. I would contend, however, that Ritchie's reliance on sexual metaphor and posts as markers and monuments is but one reading. The canoe, as vessel, as receptacle and as monument, is an equally valid metaphor. This is particularly relevant in view of Graham's use of natural and man-made objects such as plants, canoes and containers, as means of cultural transmission. What is absent from Ritchie's account is the re-emergence of Rangi as rejuvenated in the cycle between night and day. However, Ritchie's contention that the objects are translatable across cultures is an indication of the artist's familiarity with the aesthetic and cultural potential implicit in forms which exist ambiguously in the space between cultures. As such, they remain beyond capture by one culture and belong to the vernacular of a universal vision.

In 1996 Graham created *Kahukura* as a farewell to Rangimarie Hetet, a renowned weaver. Such was her stature as a Maori artist that Te Ao Mihia would surely have wept at her passing. The title of the work encapsulated Rangimarie's art (fig. 126) and her role within the Maori community as the foremost practitioner of weaving in New Zealand. Thus, *Kahukura*, as sacred garment, provided a fitting epitaph for this esteemed artist. The crescent form lacerated with grooves and bathed in the red stain of *kōkōwai* stood as metaphors of the waxing moon and the arching rainbow, which bring a promise of new hope in the future.

The inner fabric

In the art of weaving, of which Rangimarie Hetet was such an outstanding exponent, there is currently a return to customary patterns. The figurative motifs used at the turn of the century, such as ferns and birds, are edited out of the current pattern range. Museum collections are explored in search of 'authentic' patterns to anchor the woven and plaited art forms within a Maori cultural continuum. The pre-eminence of natural materials and customary techniques is a hallmark of continuity. This 'authentic' inflection also appears in the creations of Maori women artists working on the periphery of the fibre arts.

Native flax forms the basis of Heni Kerekere's wall sculptures (fig. 127). Blades of dyed flax, plaited and woven, generate a tapestry of texture and colour that recalls customary garments. A knowledge of customary forms and processes provides the inspiration but the object as art, rather than as a product of function, is paramount.

Maureen Lander, like Kerekere, employs natural fibre as part of her installations. In *Gilt Complex*, an installation created in 1995 (fig. 128), Lander uses the *pīngao*, a native fibre used in weaving, to record her concern for this dwindling native treasure. As in Graham's 1995 exhibition, here also a proverb provides the rationale for her work: *Manakitia nga tukemāta o Tāne* ('Caring for the eyebrows of Tāne').

This proverb refers to the conflict between Tāne Mahuta (God of the forest) and

128 *Gilt Complex*. An installation by Maureen Lander (Ngā Puhi, Te Hikutu) for the 1995 exhibition 'Korurangi New Maori Art' at the Auckland City Art Gallery. By permission of the Auckland City Art Gallery and M. Lander. Photo Auckland City Art Gallery.

Tangaroa (God of the sea) following the separation of their parents Papatuanuku and Ranginui – the earth and the sky. Seeking to end the strife Tāne plucked out his eyebrows and gave them to Tangaroa as a peace offering, but Tangaroa was still angry and cast them back. (Lander cited in Szekely 1996: 18)

Lander's installation lays the guilt at the feet of a marauding public pursuing the golden rays of the sun as they trample the sand-dune habitat of the *pīngao*. Gold leaf on *pīngao* stood as a metaphor for cultural treasures in collision. Pretentious gilt-edged photographs recorded the plight of the *pīngao* beneath a Doric column cloaked in a cascading twist of the golden leaf. Gilt-framed mirrors were hung as reflections of a suntan-obsessed public. An elevated crown of *pīngao* cushioned upon a royal blue pillow was placed as a reminder of a dying treasure. This element of lamentation was intensified by the semantic potency of Maori forms and words of mourning. The crown of *pīngao*, as crown of thorns, was fashioned as a *pōtae tauā*, a form of head-dress associated with mourning in customary Maori society. *Pōtae* and *tauā* as adjectives applied to a house identify it as one of mourning, while a *kākahu tauā* is a mourning garment. On the border where wall meets floor, where sea meets land, a shadow of *pīngao* was cast as a reminder that the golden leaf must be preserved intact lest its shadow remains as the only memory.

Conclusion

Maori art today ranges across indices of customary and non-customary practice which are regulated by the 'styles, canons of taste and values of Maori culture' (Mead 1997: 232). A structure such as a house is composed of components upon which forms may be carved, woven or painted. Media employed within this structure include wood, paint and fibre. Ritual may be employed as the work is created and when it is unveiled. Cosmological, genealogical or polemic narratives often define the order in which the components are arranged and images are rendered.

Harrison's meeting house, Tane-nui-a-rangi, and Hetet's cloak are placed firmly within the customary index. However, components within Tane-nui-a-rangi may fall within the non-customary index. John Hovell, as a contributing artist to the scheme of Tane-nui-a-rangi, has employed non-customary colours (blues, greens, greys, oranges) and technique (tonal modelling) to render the rafter patterns rather than employing the customary colour range of red, white and black and the application of paint in solid planes of colour in the customary manner (figs 38, 123). European-inspired leaf shapes within the rafter patterns reveal a further non-customary inflection. *Tukutuku*, like rafter painting, was subject to the incursion of figurative imagery within the meeting house from the 1870s. Peter Boyd and Hinemoa Harrison, as the artists responsible for the *tukutuku* scheme in Tane-nui-a-rangi, have maintained this 1870s tradition of figurative imagery (fig. 129). In this case, the customary index has been realigned to encompass late-nineteenth-century developments.

In *tukutuku* panels with customary designs, patterns once reserved for separate panels are combined together on a single panel. Even the carved wall panels in Tane-nui-a-rangi were subjected to an expansion of iconography beyond past models. Canoe prow, paddle and whale extend the previous iconographical range. While these departures appear minimal, even insignificant, they do demonstrate that contemporary practice within the tradition of meeting house art is by no means static. More important, these examples demonstrate the flexibility of the customary index which may change according to an individual artist's construction of the customary paradigm.

It is often asserted that communal enterprise distinguishes customary from contemporary Maori art. This argument, however, is rendered invalid by an artist like Cliff Whiting who has often involved the community in his creative projects both within and beyond the *marae* environment. Of course, distinctions will continue to be made between customary Maori art and Maori art that slides precariously towards the non-customary.

129 Side wall panels in Tane-nui-a-Rangi, Auckland University *marae*, Auckland. The design of the the *tukutuku* panel on the right includes the figure of the deity Uenuku, whose carved image is shown in fig. 57. Published by courtesy of the Photographic Archive, Department of Anthropology, University of Auckland, and Pakariki Harrison (Ngāti Porou). Photo M. Lander.

However, it should be evident in the work of Brett Graham that wood and stone are conventional media and wood carving is a customary practice. His arrangement of sculptures in narrative sequences accords with similar practice within the meeting house, while the purpose that informs his work is grounded within a cultural paradigm of customary story or proverb. It is only in the materialisation of the sculptural forms that customary alignment becomes allusive. However, this happens only if one's customary index remains static. The very notion of customary art is one that is susceptible to involuntary dislocation as cultures adopt, adapt and appropriate according to their needs within the context of their world realities at the time. Consequently, a critical examination of Maori art will reveal customary and non-customary elements coexisting with apparent ease even in Te Hau-ki-Tūranga, the prime example of the nineteenth century meeting house (fig. 38).

As artists creating work for *marae* or galleries, Kahukiwa and her contemporaries share in common a Maori *whakapapa* that is acknowledged either individually or communally. They also use cultural paradigms as points of continuity or departure in their attempt to give form to their positions as Maori, as artists, and as Maori artists. I would not be surprised if they would prefer to be acknowledged as such rather than as assimilated practitioners of fine arts.

Map of New Zealand
Drawn by Hans Rashbrook.

NORTH CAPE

Kaitaia

Bay of Islands

Whangarei

NORTH ISLAND

*Hauraki
Gulf*

COROMANDEL
PENINSULA

AUCKLAND

Thames

Wakaito River

HAMILTON

Tauranga

*Bay of
Plenty*

EAST CAPE

Te Awamutu

Rotorua

EAST COAST

Te Kuiti

Lake Taupo

Taupo

Gisborne

New Plymouth

Turangi

*Poverty
Bay*

▲ MT. TARANAKI

Napier

*Hawkes
Bay*

Hastings

Wanganui

Palmerston
North

*Tasman
Bay*

SOUTH ISLAND

Nelson
Blenheim

Cook Strait

WELLINGTON

Greymouth

S O U T H E R N   A L P S

MT. COOK ▲

CHRISTCHURCH

BANKS PENINSULA

Timaru

Queenstown

CHATHAM ISLANDS

DUNEDIN

Invercargill

Foveaux Strait

STEWART ISLAND

NORTH ISLAND

1. Te Aupōuri
   Te Rarawa
2. Ngāpuhi
3. Ngāti Whātua
   Te Kawerau-ā-Maki
   Te Wai-o-Hua
4. Ngāi Tai
   Ngāti Paoa
   Ngāti Whanaunga
   Ngāti Tamaterā
   Ngāti Maru
5. Waikato
6. Ngāi Te Rangi
   Ngāti Ranginui
   Ngāti Haua
   Ngāti Raukawa
7. Te Arawa
8. Ngāti Awa
   Whakatōhea
9. Tūhoe
10. Ngāi Tai
    Te Whānau-a-Apanui
11. Ngāti Porou
12. Rongowhakaata
    Te Aitanga-a-Māhaki
13. Ngāti Maniapoto
14. Ngāti Tūwharetoa

15. Ngāti Kahungunu
16. Ngāti Tama
    Ngāti Mutunga
    Ngāti Maru
    Te Ati Awa
17. Taranaki
18. Ngāti Ruanui
    Ngā Rauru
19. Te Ati-Haunui-a-
    Pāpārangi
20. Ngāti Raukawa
    Ngāti Apa
    Rangitāne
21. Muaūpoko
    Ngāti Toa
    Te Ati Awa

SOUTH ISLAND

1. Ngāti Kuia
   Ngāti Koata
   Te Ati Awa
2. Rangitāne
3. Kai Tahu
4. Poutini Kai Tahu
5. Kai Tahu
   Kati Mamoe

Tribal Map of New Zealand
Simplified tribal map.
By Roger Neich and Te Warena Taua.

THE AUTHORS

DR JANET DAVIDSON is an experienced New Zealand archaeologist and prehistorian who is currently developing exhibitions for the new Museum of New Zealand Te Papa Tongarewa in Wellington. She is a Fellow of the Royal Society of New Zealand.

PROF. NGAHUIA TE AWEKOTUKU is Chair of Maori Studies at Victoria University, Wellington. She was previously in the Department of Art History, University of Auckland.

ARAPATA HAKIWAI is Curator of the Maori Collections at the National Museum of New Zealand and is currently working as a Conceptual Developer planning exhibitions for the new Museum of New Zealand Te Papa Tongarewa.

DR ROGER NEICH has been curator of Ethnology at the Auckland Institute and Museum, Auckland, since 1986, and previously spent 15 years as Ethnologist at the National Museum of New Zealand, Wellington.

MICK PENDERGRAST, recently retired, was Ethnology Assistant at the Auckland Institute and Museum, Auckland and has spent many years researching and writing about New Zealand fibre arts.

DOROTA. C. STARZECKA is Assistant Keeper at the Museum of Mankind (the Department of Ethnography of the British Museum) with responsibility for the Oceanic collections.

ROBERT JAHNKE is a well-known Maori artist and co-ordinator of Maori Visual Arts in the Maori Studies Dept, Massey University, Palmerston North.

Parts of the Maori Meeting House

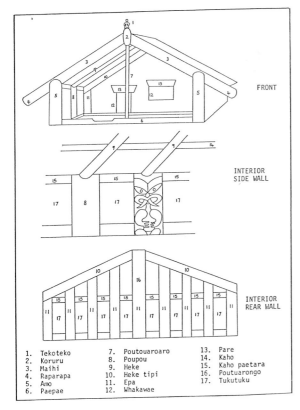

1. Tekoteko	7. Poutouaroaro	13. Pare	
2. Koruru	8. Poupou	14. Kaho	
3. Maihi	9. Heke	15. Kaho paetara	
4. Raparapa	10. Heke tipi	16. Poutuarongo	
5. Amo	11. Epa	17. Tukutuku	
6. Paepae	12. Whakawae		

Parts of the Maori, meeting house. From *Painted Histories: early Maori figurative painting*, 1993, by R. Neich, published by Auckland University Press, Auckland, reproduced with permission.

Glossary of Maori Terms

aho weft in weaving

aho poka short weft used to shape garment

amo front side panels supporting the bargeboards of a house

Aotearoa Land of the Long White Cloud, a contemporary Maori name for New Zealand

ariki paramount chief

aurei cloak pin

hā air, breath

haka posture dance

hapū sub-tribe, section of tribe

harakeke New Zealand flax, *Phormium tenax*, plant most used for Maori fibre work

hei matau pendant in form of fish-hook

hei tiki pendant in form of stylised human figure

heke rafter

heru comb

hīnau tree, *Elaeocarpus dentatus*, bark of which produces mordant used on flax and **kiekie** with black mud dye

hoeroa long, slightly curved, staff or club of whalebone

hongi pressing noses together, Maori greeting

huahua to sketch out a pattern before carving

huaki kaitaka cloak with double **tāniko** borders on three sides

hui gathering, meeting

huia wattlebird, *Heteralocha acutirostris*

hukahuka tag attachments on cloak, either rolled cords or strips of leaf

iwi tribe

kahu huruhuru feather cloak

kahu kurī dog-skin cloak

kahu tōī warrior's cloak of black dyed fibre of **tōī**, mountain cabbage tree

kai food

kāinga settlement, village

kaitaka cloak of finest flax, with **tāniko** borders

kākā native parrot, *Nestor meridionalis*

kākahu garments, clothing

kākahu raranga plaited garment

kanono small tree, *Coprosma grandifolia*, bark of which is used to produce yellow dye; also known as *manono*

kapeu pendant with curved lower end

karaka tree, *Corynocarpus laevigata*

karakia chant, prayer

kāretu sweet-scented grass, *Hierochloe redolens*

kārure cord with unravelled appearance; cloak decorated with such cords

kaumātua patriarchal head of household, elder

kaupapa foundation, body, main surface of cloak

kauri large tree, *Agathis australis*, used in Maori carving

kāwanatanga governorship

kererū *Hemiphaga novaeseelandiae*, bush pigeon

kete basket or bag, plaited from strips of flax or other material

kete muka basket or bag, woven of flax or other material

kete whakairo basket with decorative pattern

kiekie climbing plant, *Freycinetia baueriana*, used in cloak, basket and mat making

Kīngitanga Maori King Movement

kōauau straight flute

kōhanga reo Maori language programme; kindergartens providing total-immersion Maori language and culture education

kōkōwai red ochre pigment

kōrere feeding funnel

kōrero speak, talk, conversation, story

koropepe spiral pendant

korowai cloak ornamented with black rolled cords

koruru carved face at apex of bargeboards of a house

kōtaha whipsling, dart thrower

Kotahitanga unofficial Maori Parliament; lit. oneness, unity

kotiate short club, figure-of-eight shaped

kōwhaiwhai abstract curvilinear painted patterns

kuia elderly woman

kūmara sweet potato, *Ipomoea batatas*

kura red, precious, something treasured and excellent

kurī Polynesian dog, introduced to New Zealand by the Maori

kuru straight pendant

māhiti fine cloak with tassels of fur from **kurī**'s tail

maihi bargeboard of a house

maire tree, *Nestegis cunninghami*

mana power, prestige, authority

manaia   an art figure in which the face and sometimes the body is shown in profile

mānuka   small tree, *Leptospermum scoparium*

māori   clear, natural, ordinary

Māoritanga   'Maoriness', Maori ways

marae   open space in front of a meeting house

marakihau   fabulous sea-monster with fish tail and tubular tongue

māripi   knife with inserted shark teeth

matā   large tanged flake tool of stone

mātuhi   fernbird, *Bowdleria punctata*

mauri   essential spirit, life force

mere pounamu   nephrite club

moko   tattoo

mokopuna   grandchild; descendant

mōteatea   song-poem

mua   the front

muka   flax fibre

muri   the back, rear

ngā mahi whakairo   the art of carving

ngore   cloak decorated with pompoms

nguru   short flute with curved end

noa   free from religious restriction, common

pā   fortified settlement

paepae   threshold beam of a house

paepaeroa   kaitaka   cloak with vertical wefts

paheke   cloak ornamentation of rolling and running coloured cords

pahū   tree gong

pākati   notched ridge of **rauponga** surface pattern

Pākehā   person of European descent

pākura   wood-carving surface pattern in which a plain spiral is extended by repeating curved or angular sections of the spiral

papahou   rectangular carved container for valued items

para   commonly used for a rough rain cape

pāraerae   footwear

pare   lintel panel over door or window

paru   dense black swamp sediment used to produce black dye

pātaka   raised storehouse

pātea   kaitaka   cloak with wide **tāniko** border along bottom and narrower ones on each side

patu   short thrusting club

patu muka   stone beater for pounding flax fibre

patu ōnewa   short club of stone

patu parāoa   short club of whalebone

pāua   iridescent shell of *Haliotis sp.*

pekapeka   bat-shaped pendant

pīngao   sedge, *Desmoschoenus spiralis*, with bright yellow leaves used in Maori plaiting

pītau   openwork spiral; canoe prow with openwork spirals

piupiu   flax skirt with **pokinikini** tags

pōhutukawa   tree, *Metrosideros excelsa*

poi   light ball on string, swung rhythmically in song or dance

pokinikini   strips of flax leaf, which have rolled into cylinders while drying, with intervals of exposed inner fibre dyed black

pōria kākā   ring for tame bird

pounamu   New Zealand nephrite; the term is used more broadly to cover also bowenite (**tangiwai**) used for ornaments; often loosely translated as greenstone or jade

Porourangi   the ancestor from whom the *iwi* of Ngāti Porou take their name

pōtae tauā   cap associated with mourning

poupou   side wall panel of a house

poutokomanawa   interior central post of a house, supporting the ridgepole

pouwhenua   long club with widening head

puhi   young woman of high birth, with a ceremonial role

pūkāea   long wood trumpet

pūkeko   swamp hen, *Porphyrio porphyrio*

pukupuku   compacted single-pair twining

pūtātara   conch-shell trumpet

pūtōrino   bugle flute

pūwerewere   spiral form of **ritorito** wood-carving surface pattern

rāhui   seasonal restriction on food gathering

rangatira   aristocrat, chief

rangatiratanga   chieftainship

raranga   plaiting technique used for making baskets and mats

raumoa   plain ridge of wood-carving surface pattern

rauponga   wood-carving surface pattern in which a notched ridge is bordered by parallel plain ridges and grooves

rei puta   whale-tooth pendant, tongue-shaped

Rēkohu   Maori name for Chatham Islands

ritorito   wood-carving surface pattern in which short curved ridges radiate across a plain groove

taha wairua   spiritual element

tāhuhu   ridge-pole of a house; main line of genealogy

taiaha   long staff or club used for close combat

tānekaha   tree, *Phyllocladus trichomanoides*, bark of which is used to produce reddish brown dye

tangata (plural **tāngata**)   man, human being

tangata whenua   people of the land, original inhabitants

tangihanga   funeral wake

tangiwai   bowenite, used to make ornaments

tāniko   decorative Maori weaving technique

taonga   possession, property, anything highly prized, particularly cultural property, treasure

tapu   under religious restriction, sacred

taratara-a-kae/kai   wood-carving surface pattern in which a zigzag ridge runs between plain ridges

tātua   man's belt

taurapa   war canoe sternpost

tekoteko   carved figure on the front apex of the bargeboards of a house

tewhatewha   long club with axe-like blade

tīheru   canoe bailer

tikanga   custom, way of doing things

tī kāuka   cabbage tree, *Cordyline australis*

tiki   human figure form in carving

tiki wānanga   god stick used by the ritual expert to communicate with the gods

toetoe   tall grass, *Cortaderia spp.*

tohunga   an expert in either ritual or practical matters

tohunga whakairo   wood-carving expert

tōī   mountain cabbage tree, *Cordyline indivisa*

toki poutangata   ceremonial adze

tōtara   tree, *Podocarpus totara*, used in carving

tū   woman's belt of multiple cords

tuere   type of war canoe prow with central longitudinal panel

tūī   bird, honeyeater, *Prosthemadera novaeseelandiae*

tuia   bind, knit together

tukutuku   decorative knotted latticework panels of a house

tūrangawaewae   lit. standing place for the feet

turuturu   weaving stick

unaunahi   wood-carving surface pattern in which a series of short curved ridges cross a plain groove at spaced intervals

utu   return for anything, reciprocity

wahaika   short club, with crescent-shaped blade

waiata   song, song-poem

wairua   spirit, soul

waka   canoe; loose association of tribes

wakahuia   small carved container for valued items

waka kōiwi   carved container for the bones of a dead person

waka taua   war canoe

whaikōrero   oratory, formal speech-making

whakairo   ornament with a pattern

whakairo kākahu   design woven in garments

whakairo rākau   design carved in wood, wood-carving

whakairo tangata   design tattooed on body

whakakai   long earrings

whakapapa   genealogy, line of descent

whakarare   variety of **rauponga** wood-carving surface pattern in which the plain ridges of one side curve across the notched ridge

whanake   cabbage tree, *Cordyline australis*

whānau   extended family

whanaungatanga   kinship

wharariki   mountain flax, *Phormium cookianum*

whare   house

wharenui   large house, meeting house

whare manuhiri   house for visitors

whare rūnanga   meeting house

whare wānanga   higher school of learning, college of priests

whare whakairo   carved house, meeting house

whāriki   plaited sleeping or floor mat, floor covering

whatu   twining technique used to weave Maori garments

whatu aho pātahi   single-pair twining

whatu aho rua   double-pair twining

whatu kākahu   cloak-weaving

whenu   warp

whenua   land

whiringa tāngata   patterns of society

References

Abbreviations:
BM Ethno British Museum, Dept. of Ethnography (Museum of Mankind)
BM M&LA British Museum, Dept. of Medieval and Later Antiquities
ML Mitchell Library, Sydney
PRO Public Record Office, London
RAI Royal Anthropological Institute of Great Britain and Ireland, London
TL Turnbull Library, Wellington

ANDERSEN, J.C. 1934. *Maori Music with its Polynesian Background.* New Plymouth: Polynesian Society Memoir 10.

ANDERSON, A.J. 1989. *Prodigious Birds: Moas and Moa-Hunting in Prehistoric New Zealand.* Cambridge: Cambridge University Press.

ANDERSON, A.J. 1991. The chronology of colonization in New Zealand. *Antiquity* 65: 767–95.

ANDERSON, A.J. and M. McGLONE. 1992. Living on the edge – Prehistoric land and people in New Zealand. In J. Dodson (ed.) *The Native Lands. Prehistory and environmental change in Australia and the Southwest Pacific*, pp. 198–241. Melbourne: Longman Cheshire.

ANGAS, G.F. 1847. *The New Zealanders Illustrated.* London: T. McLean.

ANGAS, G.F. 1972. *Portraits of the New Zealand Maori Painted in 1844.* With a modern text by G.C. Petersen and S.M. Mead. Wellington, Sydney, London: A.H. and A.E. Reed.

ARCHEY, G. 1933a. Wood carving in the North Auckland area. *Records of the Auckland Institute and Museum* 1 (4): 209–18.

ARCHEY, G. 1933b. Evolution of certain Maori carving patterns. *Journal of the Polynesian Society* 42: 171–90.

ARCHEY, G. 1936. Maori carving patterns. *Journal of the Polynesian Society* 45: 49–62.

ARCHEY, G. 1977. *Whaowhia. Maori Art and its Artists.* Auckland: Collins.

BARROW, T. 1969. *Maori Wood Sculpture of New Zealand.* Wellington: Reed.

BARROW, T. 1972. *Art and Life in Polynesia.* Wellington: Reed.

BEAGLEHOLE, J.C. (ed.) 1955, 1961, 1967. *The Journals of Captain James Cook on his Voyages of Discovery.* 3 vols in 4. Cambridge University Press for the Hakluyt Society.

BEAGLEHOLE, J.C. (ed.) 1963. *The Endeavour Journal of Joseph Banks, 1768–1771.* 2nd edn. 2 vols. Sydney: Trustees of the Library of New South Wales in association with Angus and Robertson.

BECK, R. 1984. *New Zealand Jade.* Wellington: Reed.

BEST, E. 1898. The art of the whare pora: notes on the clothing of the ancient Maori. *Transactions and Proceedings of the New Zealand Institute* 31: 625–58.

BEST, E. 1924. *Maori Religion and Mythology.* Wellington: Dominion Museum Bulletin 10.

BEST, E. 1925. *Tuhoe, the Children of the Mist.* Wellington: Polynesian Society Memoir 6.

BEST, E. 1927. *The Pa Maori.* Wellington: Dominion Museum Bulletin 6.

BEST, E. 1928. The story of Rua and Tangaroa. An origin myth. How the art of woodcarving was acquired by man. *Journal of the Polynesian Society* 37: 257–60.

BEST, E. 1952. *The Maori As He Was.* 3rd impression. Wellington: Government Printer; originally published 1924.

BEST, E. 1976. *The Maori Canoe.* Wellington: Dominion Museum Bulletin 7. Reprint of 1925 edn.

BIDWILL, J.C. 1841. *Rambles in New Zealand.* Wellington: Orr.

BIGGS, B. 1960. *Maori Marriage: An Essay in Reconstruction.* Wellington: Reed.

BINNEY, J. 1968. *The Legacy of Guilt: A Life of Thomas Kendall.* Auckland: Oxford University Press.

BINNEY, J. 1980. The lost drawing of Nukutawhiti. *New Zealand Journal of History* 14 (1): 3–24.

BINNEY, J. 1986. 'At every bend a taniwha': Thomas Kendall and Maori carving. *New Zealand Journal of History* 20 (2): 132–46.

BINNEY, J. 1995. *Redemption Songs. A Life of Te Kooti Arikirangi Te Turuki.* Auckland: Auckland University Press/Bridget Williams Books.

BOAS, F. 1955. *Primitive Art.* New York: Dover.

BRAUNHOLTZ, H.J. 1938. Ethnographical museums and the collector: aims and methods. *Journal of the Royal Anthropological Institute* 68: 1–16.

BRITISH MUSEUM. Department of Ethnography (Museum of Mankind). Archives. Correspondence. Eth. Docs.

BRITISH MUSEUM. Department of Medieval and Later Antiquities. Archives. Departmental Correspondence.

BRITISH MUSEUM. 1808–1903. *Synopsis of the contents of the British Museum,* later *Guide to the Exhibition Rooms.* Various edns.

BROWN, D.S. 1996. Te Hau ki Turanga. *Journal of the Polynesian Society* 105: 7–26.

BROWN, G.H. and H. KEITH 1982. *An Introduction to New Zealand Painting 1839–1980.* Auckland: Collins.

BROWN, W. 1995. *100 New Zealand Artists.* Auckland: Godwit.

BROWN, W. 1996. *Another 100 New Zealand Artists.* Auckland: Godwit.

BULMER, S.E. in preparation. City without a state? Urbanisation in pre-European Taamaki-makau-rau (Auckland. New Zealand). In P. Sinclair (ed.) *Urbanism in East Africa from a World Perspective.* London: Unwin Hyman.

BURANARUGSA, M. and B.F. LEACH. 1993. Coordinate geometry of Moriori crania and comparisons with Maori. *Man and Culture in Oceania* 9: 1–43.

CAPE, P. 1979. *New Zealand Painting since 1960: a Study in Themes and Developments.* Auckland: Collins.

CASSELS, R. 1979. Early prehistoric wooden artefacts from the Waitore site (N 136/161), near Patea, Taranaki. *New Zealand Journal of Archaeology* 1: 85–108.

CAYGILL, M. 1981. *The Story of the British Museum.* London: British Museum Publications Ltd.

COLENSO, W. 1879. Contributions towards a better knowledge of the Maori race. *Transactions and Proceedings of the New Zealand Institute for 1878.* 11: 108–47.

COLENSO, W. 1892. Vestiges: reminiscences, memorabilia of works, deeds and sayings of the ancient Maoris. *Transactions and Proceedings of the New Zealand Institute for 1891.* 24: 445–67.

COLENSO COMMUNICATIONS (ed.) 1990. *Welcome To Our World; Threads That Weave Our Nation.* New Zealand 1990 Commission.

COX, L. 1993. *Kotahitanga: The Search for Maori Political Unity.* Auckland: Oxford University Press.

CRUISE, R.A. 1823. *Journal of a Ten Months' Residence in New Zealand.* London: Longman, Hurst, Rees, Orme and Brown.

DANSEY, H. 1977. A View of death. In M. King (ed.) *Te Ao Hurihuri: The World Moves On.* Revised edn, Auckland: Methuen.

DAVIDSON, J.M. 1984. *The Prehistory of New Zealand.* Auckland: Longman Paul.

DAVIDSON, J.M. 1987. The *Paa Maori* revisited. *Journal of the Polynesian Society* 96 (1): 7–26.

DAVIDSON, J.M. (ed.) 1989. *Taonga Maori: Treasures of the New Zealand Maori People.* Sydney: Australian Museum.

DAVIS, C.O.B. 1855. *Maori Mementoes: being a Series of Addresses, Presented by the Native People, to His Excellency Sir George Grey . . .* Auckland: Williamson and Wilson.

DAVIS, F. 1976. Maori art and artists, *Education* 25. Wellington Department of Education.

DAVIS, F. 1976. Bicultural artists and the modern community. In *Education* 25. Wellington: Department of Education.

DAVIS, T. 1951. *John Fowler and the business he founded.* Privately printed.

DENNAN, R. 1968. *Guide Rangi of Rotorua.* Wellington: Whitcombe and Tombs.

DEWES, TE K. 1977. The Case of oral arts. In M. King (ed.), *Te Ao Hurihuri: The World Moves On.* Revised edn. Auckland: Methuen.

DOCKING, G. 1971. *200 Years of New Zealand Painting.* Auckland: Bateman.

DUFF, R.S. 1956. *The Moa-hunter Period of Maori Culture.* 2nd edn., Wellington: Government Printer.

DUNN, M. 1972. *Maori Rock Art.* Wellington: Reed.

DUNN, M. 1996. *Contemporary Painting in New Zealand.* Roseville, N.S.W.: Craftsman House.

DURIE, E.T. 1990. Perspectives from the past. In H. Bower (ed.), *New Zealand 1990: Official Souvenir Publication,* pp. 18–19. Auckland: Dow Publishing Ltd.

DURIE, M.H. 1995. Principles for the development of Maori policy. In *Maori Policy Development: Conference Proceedings.* Wellington: A.I.C. Conferences Ltd.

ELSMORE, B. 1989. *Mana from Heaven: A Century of Maori Prophets in New Zealand.* Tauranga: Moana Press.

FAGG, W. (ed.) 1970. *Sir Hans Sloane and Ethnography.* London: Trustees of the British Museum.

FIRTH, R. 1959. *Economics of the New Zealand Maori*. Wellington: Government Printer.

FIRTH, R. 1992. Art and anthropology. In J. Coote and A. Shelton (eds) *Anthropology, Art and Aesthetics*. Oxford: Clarendon Press.

FOX, A. 1976. *Prehistoric Maori Fortifications in the North Island of New Zealand*. Auckland: Longman Paul.

FRASER, D.W. 1989. *A Guide to Weft Twining and Related Structures with Interlacing Wefts*. Philadelphia: University of Pennsylvania.

FUREY, L. 1996. *Oruarangi*. Bulletin of the Auckland Institute and Museum 17.

GARDINER, W. 1992. *Te Mura o te Ahi: The Story of the Maori Battalion*. Auckland: Reed.

GARDINER, W. 1993. Te Ture Whenua Maori – an overview of the social economic and commercial implications of the Maori Land Act. Paper presented at the Today Tomorrow Aotearoa Conference, Wellington, 30 June–1 July 1993.

GOSDEN, C., J. ALLEN, W. AMBROSE, D. ANSON, J. GOLSON, R. GREEN, P. KIRCH, I. LILLEY, J. SPECHT and M. SPRIGGS. 1989. Lapita sites of the Bismarck Archipelago. *Antiquity* 63: 561–86.

GRANT, S. 1977. *Waimarama*. Palmerston North: Dunmore Press.

GRAVES, R. 1971. *The White Goddess*. London: Faber and Faber.

GREENHALGH, P. 1988. *Ephemeral Vistas. The Expositions Universelles, Great Exhibitions and World's Fairs, 1851–1939*. Manchester: Manchester University Press.

GREY, G. 1885. *Polynesian Mythology*. 2nd edn, 2 vols in 1. Auckland: H. Brett.

HAKIWAI, A.T. 1992. The search for legitimacy. Paper presented to the World Anthropology Conference, Taipei, Taiwan 1992.

HAKIWAI, A.T. and J. TERRELL 1994. *Ruatepupuke: A Maori Meeting House*. Chicago: The Field Museum Centennial Collection.

HAKIWAI, A.T. 1995. Ruatepupuke – working together, understanding one another. *New Zealand Museums Journal* 25 (1): 42–4.

HANSON, A. 1990. The eye of the beholder: a short history of the study of Maori art. In A. and L. Hanson (eds) *Art and Identity in Oceania*. Honolulu: University of Hawaii Press.

IHIMAERA, I. (ed.). 1996. *Mataora:*

The Living Face. Auckland: Bateman.

IMPERIAL INSTITUTE. 1902. *Catalogue of the Gifts and Addresses Received by Their Royal Highnesses the Duke and Duchess of Cornwall and York During their Visit to the King's Dominions Beyond the Seas, 1901*. London: William Clowes & Sons Ltd.

IRWIN, G. 1992. *The Prehistoric Exploration and Colonisation of the Pacific*. Cambridge: Cambridge University Press.

JACKSON, M. 1972. Aspects of symbolism and composition in Maori art. *Bijdragen Tot de Taal-Land-, en Volkenkunds* 128: 33–80.

JACKSON, M. 1995. A Responsibility for the past. Wellington: *The Dominion*, 10 May 1995, p. 12.

JOHANSEN, J.P. 1954. *The Maori and His Religion in its Non-Ritualistic Aspects*. Copenhagen: Munskgaard.

JONES, K.L. 1981. New Zealand mataa from Marlborough, Nelson, and the Chatham Islands. *New Zealand Journal of Archaeology* 3: 89–107.

JONES, T.M. 1970. H.M.S. Pandora in the Bay of Plenty 1852. Extracts from the journal of Lieutenant T.M. Jones, R.N. *Historical Review* 18 (2): 62–79.

KAEPPLER, A.L. 1978. "*Artificial Curiosities*" . . . Honolulu: Bishop Museum Press. Bernice P. Bishop Museum Special Publication 65.

KARETU, T. 1977. Language and protocol of the marae. In M. King (ed.) *Te Ao Hurihuri: The World Moves On*. Revised edn. Auckland: Methuen.

KARETU, T. 1978. Kawa in crisis. In M. King (ed.) *Tihe Mauri Ora: Aspects of Maoritanga*. Auckland: Methuen.

KARETU, T. 1993. *Haka! Te Tohu o Te Whenua Rangatira: The Dance of a Noble People*. Wellington: Reed.

KAWHARU, I.H. 1977. *Maori Land Tenure: Studies of a Changing Institution*. Oxford: Clarendon Press.

KAWHARU, H. (ed.) 1989. *Waitangi: Maori and Pakeha Perspectives on the Treaty of Waitangi*. Auckland: Oxford University Press.

KELLY, L.G. 1949. *Tainui: The Story of Hoturoa and His Descendants*. Wellington: Polynesian Society Memoir 25.

KERNOT, B. 1984. Maori artists of time before. In S.M. Mead (ed.) 1984. *Te Maori: Maori Art from New Zealand Collections*. Auckland: Heinemann.

KING, J. 1995. Who shall reign over us? Wellington: *The Evening Post*, 11 July 1995, p. 7.

KING, J.C.H. 1981. *Artificial Curiosities from the Northwest Coast of America*. London: British Museum Publications Ltd.

KING, J.C.H., 1997. Franks and ethnography. In M. Caygill and J. Cherry (eds) *A. W. Franks: Nineteenth-century collecting and the British Museum*. London: British Museum Press.

KING, M. 1990. Perspectives from the past. *New Zealand 1990: Official Souvenir Publication*, p. 10. Auckland: Dow Publishing Ltd.

KIRCH, P.V. and R.C. GREEN. 1987. History, phylogeny and evolution in Polynesia. *Current Anthropology* 28 (4): 431–56.

LANDER, M. 1996. Maureen Lander. In C. Szekely (ed.). *Korurangi New Maori Art*. Auckland: Auckland City Art Gallery.

LEACH, B.F. 1969. *The Concept of Similarity in Prehistoric Studies*. University of Otago Anthropology Department, Studies in Prehistoric Anthropology 1.

LEACH, B.F. 1979. Excavations in the Washpool Valley, Palliser Bay. In B.F. Leach and H.M. Leach (eds) *Prehistoric Man in Palliser Bay*, pp. 67–136. Wellington: National Museum of New Zealand Bulletin 21.

LEACH, B.F. and H.M. LEACH (eds). 1979. *Prehistoric Man in Palliser Bay*. Wellington: National Museum of New Zealand Bulletin 21.

LEACH, B.F., A.J. ANDERSON, D.G. SUTTON, R. BIRD, P. DUERDEN and E. CLAYTON. 1986. The origin of prehistoric obsidian artefacts from the Chatham and Kermadec Islands. *New Zealand Journal of Archaeology* 8: 143–70.

LEACH, H.M. 1984. *1,000 Years of Gardening in New Zealand*. Wellington: A.H. & A.W. Reed.

LEVI-STRAUSS, C. 1963. *Structural Anthropology*. New York: Basic Books.

LOUGHNAN, R.A. 1902. *Royalty in New Zealand: the Visit of Their Royal Highnesses the Duke and Duchess of Cornwall and York to New Zealand, 10th to 27th June, 1901*. Wellington: Government Printer.

McEWEN, J.M. 1947. The Development of Maori culture since the advent of the Pakeha. *Journal of the Polynesian Society* 56 (2): 173–87.

McEWEN. J.M. 1966. Maori art. In A.H. McLintock (ed.) *An*

Encyclopaedia of New Zealand. Vol. 2. Wellington: Government Printer.

McFADGEN, B.G. 1982. Dating New Zealand archaeology by radiocarbon. *New Zealand Journal of Science* 25: 375–92.

McHUGH, P. 1991. *The Maori Magna Carta, New Zealand Law and the Treaty of Waitangi*. Auckland: Oxford University Press.

MAHUIKA, A. 1977. Leadership: inherited and achieved. In M. King (ed.) *Te Ao Hurihuri: The World Moves On*. Revised edn. Auckland: Methuen.

MAHUTA, R. 1978. The Maori King Movement Today. In M. King (ed.) *Tihe Mauri Ora: Aspects of Maoritanga*. Auckland: Methuen.

MAKERETI, P. 1986. *The Old Time Maori*. With an introduction by Ngahuia Te Awekotuku. Auckland: New Women's Press; originally published 1938.

MANE-WHEOKI, J. 1997. Buck Nin and the Origins of Contemporary Maori Art. *Art New Zealand* 82: 61–5.

MARSDEN, M. 1988. The Natural world and natural resources: Maori value systems and perspectives. Paper presented to the Waitangi Tribunal, July 1988.

MEAD, S.M. 1969. *Traditional Maori Clothing: A Study of Technological and Functional Change*. Wellington: Reed.

MEAD, S.M. 1975. The origins of Maori art: Polynesian or Chinese. *Oceania* 45 (3): 173–211.

MEAD, S.M. 1976. The Production of native art and craft objects in contemporary New Zealand society. In N.H.H. Graburn (ed.) *Ethnic and Tourist Arts. Cultural Expressions from the Fourth World*. Berkeley: University of California Press.

MEAD, S.M. (ed.). 1984. *Te Maori: Maori Art from New Zealand Collections*. Auckland: Heinemann.

MEAD, S.M. 1985. Te Maori: a journey of rediscovery for the Maori people of New Zealand. In *Triptych*, June–July 1985, pp. 11–18.

MEAD, S.M. 1986a. *Magnificent Te Maori: Te Maori Whakahirahira*. Auckland: Heinemann.

MEAD, S.M. 1986b. *Te Toi Whakairo: The Art of Maori Carving*. Auckland: Reed Methuen.

MEAD, S.M. 1990a. Maori art: sharing a taonga. In Colenso Communications (ed.) *Welcome To Our World: Threads That Weave Our Nation*, pp. 144–47. New Zealand 1990 Commission.

MEAD, S.M. 1990b. The Nature of taonga. In *Taonga Maori Conference, New Zealand, 18–27 November 1990*, pp. 164–9. Wellington: Department of Internal Affairs.

MEAD, S.M. 1997. *Maori Art on the World Scene*. Wellington: Ahua Design and Illustration and Matau Associates.

MEINERTZHAGEN, R. 1964. *Diary of a Black Sheep*. Edinburgh and London: Oliver and Boyd.

MELBOURNE, H. 1991. *Toiapiapi*. Wellington: Government Printer Books.

METGE, J. 1980. Multi-culturalism: problem or goal? In *He Huarahi: Report of the National Advisory Committee on Maori Education*, pp. 63–72. Wellington: Department of Education.

MILLER, E. 1973. *That Noble Cabinet*. London: André Deutsch.

MITCHELL LIBRARY, SYDNEY. William Strutt: autobiography and other papers 1778–1955. MS 867.

MONTGOMERY, J. 1831. *Journal of the Voyages and Travels by the Rev. Daniel Tyerman and George Bennet, Esq. deputed from the London Missionary Society . . . between the years 1821 and 1829*. Vol. 2. London: Frederick Westley and A.H. Davis.

MURU, S. 1990. The Power of te reo. *New Zealand Geographic* 5: 99–106.

NAUMANN, R., L. HARRISON and TE K. WINIATA. 1990. *Te Mana o Te Tiriti: The Living Treaty*. Auckland: New House Publishers.

NEICH, R. 1983. The veil of orthodoxy: Rotorua Ngati Tarawhai woodcarving in a changing context. In S.M. Mead and B. Kernot (eds) *Art and Artists of Oceania*. Palmerston North: Dunmore Press.

NEICH, R. 1990. The Maori carving art of Tene Waitere, traditionalist and innovator. *Art New Zealand* 57: 73–9.

NEICH, R. 1991. Jacob Heberley of Wellington: a Maori carver in a changed world. *Records of the Auckland Institute and Museum*. 28: 69–148.

NEICH, R. 1993. *Painted Histories: Early Maori Figurative Painting*. Auckland: Auckland University Press.

NEW ZEALAND, DEPARTMENT OF INTERNAL AFFAIRS. 1990. *Taonga Maori Conference, New Zealand, 18–27 November 1990*. Wellington: Department of Internal Affairs.

NEW ZEALAND 1990 COMMISSION. 1990. *The 150 Year Debate: A Selection of Quotations of the Treaty of Waitangi*. New Zealand 1990 Commission.

NEW ZEALAND GEOGRAPHIC. 1990. The Living past. *New Zealand Geographic* 5: 75–86.

NGATA, A.T. 1940. Maori arts and crafts. In I.L.G. Sutherland (ed.) *The Maori People Today, A General Survey*. Christchurch: Whitcombe and Tombs.

NGATA, A.T. 1958. The origin of Maori carving. *Te Ao Hou* 22: 30–7; 23: 30–4.

NGATA, A.T. 1959. *Nga Moteatea I*. Wellington: Polynesian Society Maori Texts 1.

NGATA, A.T. 1961. *Nga Moteatea II*. Wellington: Polynesian Society Maori Texts 2.

NGATA, A.T. 1970. *Nga Moteatea III*. Wellington: Polynesian Society Maori Texts 3.

ORANGE, C. 1987. *The Treaty of Waitangi*. Wellington: Allen & Unwin.

ORANGE, C. 1990. *An Illustrated History of the Treaty of Waitangi*. Wellington: Allen & Unwin.

PARKINSON, S. 1773. *A Journal of a Voyage to the South Seas in His Majesty's Ship Endeavour*. London: Stanfield Parkinson.

PENDERGRAST, M.J. 1987. *Te Aho Tapu, The Sacred Thread*. Auckland: Reed Methuen.

PHILLIPPS, W.J. 1963. Notes on the owl and shag as guardians or familiar spirits. *Journal of the Polynesian Society* 72 (4): 411–14.

POOL, I. 1991. *Te Iwi Maori. A New Zealand Population Past, Present & Projected*. Auckland: Auckland University Press.

POUND, F. 1985. *Forty Modern New Zealand Paintings*. Auckland: Penguin.

PRICKETT, N.J. 1979. Prehistoric occupation in the Moikau Valley, Palliser Bay. In B.F. Leach and H.M. Leach (eds) *Prehistoric Man in Palliser Bay*, pp. 29–47. Wellington: National Museum of New Zealand Bulletin 21.

PRICKETT, N.J. 1982. An archaeologists' guide to the Maori dwelling. *New Zealand Journal of Archaeology* 4: 111–47.

PUBLIC RECORD OFFICE. London. CO 406/14 f.67v.

RANGIHAU, J. 1981. Being Maori. In M. King (ed.) *Te Ao Hurihuri: The World Moves On*. Revised edn. Auckland: Longman Paul.

RITCHIE, J. 1995. Through the eye of the needle, recent work by Brett Graham. *Art New Zealand* 76: 58–61.

RITCHIE, J. & J. 1979. *Growing Up In Polynesia*. Sydney: Allen & Unwin.

ROBLEY, H.G. 1896. *Moko; or Maori Tattooing*. London: Chapman and Hall.

ROGERS, L.R. 1974. *Relief Sculpture*. New York: Oxford University Press.

ROTH, H.L. 1979. *The Maori Mantle*. Bedford: Ruth Bean; originally published 1923.

ROYAL ANTHROPOLOGICAL INSTITUTE OF GREAT BRITAIN AND IRELAND, LONDON. Archives. Diaries of Capt. J. P. Luce. MS 208.

ROYAL ARCHIVES. WINDSOR CASTLE. Diary of King George V.

RYDÉN, S. 1963. *The Banks Collection: An Episode in 18th-century Anglo-Swedish Relations*. Stockholm: Ethnographical Museum of Sweden Monograph Series, Publication No. 8.

SALMOND, A. 1991. *Two Worlds. First Meetings Between Maori and Europeans 1642–1772*. Auckland: Viking.

SCHAFER, H. 1974. *Principles of Egyptian Art*. Oxford: Clarendon Press.

SHAWCROSS, W. 1976. Kauri Point swamp: the ethnographic interpretation of a prehistoric site. In G. de G. Sieveking, I.H. Longworth, and K.E. Wilson (eds) *Problems in Economic and Social Archaeology*, pp. 277–305. London: Duckworth.

SIMMONS, D.R. 1981 Stability and change in the material culture of Queen Charlotte Sound in the 18th century. *Records of the Auckland Institute and Museum*. 18: 1–16.

SIMMONS, D.R. 1984. Tribal art styles. In S.M. Mead (ed.) *Te Maori: Maori Art from New Zealand Collections*. Auckland: Heinemann.

SIMMONS, D.R.1985. *Whakairo: Maori Tribal Art*. Auckland: Oxford University Press.

SIMMONS, D.R. n.d. Draft catalogue of the British Museum Maori collections. British Museum, Dept of Ethnography. Archives.

SKINNER, H. D. 1917. Maori and other Polynesian material in British museums. *Journal of the Polynesian Society*. 26: 134–7.

SKINNER, H.D. 1923. *The Moriois of Chatham Islands*. Honolulu: Bernice P. Bishop Museum Memoir 9 (1).

SKINNER, H.D. 1932–6, 1943. Maori amulets in stone, bone and shell. *Journal of the Polynesian Society* 41–5, 52.

SKINNER, H. D. 1974. *Comparatively speaking: Studies in Pacific Material Culture 1921–1972*. Dunedin: University of Otago Press.

SMITH, S.P. 1910. *Maori Wars of the Nineteenth Century*. Christchurch: Whitcombe and Tombs.

SPARROW SIMPSON, W.J. 1899. *Memoir of the Rev. W. Sparrow Simpson, D.D.* London: Longmans, Green and Co.

STACK, J.W. 1876. An Account of the Maori house attached to the Christchurch Museum. *Transactions and Proceedings of the New Zealand Institute* 8: 172–6.

STAFFORD, D. 1994. *Landmarks of Te Arawa*. Wellington: Reed.

SUTTON, D.G. 1980. A Culture history of the Chatham Islands. *Journal of the Polynesian Society* 89 (1): 67–93.

SUTTON, D.G. 1987. A Paradigmatic shift in Polynesian prehistory: implications for New Zealand. *New Zealand Journal of Archaeology* 9: 135–55.

SUTTON, D.G. 1990. Organisation and ontology: The origins of the northern Maori chiefdom. *Man* 25: 667–92.

SZEKELY, C. (ed.). 1996. *Korurangi New Maori Art*. Auckland: Auckland City Art Gallery.

TAUROA, H. and P. 1986. *Te Marae: A Guide to Customs & Protocol*. Wellington: Reed Methuen.

TE AWEKOTUKU, N. 1990. Art and the spirit. *New Zealand Geographic* 5: 93–7.

TE AWEKOTUKU, N. 1991. *Mana Wahine Maori: Selected Writings in Maori Women's Art, Culture and Politics*. Auckland: New Women's Press.

TE RANGIHIROA (P.H. BUCK). 1926. *The Evolution of Maori Clothing*. New Plymouth: Polynesian Society Memoir 7.

TE RANGIHIROA (P.H. BUCK). 1950. *The Coming of the Maori*. 2nd edn. Wellington: Whitcombe and Tombs.

TREGENZA, J. 1980. *George French Angas: Artist, Traveller and Naturalist 1822–1886*. Adelaide: Art Gallery Board of South Australia.

TROTTER, M. and McCULLOCH, B. 1981. *Prehistoric Rock Art of New Zealand*. 2nd edn. Wellington: Reed.

TROTTER, M. and McCULLOCH, B. 1989. *Unearthing New Zealand*. Wellington: Government Printer Books.

TURNBULL LIBRARY, WELLINGTON. J.H. Meinertzhagen letters. MSP-37, fold.119.

VAYDA, A.P. 1960. *Maori Warfare*. Wellington: Polynesian Society Maori Monograph No. 2.

WILLIAMS, H.W. 1975. *A Dictionary of the Maori Language.* Reprint of 7th edn. 1971. Wellington: Government Printer.

WILLIAMS, J. 1990. Back to the future. In *Puna Wairere: Essays by Maori*, pp. 14–18. Wellington: New Zealand Planning Council.

WILSON, D.M. 1984. *The Forgotten Collector: Augustus Wollaston Franks of the British Museum.* London: Thames and Hudson.

WILSON, D.M. 1989. *The British Museum: Purpose and Politics.* London: British Museum Publications Ltd.

WINIATA, M. 1967. *The Changing Role of the Leader in Maori Society.* Auckland: Blackwood and Janet Paul.

WINITANA, C. 1994. From Words to Wood. *Mana* 6: 12–21.

YEN, D.E. 1961. The adaptation of kumara by the New Zealand Maori. *Journal of the Polynesian Society* 70 (3): 338–48.

Index

Page numbers in italics refer to illustrations.